She's
Tricky
Like
Coyote

Four-generation photo: Annie Miner Peterson (standing, right), her daughter, Nellie Aasen (seated), her granddaughter, Iola Edmonds (standing left), and her great-granddaugher, Urla (in Nellie's lap) in 1929. Photo courtesy Iola Larson.

On the preceding page: Annie wearing part of her collection of Native American clothing items, ca. 1910. Photo courtesy Esther Stutzman.

She's Tricky Like Coyote

Annie Miner Peterson,
an Oregon Coast Indian Woman

by Lionel Youst

The Civilization of the American Indian Series

University of Oklahoma Press : Norman and London

"The Trickster Person Who Made the Country," a Coos myth dictated in Muluk by Annie Miller Peterson to Melville Jacobs in 1922 and published in *Coos Myth Texts* by the University of Washington (1940), is reprinted in its English version with grateful acknowledgment to the University of Washington Press.

All maps are by Lionel Youst.

Library of Congress Cataloging-in-Publication Data

Youst, Lionel, 1934–
  She's tricky like coyote : Annie Miner Peterson, an Oregon Coast Indian woman / by Lionel Youst.
    p.   cm.
  Includes bibliographical references and index.
  ISBN 0-8061-2972-7 (cloth : alk. paper)
  1. Peterson, Annie Miner, 1860–1939. 2. Coquille women—Biography. 3. Linguistic informants—Oregon—Coos Bay—Biography. 4. Coquille language—Oregon—Coos Bay—History. 5. Anthropological linguistics—Oregon—Coos Bay—History. 6. Coos Bay (Or.)—Biography.   I. Title.
E99.C8742P479   1997
979.5'230049741—dc21
  [B]   97-12529
                                                                         CIP

Text design by Deborah Hackworth. Front-matter design by Alicia Hembekides. Text set in Caslon 540 with Antique Olive display.

She's Tricky Like Coyote: Annie Miner Peterson, an Oregon Coast Indian Woman is Volume 224 in The Civilization of the American Indian Series.

1   2   3   4   5   6   7   8   9   10

he-T'SMI•'XWN

(She's Tricky Like Coyote)

Contents

Appendix

Illustrations

MAPS

KINSHIP CHARTS

Preface

Annie Miner Peterson was born at an Indian village on a tidal slough on the southern Oregon Coast probably in May of 1860.[1] The slough was an inlet to Coos Bay, which was then a remote and obscure part of the Pacific coastal frontier. She was born during the time that the few hundred Indians who lived on the shores of that bay were being replaced by a few hundred whites from elsewhere. It was the time predicted in the mythology of her maternal ancestors.[2] It was the time of the coming of a people to arrive after the Indians: the time of the coming of the Moving People.

Annie lived a full and fascinating seventy-nine years in western Oregon. As a child, she absorbed the culture of her maternal ancestors and mastered the traditional arts of basketmaking and storytelling. She learned English after she was twenty years old, but from childhood she had been bilingual in Hanis and Miluk, the languages of her maternal relatives, and she was probably also conversant in Alsea. She lived to become the last person who was fluent in Miluk.

Between 1900 and 1942 a half-dozen professional anthropologists worked with linguistic informants in the languages of the Oregon Coast. They studied the Penutian languages of Alsea, Suislaw/Umpqua, Hanis Coos, and Miluk Coos. Perhaps a dozen native informants did significant work in those languages with the anthropologists.

At least ten of these linguistic informants were related by blood or by marriage to Annie, who had been married to men descended from the Alsea, the Coos, and the Tututni. As a result, her knowledge of the several cultures of the Oregon Coast was probably without equal among her contemporaries.

It was Annie who preserved for posterity a glimpse of the culture of her mother and her ancestors before the coming of the Moving People. Unlike many of her contemporaries, Annie did not filter her narratives through the inhibitions and taboos instilled by Christian white culture. As a linguistic informant to the anthropologist Melville Jacobs, she gave to science virtually all that is known of the Miluk language.

Annie was one of the very few American Indian women of the transitional generation to have left an account of her own life. As such, she is in the select company of Sarah Winnemucca of the Northern Paiute and Lucy Thompson of the Yurok, each of whom dictated autobiographies that were subsequently published.[3] Unlike those two women, who recorded their material in English, Annie dictated her autobiography in her native language of Miluk Coos.

She dictated her story to a professional anthropologist, and it was translated into English with a scholarly emphasis on the nuances of meaning.[4] The result is an account that, more accurately than any other, reveals the mind of a bright and extraordinary woman who was raised as a traditional Indian but whose adult life was spent in the white world. Her autobiography, regrettably, is only a few pages.

Annie's Indian name was a long—and, to us, unpro-nounceable—Hanis word, he-T'SMI•'XWN, which meant "she's tricky like coyote." She had been named after a deceased aunt, and it seemed to fit her quite well. Through-out her life she was known to be fiercely independent and outspoken. As is often the case with people of exceptionally strong character, her contemporaries were divided between those who loved and those who hated her. The heat of that division has sometimes obscured the person and her contri-butions to anthropology, linguistics, and folklore.

I was only five years old when Annie Miner Peterson died in 1939, and I do not remember anything about her death. I do remember, however, that we lived on North Slough of Coos Bay then and that an old Coos Indian woman named Mrs. Waters lived next door. Her son, Johnny Waters, worked for my dad and became a lifelong family friend. Mrs. Waters's nephew, Jim Siestrom, and his family lived down the road a bit, and they too were longtime family friends. About a mile from our house were the bogs where Annie, Mrs. Waters, and many of the other Indians of the Oregon Coast had met each September to pick cranberries.

I was ten years old when Annie's niece, Lottie Evanoff, died in 1944. My dad read about it in the newspaper and announced solemnly: "There are no more Coos Indians. The last one died yesterday." I asked: "What about Mrs. Waters and Jim Siestrom? They are still around." My dad answered that they were only part Indian and that Lottie had been the last full-blood. I can remember to this day the empty feeling I had in the pit of my stomach at that time. Something had changed utterly.

In my youth I worked in logging camps with descen-dants of the Coos Indians. It was Johnny Waters who taught me how to run a Caterpillar tractor. I tramped for a while from camp to camp in Oregon and California with Guy Martin, a Coos descendant who had been raised at Siletz, and with Glen Miller, a Coquille descendant who had been raised at South Slough of Coos Bay. We were loggers and we were buddies.

Later, I joined the U.S. Air Force. Over the years I lived in North Africa and Southeast Asia and in Nebraska, Texas, and California. During that time I developed an avocational interest in the subject matter of anthropology. The further I got into it, the more I regretted not having learned more about the descendants of the native people who had lived around me during my childhood.

Eventually I moved back to Oregon. Insofar as I had the leisure to do so, I explored the published literature of the coastal Indians. Most significant for me were the two volumes by Melville Jacobs with the texts of his work with Annie Miner Peterson in 1933 and 1934, books I first read in 1971. Probably next in importance was a history of the Rogue River Wars in southwestern Oregon, Stephen Dow Beckham's *Requiem for a People* (1971). But it was not until 1988 that I was introduced to the microfilm edition of the field notes of John Peabody Harrington. Those raw field notes made me feel that I was at last coming to know those long-dead people.

I noticed, in the course of my reading, that the historians seldom used the excellent and priceless oral records (both published and unpublished) that the anthropologists had gleaned from their informants. On the other hand, anthropologists rarely referred to the relevant works of history. Each of the disciplines seemed quite content to ignore the other.

The more I studied the material about Annie Miner Peterson, the more I was attracted to her. She exemplified for me all that was best about the hardy and independent working-class women of the Oregon Coast. These were

outspoken women, without pretensions, who were comfortable around men and had no obvious problems with
themselves. In a barroom or a dance hall, in the cookhouse
of a logging camp or at the waterfront of a coastal town, at
home with a family or in a mill at work, these women were
quintessentially of the Northwest. Some of them were Native
American, some were of mixed parentage, some were
second-generation Scandinavians, but most were probably
of pioneer Yankee stock. What they had in common was
their ironic view of their situation, whatever that might have
been, and their indestructible ability to survive. What set
them apart from more modern trends was their refusal ever
to see themselves as victims of anything. They just kept
going. In Annie's case, she just kept going for seventy-nine
years.

From time to time I would mention Annie Miner
Peterson to someone with a professional interest in the
subject. I found that none of them shared my view of her.
She had been vilified by certain influential spokespeople
within the newly restored tribal entities. As a result, various
professionals had begun to repeat what can be described
only as defamatory attacks on her credibility.

In their most extreme form, these attacks alleged that
nothing Annie Miner Peterson had contributed to the record
could be accepted because she was a congenital liar. It was
said that she had fabricated the myths and ethnological
texts, that she could not speak Miluk, and that she was not
even an Indian. To hear such outrageous misrepresentations
from someone who was jockeying for a position of influence
within a newly restored tribal entity might be understand-
able. But to hear this nonsense repeated by university-
trained professionals was, to me, depressing.

I began to assemble all that was actually known about
Annie from existing records. As I did, I realized that neither
the tribal spokespeople who were generating the misinfor-
mation nor the professionals who were repeating it had ever

read the relevant material, at least not critically. I eventually decided that I would compile what I had found into a biography, but I lacked one essential source. I needed to hear firsthand just what kind of person she had been; I needed to talk to someone who had actually known her.

My breakthrough came when an old-time logger named Wally Anderson told me that he had grown up next door to and had gone to school with Annie's grandchildren. He had been close friends with them and had worked in logging camps with her grandson. He knew her granddaughter, Iola Larson, who was still living and to whom he would be happy to introduce me.

When I met Iola, I liked her immediately. She had those qualities that I had so admired in women I had known in my youth. I told her that I thought her grandmother was a very important person locally, and I asked if she would help me with a biography of Annie. Iola enthusiastically agreed, and the result is the present book.

The communities of which Annie Miner Peterson was a part during her lifetime comprised survivors of the native peoples who had lived in what is now Coos County, Oregon. Before Euro-American contact, those communities subsisted on the relatively abundant resources of the tidal sloughs, the ocean beaches, and the rivers of that part of southwestern Oregon. There are two major river drainages here: the Coos River in the northern third and the Coquille River in the southern two-thirds of the county. The peoples who had originally lived on those two river drainages were culturally quite similar and very much intermarried, but they spoke three mutually unintelligible languages. Each of the two river drainages had its own history during the period of white contact and settlement. Consequently, the native peoples who had lived on those two river drainages ended up with separate legal statuses vis-à-vis the U.S. government.

The descendants of the native peoples of Coos County are currently formed into two tribal entities: the Confederated Tribes of Coos, Lower Umpqua, and Siuslaw Indians; and the Coquille Indian Tribe. The Confederated Tribes achieved full federal recognition in 1984 under Public Law 98–481. They are composed of descendants of speakers of the extinct languages of the Siuslaw, the Hanis, and those Miluk who were from around the mouth of Coos Bay. The Coquille Tribe achieved full federal recognition in 1989 under Public Law 101–42. It comprises descendants of the Athapaskan-speaking Upper Coquille and those Miluk who were from around the mouth of the Coquille River.

No native speakers of these languages remain in the current generation. However, the two tribal entities both have Miluk as a focal point in their respective cultural restoration projects, and the focal texts are those of Annie Miner Peterson. Each of the tribes has a tribal member who has had university training in linguistics. A part of their respective cultural restoration programs involves an attempt to introduce a knowledge of the language to the present generation.

The linguistic view of the relationship of Miluk with Hanis is a matter of some interest but one that has remained essentially unchanged since the 1890s. For over one hundred years linguists have agreed that there seems to be a relationship between the two. However, the nature of that relationship has been, and still is, problematical. The languages are currently classified as the Coos, or Kusan, family of the Penutian phylum of the Amerind languages. Although they both seem to have derived from a Kusan parent, this has never been conclusively demonstrated. Whether they are distinct languages that came closer together through time or dialects of the same language that drifted apart has been debated, but neither theory has been demonstrated. The only significant data that can be used to solve those questions lie in the work that Melville Jacobs did with Annie Miner Peterson during 1933 and 1934. The answers, no doubt hidden in the data, have not yet revealed themselves.

Acknowledgments

Thanks go first to Wally Anderson, who introduced me to his childhood friend, Iola Larson, the granddaughter of the subject of this book and the only living person who knew her; thanks are due Iola for the pleasant visits during which she shared her memories of her grandmother. She read the very first draft of the manuscript and gave me most valuable critical comments.

I would also like to thank the following: Troy Anderson, Miluk Language Teacher for the Coquille Indian Tribe and a member of its Cultural Committee, for reading an early draft and giving me valuable suggestions; William R. Seaburg, Acting Assistant Professor at the American Indian Studies Center, University of Washington, for reading a second draft and giving me important ideas and encouragement; Jim Thornton, Indian Education Coordinator at the Coos County Education Services District, for first introducing me to the fascinating world of the Alsea/Siuslaw/Coos field notes of John Peabody Harrington several years ago; Esther Stutzman, formerly of the Coos and presently of the Confederated Tribes of Siletz, for encouraging my work; Melody Caldera, for sharing with me all of her extensive research on South Slough of Coos Bay; Gary Lundell, Reference Specialist for the Manuscripts and University Archives at the University of Washington; and the trustees of the Melville Jacobs Collection, for allowing me access to the collection.

Many others helped me, among whom I must mention Melissa Huppi, the Alaska bush pilot who flew me up and down the Oregon Coast in her Cessna floatplane so that I could see the entire stage upon which the drama of our subject's life was played out; Jan Bone, who put my maps in her computer and made them really look good; and my editor, D. Teddy Diggs, who saved me from a couple hundred stupid mistakes. Finally, there are my two daughters, Alice and Julia, who helped in many ways, and my wife, Hilda, without whose support I would not get anything done.

She's Tricky Like Coyote

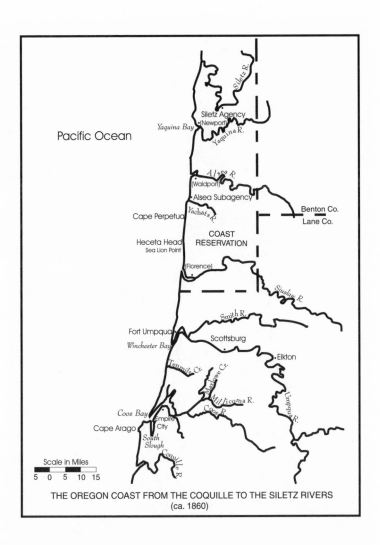

THE OREGON COAST FROM THE COQUILLE TO THE SILETZ RIVERS
(ca. 1860)

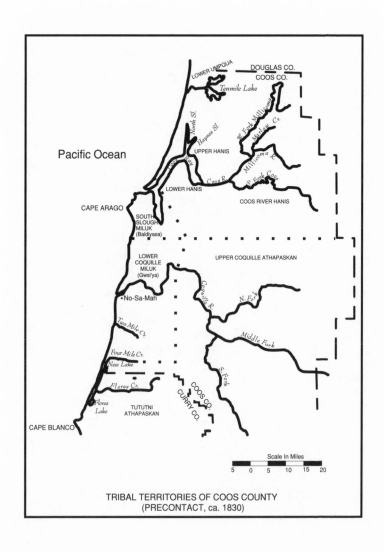

Pacific Ocean

LOWER UMPQUA

DOUGLAS CO.
COOS CO.

Tenmile Lake

North Sl.

Haynes Sl.

W. Fork Millicoma

Marlow Cr.

UPPER HANIS

Millicoma R.

E. Fork Coos

Coos R.

LOWER HANIS

CAPE ARAGO

COOS RIVER HANIS

SOUTH
SLOUGH
MILUK
(Baldiyasa)

LOWER
COQUILLE
MILUK
(Gwsl'ya)

UPPER COQUILLE ATHAPASKAN

•No-Sa-Mah

Coquille R.

N. Fork

Two Mile Cr.

Middle Fork

Four Mile Cr.

New Lake

S. Fork

Flores Cr.

Flores Lake

TUTUTNI
ATHAPASKAN

COOS CO.
CURRY CO.

CAPE BLANCO

Scale In Miles

5   0   5   10   15   20

TRIBAL TERRITORIES OF COOS COUNTY
(PRECONTACT, ca. 1830)

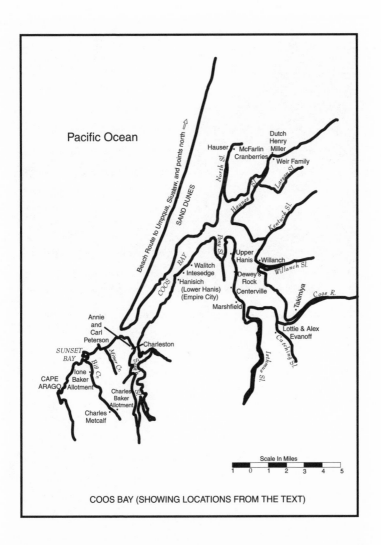

Pacific Ocean

Beach Route to Umpqua, Siuslaw, and points north ⇨

SAND DUNES

North Sl.

Haynes Sl.

Larson Sl.

Kentuck Sl.

Willanch Sl.

Coos R.

Takimiya

COOS BAY

Pony Sl.

Hauser

McFarlin
Cranberries

Dutch
Henry
Miller

Weir Family

Walitch

Intesedge

Hanisich
(Lower Hanis)
(Empire City)

Upper
Hanis

Willanch

Dewey's
Rock

Centerville

Marshfield

Lottie & Alex
Evanoff

Cushing Sl.

Annie
and
Carl
Peterson

Charleston

SUNSET
BAY

Miner Cr.

Big Cr.

South Sl.

Isthmus Sl.

CAPE
ARAGO

Ione
Baker
Allotment

Charles
Baker
Allotment

Charles
Metcalf

Scale In Miles

1   0   1   2   3   4   5

COOS BAY (SHOWING LOCATIONS FROM THE TEXT)

Mouth of Willanch Slough, on the eastern shore of upper Coos Bay. The photo views the bay as seen from the site of the Indian village of Willanch, where Annie was born in 1860. Photo by the author.

1

Contact

In the days before Annie was born, the passage of time was marked by fish and leaves. When the willows had just started to bloom, her people would go to catch herring, which were guided by fences of fir limbs and caught in dip nets.[1] Later, when the smelt were spawning on the ocean beach, all of the leaves were out and everything was in bloom: again, the dip nets.

Upriver when the eels were running, the vine maple had their first streaks of red. Far downstream the seasonal salmon dams were being built while the big-leaf maple were coming into a full, bright golden-yellow. When the dip nets had taken the salmon from in front of the dams, the red and gold of the maple had been replaced by the dull, monotonous brown of the alder.

All of the leaves were gone and the hills had only the evergreen hue of the Douglas fir when the cycle came to a close and the rains set in. At that time the elders told the stories that they themselves had learned as children.

The Coos River and the various inlets to Coos Bay drained about nine hundred square miles of mostly timbered hinterland. Periodic fires changed the character of the land from time to time. After a burn the elk herds would move into the richer browsing of the open spaces, and there they could be more easily hunted. The elk trails, usually following the ridges, made human travel possible across the rugged and brushy mountains of this part of the Coast Range.

In some areas no fires had burned for over five hundred years. In those places the pure stands of Douglas fir blocked out the sun and prevented the growth of underbrush. The carpeted floor of those great dark forests created a hushed and awesome cathedral, seldom visited by man or beast.

The people lived along the waters of the bay and its inlets, of the Coos River and its tributaries, of the coastal lakes, and of the ocean beach. Life had continued in the Coos country for perhaps a hundred generations, following traditions that supposedly ensured that the people would survive. The climate was wet and mild, and the danger of periodic famine was slight. Clams and native oysters and mussels and elk and deer and ducks and geese and, above all, salmon and other fish provided a more than ample supply of protein. Berries in season and various roots and shoots gave variety to the diet. Few other natives in all of North America had a better life at the time the Moving People began coming through the region.

About two years before the first of the Moving People came through, there had been a "visit" of the smallpox. That was probably in 1824.[2] The Hanis Coos villages on Tenmile Lake were hardest hit; their entire population was wiped out.[3] Some of the villages around the bay were also depopulated.

On October 25, 1826, Alexander McLeod and a party
of trappers from the Hudson's Bay Company traveled through
the area, moving from north to south. They may have been
the first whites ever at Coos Bay, but they did not stay long.
About a year and a half later, in July 1828, Jedediah Smith
and his party of fur trappers came through, traveling from
south to north.[4] They did not stay long either.

Then in 1836, some twelve years after the smallpox
outbreak, another disease, probably measles, struck. These
epidemics reduced the Coos Bay population from something
over two thousand at its peak to about eight hundred by the
time the first permanent white settlers arrived in 1853.

The fur traders had not come to settle in the 1820s.
They wanted pelts from the beaver so that fashionable hats
could be made for wealthy men in the East and in Europe.
The beaver were fairly numerous on some of the sloughs of
Coos Bay.[5] The traders introduced dentalium shells from
Canada and trade beads from Europe as a circulating medium
of exchange with the natives. They used these items, as well
as iron pots and kettles, steel needles, axes, knives, and
even flint ignition guns, to trade for the beaver hides. The
Indian women benefited the most from the new labor-saving
devices, but for the men the prestige of owning a gun or an
iron ax was paramount.[6]

The impact of the fur trade on the Indians of Coos Bay
was much less than on the Umpqua people, who lived to the
north.[7] William Harris, who came to Coos Bay with the first
white settlers in 1853, estimated that at that time—twenty-
seven years after the first fur traders had come through—
there were only six guns in the entire county.[8] All six were
old, obsolete Hudson's Bay Company flintlocks.

The Coos country was on the periphery of the fur
trade. The trading post was about sixty miles away on the
Umpqua River, near the present-day town of Elkton. The
chief trader at the post was a Frenchman named Jean

Gagnier, who had followed the Hudson's Bay Company custom of marrying into a prominent Indian family within the trading area. The ties of the Hudson's Bay Company with the Lower Umpqua Indians were thus fixed, and the trade in furs dominated their economy from 1836 to 1852.

A Lower Umpqua relative of Jean Gagnier's wife, interviewed as an old woman in 1911, described the place that trapping had held in the lives of her people during her childhood: "My step-father was setting traps. . . . The hides would be packed and carried away. . . . Some of our relatives would sometimes bring in a canoe a great quantity of hides. . . . Everybody wanted hides."[9]

Although the Indians of Coos County were far from the market, there were beaver on the slough near the village of Willanch, on the east side of the bay.[10] From there it was an easy fifteen miles with the tide upstream to Marlow Creek near the present site of Allegany. From Marlow Creek (the head of tide on the Millicoma River) to Scottsburg (the head of tide on the Umpqua River) was a rough thirty-three miles over which the heavy beaver hides had to be packed.

One of the young men who packed a load of beaver hides over that trail and sold them to Jean Gagnier of the Hudson's Bay Company was Daloose Jackson. Daloose later became Annie's brother-in-law by marrying her half-sister Fannie. He was a son of the headman of the village of Hanisich, one of the three Lower Hanis villages at what later became the town of Empire. He later said that with the money he got from the sale of the hides, he bought clothes, the first clothes he had ever put on.[11] All the rest of his life—and he lived a long, long time—he dressed in fine regalia and was considered by the whites to be a "cock of the walk!"[12]

Annie's mother was probably born a little after the first of the fur traders had visited Coos Bay back in 1826. Annie's grandfather, Minkws, was from Intesedge, a Lower Hanis Coos village a few hundred yards to the north of Hanisich.

He was probably the headman at the village, which was where Annie's mother was born. A few hundred yards north of Intesedge was the third village, Wallitch. These three villages lay along the eastern shore of the lower bay about six miles from its mouth.

Annie's grandmother was from a village that did not speak the Hanis Coos. Her village spoke Miluk Coos, a language that was related to but quite different from Hanis. At the time Annie's grandmother was born, Miluk was spoken by the people who lived on South Slough of Coos Bay and along the ocean beaches to the west as well as at the mouth of the Coquille River twenty miles to the south. The people of the villages on South Slough and the ocean beaches were known as Baldiyasa, or "Beach Shore People." The people of the "Mouth of the Coquille" villages were known collectively as Gwsi'ya.[13]

The anthropologist Melville Jacobs wrote in his notebook that Annie's grandmother had come from one of the Miluk-speaking Gwsi'ya villages at the mouth of the Coquille River.[14] The people of those villages were called "Miluk-gwsiya."[15] Annie's grandmother was known as "Miluk-w'mae," which meant "Miluk-Person." Names of people were often based on where they were from. She could have had the same name, however, had she come from South Slough because the villages there were also Miluk-speaking. Her modern name was Susan, with no surname.[16]

It was considered a matter of prestige to seek one's wife from a distance.[17] Annie's grandmother, evidently a person of exotic beauty, was able to confer such prestige upon Minkws. Her hair was said to have been dark brown and slightly wavy. The majority of Indians in the Northwest had straight black hair, but occasionally, as in Susan's case, one was born with wavy brown hair. Annie's mother inherited that trait.[18]

Annie's grandfather had grown up on the bay before the first of the Moving People had come through. When Annie was young she learned from him certain incidents in the history of his people. One is the story he told of the time "the water got high."[19] This story, well known to most of the Coos, illustrates the significance of the quasi-historical narratives and tales that formed a part of their literature.

According to the story, there had evidently been a long, continuous, light rain. At a certain time during this unremarkable rain the ocean and all the waters rose quite rapidly and unaccountably. All the villages were near the water's edge, and as the water rose, the villages were flooded. Everyone who could get into a canoe did so. Those who did not soon drowned.

When Minkws was a young man he met an elderly woman who had been one of the survivors of that flood. She had been just a girl at the time and had been hung up in a tree by the rising waters. When the water receded she tried to get down, but she fell. Minkws said that the resulting injury gave her a humped back for the rest of her life.

Geologists tell us that after about the year 1400, several catastrophic earthquakes and tsunamis occurred along the northwest coast.[20] This narrative most probably described a tsunami sometime between 1750 and 1780.[21] Minkws was able to pass along, through his granddaughter Annie, a secondhand account of it. When she was a child, Annie became a repository of a large body of such cultural and historical information.

Almost everywhere along the shore and up the various inlets were small villages of perhaps ten to one hundred persons. Within each village the males were closely related, either as descendants or as siblings of the headman. The wives of all but the very lowest classes were from other villages, and all the daughters married out. The social and economic ties among these settlements were cemented through marriage and blood relationships. All of politics began and ended with marriage and lineal descent.

According to Annie (and she may have been exaggerating here), illegitimate conception was not a problem within the villages. She said that abortion was unknown and unnecessary.[22] The reasons behind such rigorous adherence to the sexual mores of the community were related to the strict sanctions imposed for any violation.

Annie told of an incident that had occurred only a few years before the arrival of the white settlers. A young couple had been caught in the act of "being together"—"spooning" was the word Annie used to describe it. Both were unmarried, and his parents were well-off. All of the people of the Lower Hanis villages assembled to watch while a post was driven into the mud flats far out at the water's edge during low tide. The unfortunate couple was bound securely to the post.[23] The six hours that it took for the tide to come in and drown the couple provided ample time for the community to reflect on the seriousness of the matter. One can only imagine the profound effect this had on community morals. The incident might have been witnessed, from the village of Intesedge, by Annie's mother before she was married.

Marriages were usually negotiated by the parents, and a bride-price was paid by the family of the groom to the family of the bride.[24] The higher the price, the more prestige was attached to the marriage. Such marriages usually took place about a year after first menses. When Annie's mother was of age she was betrothed in such a negotiated marriage to the headman of the Coos River village of Takimiya. Takimiya may have been a satellite of Intesedge or perhaps of one of the other Lower Hanis villages.

Each of the Lower Hanis villages had its own headman, and each had satellite villages farther up the bay or on Coos River. Some of these satellite villages were seasonal, with grass or brush houses, but others were occupied year-round with wooden dugout houses. According to Annie, the people of the village of Intesedge liked living at their upriver villages and tended to stay in them year-round.²⁵ Takimiya was probably one of the year-round upriver villages.

Takimiya held enormous economic importance because it was situated at the first site on Coos River where salmon weirs could be placed from bank to bank. The salmon weir would reach from Takimiya several hundred feet across the river, with only a gap large enough for a canoe to pass. The salmon were thus easily caught in unlimited numbers during the early fall runs. After the men had caught as many salmon as they needed, they would remove the weir.²⁶ Annie's niece Lottie Evanoff remembered that her father, Daloose, "went up to that place every summer, and since he was a chief would merely look on as his men were catching salmon there."²⁷ Annie's mother had three children by the headman of the village of Takimiya: two girls, whose modern names were Nellie and Fannie, and a third child whose name has not come down to us.²⁸

In October 1850, a two-masted brig entered Coos Bay. The *Kate Heath* had been chartered to deliver seventy-five immigrants from San Francisco to the Umpqua River. They had suffered an extraordinarily grueling voyage, having been blown by storms more than six hundred miles offshore before approaching what they thought was the Umpqua but was in fact Coos Bay.²⁹ This ship, the first to have crossed the Coos Bay bar, had four men on each oar, according to Lottie Evanoff. She said, "They rowed into Coos Bay, three oars on each side." After that, she said, "the Indians nicknamed the Whites sometimes 'Longpaddles.'"³⁰

Men from the Upper Hanis villages lay in ambush at a marsh island to destroy the ship and its passengers. Lottie described the incident, mentioning the role of her paternal uncle "Tyee Jim": "But my Uncle Jim rushed from Empire and asked them, 'Where is your cannon? Where is your gun? It ain't only here. Lots of these kinds of people all over the country. We can't kill them all.' So the Upper Hanis reluctantly stopped. They had planned the attack with bows only.

The Coos River Hanis came downstream with elkmeat to trade to those schooner Whites."[31]

A few days after the *Kate Heath* was rowed into Coos Bay, Patrick Flanagan, who had arrived at the Umpqua River two months earlier on board the *Samuel Roberts*, heard that a ship had entered Coos Bay by mistake. Out of curiosity he went down to see it. He followed the beach route, then crossed the sand dunes to the head of tide at North Slough. When he came down North Slough in a canoe, the ducks were so thick on the water and so tame that they merely parted for the canoe to paddle by.

Patrick's son, J. W. Flanagan, told the story as it was related to him. He said that the *Kate Heath* had been anchored at the north bend of the bay, at the point where the highway bridge today stands. "The Indians were paddling a circle around the boat while the crew stood with guns at the bulwarks to keep them off." As Flanagan's canoe came close to the ship, the captain waved it away. Flanagan had a dark beard, and when he stood up in the canoe the skipper exclaimed, "My God, a white man!" According to J. W. Flanagan, "Father went aboard the ship, sailed her down the bay, out over the bar and up the coast to the Umpqua."[32]

The ship continued north to the Umpqua, where five of its crew drowned while crossing the bar. Some of its passengers, after looking over the Lower Umpqua, later returned to Coos Bay, where they established themselves.[33] Patrick and his brother James were among them. Years later they both became acquainted with Annie.

The next ship in the Coos Bay area was the *Captain Lincoln*, a three-masted schooner, on January 3, 1852. An army resupply ship, the *Captain Lincoln* could not get into Port Orford because of a storm and was trying to reach the Umpqua. It crashed on the north spit of Coos Bay during the night, with no loss of life or cargo. The soldiers and crew camped in the sandhills until May before hiking south to Port Orford.

Indians from villages all along the bay and up Coos
River visited the shipwreck site while the soldiers remained
camped there. Annie's mother may have seen it. Annie's
grandfather, Minkws, was certainly involved. The Indians
were generous in providing fresh fish and game as well as
labor to the castaways, who in turn were quite generous in
paying with trade goods.

The headman from the village of Hanisich did most of
the organizing and negotiating with the whites. He was
known to the whites as "Hannas," from the name of his
village. He may have been the father of Daloose. The whites
considered him to be the "Chief" of all the Coos Indians.

Relations between the castaways and the Indians were
fine except for one unpleasant incident: an Indian stole a
revolver. He was caught by the soldiers and sentenced to
twenty-five lashes with a rawhide. According to Henry H.
Baldwin, one of the soldiers, "The lash was applied heavy
and cutting, the culprit bearing it with Spartan indifference."
The Indians of the area were spectators. This was the only
encounter in which the whites found any fault with the
natives. Baldwin added wryly, "That was the first religious
teaching in Coos county for we taught them the eighth
commandment."[34]

On May 5, 1852, the schooner *Nassau* sailed into Coos
Bay from the Umpqua to pick up the cargo from the *Captain
Lincoln*. The *Nassau* has officially been listed as the first
ship to enter Coos Bay—the experiences of the *Kate Heath*
having evidently been forgotten. Virtually all of the cargo
from the *Captain Lincoln* was delivered by the *Nassau* to
Port Orford on May 20.[35]

The Indians on the bay observed the highly organized
activity of the soldiers and the unimaginable material wealth
represented by the ship and its cargo. The result was a
respect for the whites and an understanding of the benefits
that could accrue as long as good relations were maintained.
The experience of the wreck of the *Captain Lincoln* may

help explain why the Indians of Coos Bay were at peace with their white neighbors during the unfortunate Rogue River War of 1855 and 1856.

Whites intent on permanent settlement did not arrive at Coos Bay until May 1853. They had come from the gold diggings at Jacksonville, two hundred miles to the southeast, and had organized themselves as the Coos Bay Commercial Company. They were interested in land, not in beaver hides, and they were willing to be as conciliatory with the Indians as they had to be to get it.

William H. Harris, who led the Coos Bay Commercial Company into the area, later noted, "These Indians were very friendly, and be it remembered that they soon became very much attached to the white man, and during the Indian war, which soon broke out at Rogue river, commonly known as the Indian war of 1855 and 1856, the Coos bay natives were true to their newly acquired neighbors."[36] Of the nineteen men in the original Coos Bay Commercial Company, three were married to white women, who came to the area later.[37] Many of the rest married into the Indian villages. After Coos County was organized, some of the Indian-white marriages were formalized in the official records of the county clerk. Whether or not a marriage was officially recorded would become a matter of immense importance later on.

The Indians saw the advantage of marrying their daughters into these Moving People, not least because of the technologically advanced goods obtainable through them.[38] Like marriages in general, some of these arrangements were very good for both parties and some were not. As wives and mothers, Indian women very soon became an integral and influential part of the local scene, a role that was never available to the Indian men.

As noted earlier, the Indians of Coos Bay were exogamous. This custom had two major benefits, one genetic and one political. Genetically, it ensured against inbreeding and,

in that regard, evidently paid off very well. As Captain
Harris of the Coos Bay Commercial Company noted, "The
pioneers found that, physically, the natives were a fine
robust, and healthy looking people." The Indian agent J. L.
Parrish noted in his census of July 1854, "They seem to be
free from disease, with the exception of sore eyes, which is
confined exclusively to the women, and the venereal which
has been recently introduced among them by their white
neighbors."[39] Politically, exogamy provided close family ties
with other villages, ensuring good trading partners and economic cooperation. The custom also made it fairly easy for
the whites to buy a wife, though not always with honorable
intentions. In a diary entry Corporal Royal A. Bensell, a
soldier stationed later at Siletz, made the following observation about this practice: "By the way, these Indians, all (of)
them, sell their women to any persons wishing to purchase.
Prices according 'to age and appearance,' some $5 and
others $50, and the whole tribe or tribes will see that the
bargain is sustained. Should the Squaw 'vamoose' the tribes
will refund the money. Some of the Boys invest in this rather
doubtful traffic."[40]

Among the men of the Coos Bay Commercial
Company who took Indian wives was Henry Miller, also
known as "Fortnight Miller" or "Yankee Miller," who settled
at first on Coos River near the village of Takimiya.[41] He
married the sister of Annie's mother's first husband, the
headman of the village. Miller named his wife Mary, a very
common name given to the Indian women by the whites.
The marriage was made "legal" in 1865, after U.S. Army
troops visited the area.[42] The army had removed to the
reservation at Yachats some Indian women whose marriages
to their white partners were not "legal," and as a result at
least eight Indian-white marriages were solemnized and
recorded with the county clerk around that time.

Another Indian woman with the name "Mary" was
Annie's maternal aunt, from the village of Intesedge. She

married another Henry Miller on Coos River. This Henry
Miller was called "Dutch Henry" to distinguish him from
"Yankee Miller." Dutch Henry and Mary later lived many
years on what came to be known as Haynes Slough. Annie
lived with them there for several years, and her grandmother,
who by then was very old, died there.

The men of the Coos Bay Commercial Company
traded and negotiated to get control of areas they thought
would make good sites for farms, mills, towns, or coal
mines. In nearly every case these were exactly the same
sites that the Indians had been using as their villages for
centuries. Some of these village sites were vacant because
of the previous epidemics, but many were occupied.

Among the villages that were occupied was the string
of settlements known collectively as Lower Hanis.[43] William
H. Harris filed his Donation Land Claim in 1853 for the
entire site of these Lower Hanis villages, an area that looked
to be the best place for a wharf. His was the first land claim
in Coos County.[44] He worked out the arrangements with the
inhabitants, some of whom would stay and some of whom
would have to move to locations less desired by the whites.
Those who lived at the village of Intesedge had to move
because that was exactly where Henry H. Luse later put his
sawmill.

Mouth of Miner Creek at the ocean, three-fourths of a mile southwest of the entrance to Coos Bay. This creek was named for Annie's biological father, James Miner. He mined for gold here in the 1850s. Photo by the author.

2

The War

The nineteen men of the Coos Bay Commercial Company had arrived in the region in May 1853. In July word got out that two mixed-blood French-Canadians had found gold on the beach at Whiskey Run, about ten miles south of the Coos Bay bar. Those few white settlers who were already on the coast and several hundred others from outside the area converged on Whiskey Run for what turned out to be a modest gold rush. Like gold rushes elsewhere, this one proved disastrous for the native population.

The first of the disasters occurred just six months after the gold rush began. On January 29, 1854, about forty of the miners from Whiskey Run murdered at least sixteen of the Miluk-speaking Lower Coquille Indians at the mouth of that river.[1] As a result of the massacre, a number of Lower

Coquille refugees ended up living with their relatives at South Slough.[2]

The headmen of the Coos villages understood perfectly the ramifications of the incident. Some of them thought they should take action against the whites, who on Coos Bay were in the minority. Other headmen knew that to take such action would, in the end, be suicidal. Eventually the controversy reached the village of Takimiya.

Annie's mother's husband was, as stated earlier, the headman at Takimiya. We know very little about him, and even his name is lost to us. Annie had heard and remembered the names of his two elk dogs, however, and that gives us a clue to his interests. The Coos River Hanis were noted for supplying dried elk meat for trade or sale to other villages and to the whites. They were the ones who had taken dried elk meat to trade to the immigrants on board the *Kate Heath* in October 1850.[3] Each bale of meat weighed about one hundred pounds. Frank Drew* said, "It would be as heavy as one of those Indians would lift, and they were pretty stout fellows!"[4]

The names of the two elk dogs were Hanis words meaning "White Nose Stripe" and "Kinky Hair." Annie said that when hunting, a man would ideally have four dogs for driving the elk.[5] Coquille Thompson** described the elk-hunting method. He said that the dogs would grab an elk high on the thighs and hold on while the elk wheeled around. That would give the hunter time to put several arrows into the animal. As soon as the elk fell, the dogs

---

* Frank Drew, a little younger than Annie, was a stepson of Daloose Jackson's brother Cammon. Drew became an ethnologic informant to a number of anthropologists over a period of about thirty-five years.
** Coquille Thompson, several years older than Annie, was the son of the headman of a village of the upper Coquille Athapaskans. He was the only significant ethnologic and linguistic informant of the Upper Coquille people. See appendix 2.

would bite it on the throat, killing it. Those purebred Indian elk dogs would go only for elk and did not bother with deer.[6]

According to Thompson, the Miluk-speaking people at the mouth of the Coquille, the people of Annie's grandmother, were expert at breeding and training the elk dogs. The dogs were said to be black and white and very big. Thompson said that his own father had bought two of them, paying a string of dentalium—"as long as my arm"—valued at about one hundred dollars.[7]

Annie's mother's husband did not want to make friends with the white people. According to his granddaughter Lottie, he was shot and killed by an Indian who disagreed with these policies. Lottie added that her mother, Annie's half-sister Fannie, was a baby in his arms at the time he was shot "at his house on Coos River." She added, "They made his younger brother chief of the Coos River Hanis."[8]

Lottie then told the story of how the younger brother, now chief, went to Camas Valley with a few boys. On their way back they were all murdered. She said that after this incident, the whites said they no longer needed a chief for the Coos River Hanis. The chief at Lower Hanis was enough because "they were all Hanis anyway."[9]

According to Lottie, the headman of the village of Upper Hanis, at the present site of North Bend, was the last headman who wanted to kill off the white people. The others favored getting along with the whites. Lottie said that the Upper Hanis headman was having the chiefs of the other villages killed. Her paternal grandfather, Daloose's father, was the headman at Hanisich, and "he got murdered." Daloose's brother Jim asked the whites if it was all right to kill the Upper Hanis headman, "so they did," Lottie added succinctly.[10] That ended resistance to the whites on Coos Bay.

The Indians at South Slough did not speak Hanis but spoke Miluk, a completely different but related language. Lottie said that the South Slough chief went up to the Umpqua River on business and the Umpqua killed him.

Then the whites said, "What, no South Slough chief?" "So," she said, "they made Old Taylor the South Slough chief." He evidently did not work out, so they appointed another South Slough chief. He was the last one, according to Lottie.[11] After that, the whites were satisfied to deal only with the Lower Hanis chief, who by then was Annie's future brother-in-law, Daloose Jackson.

On July 31, 1854, Congress approved the Indian Appropriations Act. This gave Joel Palmer, the superintendent of Indian affairs for Oregon, the authority to conclude treaties with the Indians.[12] For those Indians who were living on the western slope of the Coast Range the government proposed to set aside a reservation, the Coast Reservation, about 120 miles long and 20 miles wide, comprising approximately one million acres, along the central Oregon Coast.

Very few whites were in this area, which had no known gold and of which very little was suitable for agriculture. The idea was that the Indians who already lived there would not have to move. Of the coastal Indians, only those in Coos, Curry, and western Douglas Counties would be removed from their homelands. Most of them would end up in areas that were not unlike what they were used to. Palmer negotiated the treaty with the understanding that he was authorized to do so and that it would ultimately be ratified by Congress.

During the summer of 1855 Palmer met in conference with the chiefs, headmen, and delegates from virtually every group of Indians along the Oregon Coast. The treaty was explained to the Indians in the Chinook jargon, the trade language of the Hudson's Bay Company. At that time none of the Coos Indians could speak either the jargon or English.

According to Frank Drew, however, one white man could speak Hanis almost like a native. The Indians called him "Hanis Atli's," which meant "Hanis Language." One of the Coos who knew a little jargon said to Hanis Atli's,

"Mayga wa wa, Tom" ("You talk, Tom").[13] And so it was Tom "Hanis Atli's," a white man living among the Coos River Hanis, who explained to them what Palmer was proposing.

On August 17, 1855, the chiefs, headmen, and delegates from nearly all the bands, villages, and individual settlements on the bay agreed to the terms of the treaty. Fifty-two of these dignitaries, including Daloose Jackson, signed their "X" to the document. On August 23 the agreement was concluded with the Lower Coquille Indians. By September 8 the chiefs, headmen, and delegates of virtually all the Indians on the Oregon Coast had agreed to the treaty.[14] Unfortunately, the treaty was never ratified by Congress.

The Indian War in the Rogue River Valley had expanded to the Curry County coast. Known as the "War of 1855 and 1856," it caused "much alarm" at Coos Bay. Fifteen volunteers went down to Gold Beach to fight, William Harris having been elected captain.[15] They returned after a few days, went to the various villages and settlements on Coos Bay, and forcibly encouraged the Indians to gather at a sandspit about a mile below Empire. As the villages were emptied, the dugout houses were burned along with the baskets, canoes, and other property.

Even with all the harsh treatment, many of the Indians of the Coos country were still very friendly with the whites. Mrs. William Waters told, many years later, about the attitude of her maternal uncle Steven, an Upper Hanis headman who had signed the treaty: "My uncle he like White people. He didn't care what they did. Burn his baskets and his Indian house but he still loves White people. He was a good Indian. He never drink. That was the only Indian who didn't drink. That was 'cause he was old-fashioned, I guess."[16]

While the Indians were at the sandspit below Empire they were given names by the volunteers. Daloose was given the name Jackson and was thereafter known as Daloose Jackson. Stephen, Dick, Taylor, Bob, John, George, Charley,

Pete, Joe, Sam, Johnson, Jack, and Jim Buchanan were among the other names that were given and that were retained. The Indians were able to accept the names given to them by the whites because these were nicknames. Most people were known either by their place of origin or by a current nickname.[17]

According to Lottie, the volunteers ran out of names, and for fun they gave one man the name of "Kiss-My-Arse." He thought that was his real name until later whites disillusioned him.[18] Although such antics were no doubt amusing to the whites, the fun was probably lost on the Indians. The attitude of the whites was summed up by Agnes Sengstacken, the daughter of one of the first white women on the bay, who merely commented, "Evidently Indians have no sense of humor."[19] Their stoic reaction to the white man's practical jokes could give that false impression.

It was probably during this time that the white men gave Annie's mother the old-fashioned pioneer name "Matilda."[20] She carried that name through the rest of her life, and she gave it to Annie as a middle name.

A fort at the north spit of the Umpqua River was being built as a southern gateway to the new Coast Reservation. It would be called Fort Umpqua, and while it was under construction, most of the Indians of the Coos Bay area were moved to the north spit of Coos Bay. There they remained until the summer of 1857, when they were moved twenty miles up the coast to Winchester Bay.

On the north spit of Coos Bay and at Winchester Bay the Indians could pretty well come and go as they wanted. The camp population kept getting smaller, however, because so many of them were going back to their original homes.[21] Many had never left their homes in the first place, and many others were living near their white in-laws at various locations. It seems that E. P. Drew, the agent at the Umpqua Subagency, did not have a lot of control over his wards.

Meanwhile, the wooden buildings at the army fort at Port Orford had been taken down and shipped to the Umpqua River, where they were rebuilt on the north spit of that river. When the new fort was ready the Indians from Coos Bay were moved in, along with the Indians of the Lower Umpqua. At peak population, almost seven hundred Coos and Lower Umpqua Indians lived there. The Siuslaw to the north did not have to move because their homeland was inside the boundaries of the new Coast Reservation.

Aside from the diseases that neither the whites nor the Indians could control, life was probably not too bad at Fort Umpqua. The government had a doctor there, the kids could go to school, and a man baked bread every day, rationing it to the Indians.[22] When the Indians built their fires in the morning at the fort, the smoke would come up all along the Umpqua River, like fog.[23] The soldiers built a dance floor, and the few whites who lived in the area would attend the dances, as would some of the Indians.[24]

At Fort Umpqua whites were always willing to sell or trade whiskey to the Indians. Annie's half-sister Fannie remembered an Umpqua Indian who would get drunk and walk up and down the beach saying, in the Lower Umpqua dialect, "I'm not whiskeyed up!" Another Umpqua Indian, when drunk, would carry a butcher knife and say that he was going to kill the "Whiteman-driven-out-ones." By this he meant all the Indians who had been moved there by the whites.[25]

During the time at Fort Umpqua, infectious diseases took a toll. Tuberculosis was particularly devastating. Successful treatment was beyond the power of Dr. John Milhau, who was stationed there, and was also beyond the power of the Indian shamans. In the case of the shamans, whenever one of their patients died of the disease, the relatives of the deceased would kill the shaman, as well as anyone else suspected of having anything to do with the death. Dr.

Milhau is said to have complained, "Between the disease and the means taken to prevent it a large number have been buried."[26]

Also among the diseases was smallpox, which could be epidemic where an unimmunized population was living in close quarters. The Indians had great faith in the beneficial effects of cold water as a general cure, but this proved fatal in the case of smallpox and some of the other infectious diseases. The standard Indian remedy was to work up a good sweat in the sweathouse and then rush into the cold water of the ocean or the river.[27] Pneumonia and a quick death very often followed.

Matilda now had a new husband, an Umpqua, who got smallpox at that time. As the story goes, he actually died and then came back to life two days later. His relatives and wives were waiting for other relatives to come from Siltcoos for the funeral, but by the time they arrived, he was up and alive again. According to Lottie he had six wives, including Matilda. They were all crying, and he said, "What are you women crying about anyway?" He got stronger every day as they took him outside to give him fresh air.

He had become so lousy, however, that the lice could be scraped off with a knife. When his wives asked how he got that way, he explained that while he was dead, he came to some old people who gave him lice to eat. The old people sent him back. They said: "You are a dead man. We don't want you." His wives changed his clothes, and one of them said, "You got so lousy, you'd better eat one." So he ate one, and afterward there were no more lice. He was the only person that Lottie had heard of who had come to life after having died from smallpox. It was said that he was "dead" for two nights, but he lived to be an old man.[28]

Some of his other wives were evidently jealous of Matilda's greater favor with him. According to Annie, they told lies about Matilda. Listening to the lies, he became jealous and shot Annie's mother with a shotgun. When she recovered from the wound, she left him and went back to Coos Bay.[29]

According to Annie, an Indian wife could divorce her husband by leaving their children with him. In effect, she had paid for herself. If she wanted another man then, she could have him. That was the arrangement for the divorce of Matilda from her Umpqua husband. She left her three Umpqua children with her husband, and nothing is known of their subsequent fate.

During the summer of 1857, most of the Coos Indians were moved from the north spit of Coos Bay twenty miles up the beach to the new Fort Umpqua. During that same summer, Coos Bay got its first industry. Two steam-powered sawmills were set up, one at the old Lower Hanis village site of Intesedge and the other at the old Upper Hanis site of Kolokaytch.[30] The first mill, established by Henry Luse, dominated the new town of Empire for the next twenty-five years. The second, established by Asa Simpson and his sons, was the major influence in the town that later became North Bend. Many of the employees at both sawmills were Indians.[31]

There was a terrible dichotomy in many of the whites' attitudes toward the Indians at that time. The white youths were certainly influenced by the fear and loathing felt by many of the adults. On the one hand, Indian men were valued and respected employees. On the other hand, Indians were being moved about with no legal rights and were considered by some of the whites to be less than human. Such attitudes were bound to have terrible consequences.

Some of those same white men who considered the Indians to be less than human had no compunction about cohabitation with Indian women. Marriages were instituted quite differently among the Indians than among the whites. Certain white men took advantage of that fact and would "purchase" wives just as men paid for prostitutes. For the Indians, the purchase constituted marriage. For these white men, the purchase carried no obligation. Some of the early pioneers abandoned their Indian families when white women became available for marriage later on.

The white children and grandchildren of those pioneers often never knew about their Indian half-brothers and half-sisters, even though some bore the names of their fathers and lived in the same community. Grandchildren almost never knew all of what their grandfathers had done when young. One story that has passed underground in Coos County since 1858 illustrates this point.

The story tells of a "tar and feathering," perhaps the first in the county.[32] Because the moral lesson to be gained is so ambiguous, because the people involved were so well-known at the time, and because the details of the incident were so shocking, it is one of those stories perhaps best forgotten. In fact it has almost been forgotten. It is, however, a story that involves a family into which Annie later married.

Bill and Cap were two eighteen-year-old white boys living in Empire in 1858. Bill, the son of a prominent businessman, was living with a young South Slough Indian woman named Sally. Cap, who did not have a girl, asked Bill if he could get him one. Bill's girlfriend, perhaps innocently, said that she knew a girl at South Slough. Fortified with whiskey, Bill and Cap stole two horses belonging to Daloose Jackson, and the three of them rode seven or eight miles to where a twelve-year-old girl was living at a place belonging to a frontiersman named Charlie Metcalf. Evidently no one else was there at the time.

When Cap attempted intercourse with the girl, he found that her vagina was too small. In their depraved drunkenness, the two boys decided they could enlarge it by cutting it with a pocketknife. One held her while the other attempted the mutilation. The girl broke loose and fought them as best she could. She was screaming and bleeding all over the room. Her paternal uncle heard the screams and came to help, but Bill knocked him out with a new ax handle. The girl escaped, running naked and bleeding to neighbors, and word of the incident spread quickly for miles. Sally, meanwhile, hid in the brush.

The two youths were immediately caught by what could be described as a lynch mob. They were taken back to Empire, the county seat at the time. Since the law at Empire had never brought a case against a white who had violated the rights of an Indian, the outraged citizens decided that it was time to take the law into their own hands. They immediately built a fire in front of the Pioneer Hotel and heated a pot of tar.

Cap was first. He was stripped, his head was shaved, and warm tar was painted over his entire body. Someone produced a sack full of chicken feathers, which were unceremoniously dumped over his head. Daloose Jackson, who was there, said afterward, "He looked like an owl."

Bill was next. The barber had just finished shaving one side of his head when his sister pushed her way through the crowd and threw her arms around his neck, sobbing and pleading. She carried on to such an extent that the crowd relented and turned him loose. He was, after all, the son of a prominent businessman. His girlfriend, Sally, would have been next, but they could not find her.

The mob then took Cap, tarred and feathered, across the bay in a rowboat and dumped him off on the north spit. He managed to walk from there to a place called Hennesy's, where old Hennesy got the feathers off of him and gave him some clothes. Later, Hennesy secretly placed Cap on a schooner bound for San Francisco. No one ever heard of him again.

The subsequent history of the other participants in this bizarre event is interesting and noteworthy. The following year Bill's sister married a prominent citizen. Bill's girlfriend, Sally, gave birth to a boy, who died. She and Bill stayed together, and Bill became proficient in the Miluk language, the only white man ever to do so. They had another boy, whom they named Jasper. He was raised at South Slough, and when he came of age he married a local mixed-blood girl. He lived into his eighties.[33]

Sally died, and Bill married a white woman. He had a large family with her, became a noted tugboat captain, among other things, and lived into his nineties. He was highly respected, and by the time of his old age the depraved incident from his youth had been obscured or forgotten.

What happened to the twelve-year-old victim? According to Lottie, she later married Charlie Metcalf, with whom she had six sons.[34] The marriage records at the Coos County Courthouse reflect that Charlie Metcalf married Susan, an Indian woman, in 1864. If this was the same girl, she would have been eighteen years old by that time. One of the sons of Charlie Metcalf and Susan was Eli, to whom Annie was married from 1898 to 1910.

The true significance of this incident is that not the law but the white citizens themselves put a stop to the depredations that had become so common against the Indians at the time. This turned out to be the last outrage against the Indians at Coos Bay for at least a generation.

When Annie's mother, Matilda, moved back to Coos Bay from Fort Umpqua, an Englishman named James Miner was working in a stave mill. The mill was at a small community called Centerville, halfway between the north bend of the bay and the Coos River delta to the south and directly across the bay from the Indian village of Willanch. The Centerville Saloon was just below the hill facing the bay. In addition to working in the mill, Miner was the bartender here.[35]

James Miner at one time attempted to find gold in the small creek that runs through Bassendorf Beach, the sandy beach immediately to the south of the Coos Bay bar. That creek, to this day, is shown on the maps as Miner Creek. According to Lottie, it was named for James Miner, who had taken up the place and "washed black sand" there.[36]

How James Miner came to know that Matilda was available is not known. He may have been acquainted with her before she went north to the Umpqua River. In any case, they moved in together at Willanch. Miner worked six days a week at the stave mill, as well as working at the saloon. He was home only on Sundays, when he would row across the bay to Willanch. But even with these frequent separations, Matilda soon became pregnant again.

According to Annie, her mother suffered with a very hard delivery. She gave birth to twins, one of whom was allowed to die. The surviving twin was Annie Matilda Miner.[37] When James Miner came home the following Sunday, no one thought to tell him that there had been twins. Perhaps no one could speak English well enough to convey such information. Someone else later told him that one of the babies had died. According to Annie, when he found out, he was angry that he had not been told earlier. Matilda was hurt that her common-law husband was scolding her about it, since she herself had almost died as a result of the hard delivery. Regardless, larger events were shaping their lives at this time.

The government had decided to close the Umpqua Subagency at Fort Umpqua and to move all of the Coos and Lower Umpqua Indians to Yachats, about fifty miles up the coast. This time the army was serious, and soldiers went around the bay forcefully removing all of the Indians who were still living there or who had returned from Fort Umpqua. The only ones who could stay were women who were legally married to white men and these couples' children. The army took Minkws and his wife, as well as Matilda's daughters Nellie and Fannie.

The Coos County Courthouse contains records of several Indian-white marriages during 1860. Matilda probably could have legally married James, and then she and her baby, Annie, could have stayed. James Miner offered to take the baby and let his sister raise her, but nearly all of Matilda's

family and friends had gone north. Matilda may also not
have been getting along very well with James at that time.
In any case, she decided to take Annie and go north after
the rest of her people. When James Miner came home to
Willanch the following Sunday, no one was there.[38]

A part of the beach route between Coos Bay and Yachats, fifty-five miles of sand beach fronting one of the world's longest stretches of coastal sand dunes. This was the highway that connected the peoples who spoke the several Oregon Coastal Penutian languages. Coos Head and Cape Arago are in distance. Aerial photo by the author.

Heceta Head and Sea Lion Point. This photograph shows "The Big Hill," over which travelers had to pass between the Siuslaw, Umpqua, and Coos Rivers to the south and the Alsea River to the north. Aerial photo by the author.

3

Annie's First Years

The sandy beach fronting the Oregon dunes is fifty miles long.* It takes two days to walk it. It had been used as a highway for people going up and down the coast for a thousand or two thousand years or more. The southern end is the entrance to Coos Bay, and the people

---

* The Oregon Department of Geology and Mineral Industries says: "The largest strip of dunes along the Oregon Coast extends about . . . 55 miles. It is divided into three segments by the Siuslaw and Umpqua Rivers." The beach route followed the northern 46 miles of the continuous sandy beach. It is 17 miles from the beginning of the beach route to the Umpqua River; 23 miles more to the Siuslaw River; 6 miles from the Siuslaw River to the end of the dunes at Sea Lion Point; and 14 miles from Sea Lion Point to Yachats, about half of which is sandy beach and half rocky headland. It is thus a total of about 60 miles along the beach, Coos Bay to Yachats. The modern highway distance is 78 miles.

living there were known to the people farther north as
Kukoos, or Southerners.[1]

As one heads north, two rivers and several creeks cross
this sandy beach, but otherwise there are no impediments
to travel until one reaches the basalt outcroppings known as
Sea Lion Point and Heceta Head. For centuries the sandy
highway along the ocean front linked the peoples who lived
on the tidewater stretches of the Coos, the Umpqua, and
the Siuslaw Rivers and the several smaller creeks and lakes
of the area. There was evidently considerable trade and
intermarriage among these peoples, whose cultures were
remarkably similar to one another.

From the northern end of the sandy beach it was
fourteen more miles across Heceta Head and Cape Perpetua
to Yachats, the reservation where the Coos and the Lower
Umpqua Indians were moved by the U.S. army. With pack
animals it took another day and a half to get there. North
of these rocky headlands were the Alsea peoples, whose
culture was intermediate between that of the Tillamook to
the north and the Siuslaw to the south.

The four- or five-day walk from Coos Bay to Yachats
was the longest walk the Indians of Coos Bay ever took
because most of them were never able to come back. The
birth rate was low and the death rate was high, and the
population declined by 50 percent during the fifteen years
the Indians spent at Yachats. Matilda and her daughters,
however, were survivors.

It is not known in whose company Matilda and her
baby, Annie, traveled up the coast. From time to time the
army escorted small groups of stragglers to Yachats. Matilda
and Annie may have been with such a group. A fairly large
number of Indians remained at Coos Bay at that time,
scattered around the bay and up the sloughs and rivers.
Some had never been rounded up in the first place, and
others had returned to Coos Bay from Fort Umpqua.

All of them were familiar with the beach route. Walking on the beach is easy in the wet, hard sand at low tide. At high tide, however, one has to walk in the soft sand nearer the seawall, making for very hard going indeed. The traveler takes one step forward and a half step back, it seems, while the wind never stops blowing.

This was the third time Matilda had traveled the route between Coos Bay and Fort Umpqua: once when she had gone to join her Umpqua husband and his other wives; once when she had returned to Willanch after leaving this husband; and this time, which was harder because she was carrying and nursing her new baby, Annie.

By midday Matilda and Annie could have rested awhile at Tenmile Creek. At low tide they could cross waist deep in the cold water. By dark they should have reached Winchester Bay near the southern bank of the mouth of the Umpqua River. They may have camped there.

The next day they moved on up the beach, and by noon they should have been at the Siltcoos River. This was the southern boundary of the Coast Reservation and the beginning of the homeland of the Siuslaw Indians. It was halfway between the mouths of the Siuslaw and the Umpqua Rivers. If they had camped at Fort Umpqua the night before, they could have gotten to the Siuslaw by evening. They were probably ferried across the river by old Jean Gagnier, formerly of the Hudson's Bay Company. Gagnier, his Lower Umpqua wife, and their son John had moved to the Siuslaw after the Hudson's Bay Company ceased operating its post at Elkton in 1852. Jean had become the principal spokesman of the Siuslaw. Later his son John, who also married a Lower Umpqua woman, was considered by some to be "chief of the Siuslaw Indians," many of whom were still living in their traditional dugout houses.[2] However, by then most of them had frame houses "weatherboarded with clapboards."[3] Probably about 130 Siuslaw Indians lived on the river at that time.

The next regular camping place was at Lily Lake, at the northern end of the sand dunes. This lake is at the foot of "The Big Hill," the basalt mountain that includes Sea Lion Point and Heceta Head. The easy part of the trip was behind them. The steep and dangerous trail now wound for about three miles along the cliff, through canyons and draws, over rotten logs, and around almost vertical hillsides. At some places a traveler could have fallen five hundred feet or more onto the rocks or into the surf below. One suspects that the indescribable beauty of the place was lost on Matilda, concerned as she was for both herself and Annie.

After crossing "The Big Hill," the group traveled about eight miles up a sandy beach before reaching Cape Perpetua, the next basaltic outcrop. They would, no doubt, have camped at one of the several creeks along that stretch. The last day of the journey to Yachats took them over and around Cape Perpetua. There were two trails, an upper and a lower. The whites generally preferred the upper trail, which was passable with pack animals and horses. The Indians liked the lower one, which was shorter and did not require as much climbing. The lower trail could be used only at low tide, but it had been traveled for hundreds of years by the Alsea and the Siuslaw Indians.[4]

The group probably reached Yachats by around noon the next day, making the journey of about sixty miles from Coos Bay to Yachats in four and one-half days. The trip would have been longer, of course, if they had stayed over at Winchester Bay, Fort Umpqua, or Siuslaw—which they may have done. It was slow going, but the rocky headlands made for slow going. On the faster parts of the trail were built-in delays for crossing rivers, waiting for tides, and stopping so that the elderly and the nursing mothers could rest. The trip would no doubt have been less stressful had it not been taken with an army escort.

When Matilda arrived at Yachats, 279 newly arrived Indians were already living there.[5] These included the bulk of the surviving Coos and Lower Umpqua Indians, as well as a few of the Lower Coquille. The location was fine. There were shellfish on the rocks, fish in the sea, and a salmon run on the Yachats River. Yet several years would pass before the location was developed enough to adequately support a concentrated population of 279. In the meantime there were many hardships.

Yachats Prairie is a flat bench that rises twenty or thirty feet above sea level and slopes toward the ocean. It is about a quarter-mile wide and extends from the mouth of the Yachats River north for a couple miles. Although the area was not suitable for the purpose, the government intended that it be turned into agricultural land.

Yachats had been the site of an Alsea settlement, but none of the Alsea were living there at the time the Coos and Lower Umpqua arrived. Nearly all of the Alsea at Yachats had succumbed to smallpox, which had been introduced at the Columbia in 1853 by ships from San Francisco. The Alsea houses, like the houses of the people to the north and south of them, were dugouts with split cedar or spruce sides and roofs. In 1860 some of the houses were said to still contain the remains of Alsea people who had died of small-pox seven years earlier.[6]

The Alsea Subagency of the Coast Reservation had three parts: at Waldport were the remaining Alsea Indians, who were living mostly in their traditional dugout houses; at Siuslaw were the Siuslaw, most of whom were living in wooden frame houses; and at Yachats were the Coos and Lower Umpqua, whose houses were yet to be built. At Yachats the Umpqua settled near the mouth of the Yachats River, and the Coos settled a little farther north, on the prairie.

The Coos and the Lower Umpqua were newcomers to the area, but they quickly adapted. They did not know the myths and traditions that went with the land, but they were on the same coast that they knew so well. The ocean, the climate, the flora, and the fauna were all about the same as at their original home.

At Yachats, Matilda was reunited with her father, her mother, and her daughters from her first marriage. Some of the Miluk-speaking Coquille people from her mother's side and most of the Hanis-speaking people from her father's side were together. A few of her sisters and aunts, married to white settlers, had remained at Coos Bay. Among them was her sister Mary, who had married "Dutch Henry" Miller and now lived on Haynes Slough.

Among Matilda's other relatives who never moved to Yachats were Old Marlow and his wife. They lived at the head of tidewater on the Millicoma River, beyond the reach of even the U.S. Army. Another name that comes down to us is Marshfield Tom. During those early years Marshfield Tom lived on the northern outskirts of the town of Marsh-field,* first at Alder Street, then farther north as the town grew.[7] During the reservation years, any adult male Indian at Coos Bay was a rarity.

Matilda was also related to some of the Lower Coquille Miluk who had been transported by ship to Portland and who had then settled at Siletz in 1856. Siletz, the head-quarters of the Coast Reservation, was about fifteen miles from the coast by traveling up the Yaquina, then over the divide to the Siletz River. While Annie was still a baby her mother moved from Yachats to Siletz to be with those Lower Coquille relatives. Later, Matilda moved with a number of them back to the coast at Yaquina.

During Annie's first three or four years she and her mother lived mostly with their Lower Coquille relatives at Yaquina. At Siletz the Coquilles had settled near the river, about a half mile south of the government buildings. They

---

* Marshfield was a settlement on the western shore of upper Coos Bay. It soon became the principal city on the bay, and in 1944 it consolidated with Empire and became the city of Coos Bay.

frequently camped and fished at Yaquina Bay and probably lived there most of the time.

It was of Yaquina that Annie had her first memories. She said: "It was as if I awakened from a sleep, and my mother was washing me. I must have been doing something in the mud and she was washing my head. I was just covered with mud. That is the first thing I remember. . . . I was never in the house, I was always doing things outside, without clothes, in brush, timber, water. But I was never in the house. Only at night was I in the house." She commented also that her mother was weeping, condoling her for being fatherless.[8]

Annie's mother was somewhat progressive in her attitude toward child rearing. For example, both she and her sister were opposed to piercing the septum of Annie's nose. Normally a rather large hole was made in the membrane of the septum. Items could then be put through the hole or hung from it. Matilda refused to let the old people do that to Annie. She said, "Go ahead, hang them from Annie's hair but don't put that hole through her nose!" Annie's ears, however, were pierced with four or five holes made with a deer or elk bone needle.[9]

As for discipline, Annie could not remember ever having been spanked. She was sure that whippings were far more rare among the Indians than among the whites. She thought that a child who had lied or had done something specifically prohibited might be whipped. However, she had never personally witnessed such punishment.[10]

The Lower Coquilles must have felt much more at home near the bay and the ocean at Yaquina than they did several miles inland on the Siletz River. The ocean had its familiar foods and sounds and smells. There were clams and native oysters and mussels, sea lions, an occasional beached whale, and saltwater fish in abundance. In short, the ocean area had everything they were used to from their homes on the Coos and the Coquille Rivers.

There were almost no Yaquina Indians left alive. Nearly all of them had succumbed to the succession of epidemic diseases that had hit the central Oregon Coast periodically between 1775 and 1853. The great and abundant bay at Yaquina had thus become, for a few short years, the inherited property of those Indians from southwestern Oregon who had been removed to Siletz and Yachats.

While living at Siletz and Yaquina, Matilda entered into another common-law marriage. This, her fourth husband, was a Lower Coquille Indian whose name has not come down to us. They had one daughter, Agnes, Matilda's ninth and last child.

A favorite fishing camp on Yaquina Bay was called Sand Point, on the southern side of the bay where a ferry slip was later built. Sometime before Annie was six years old, her mother's new husband died of neck cancer. They had been fishing at Sand Point. Near the end he said, "When I die, burn me so my child Agnes won't get cancer."[11] Because of the epidemics it had become customary to burn the bodies of the victims of infectious diseases. His body was burned as well.

One man at Yaquina was called Ma'lu'c, the Coos name for the Columbia River.[12] He got his name because for a time as a youth he had been a slave of the Chinook. Annie heard him tell his story. He had evidently been sold from one tribe to the next until he reached the Columbia River. He said he was watched all the time and so could not escape. He added: "Once we were spearing salmon. They did not know my Coos language and I did not know their Chinook language." The Chinook youths were singing songs, and so Ma'lu'c thought that he would sing too. He sang,

>   They made me go there when I was poor,
>   But I am returning well off.

He said:

They stared at me. They talked together in their
language. That is what it was like when I was there.
Then once they were not watching me. I ran away.
I traveled at night. When it became daylight I
would be beside a log. When I reached a bay, and
they had all gone to bed, I would steal a canoe, and
when I landed, I would shove off the canoe, so that
it drifted away. . . . That is the way I came back.
I fled in summer, so I ate fruits and berries. I had
Indian fire sticks. When I was a distance from the
Columbia River and I was far inland, and possibly
a creek flowed there, I would spear trout. That is
what I ate. That is the way I came back, that is how
I returned home. That is why I was named Ma'lu'c.

Because the song Ma'lu'c had sung while spearing
salmon with the Chinook youths had given him the power
to escape, it became his dream-power song. He sang it in
later years at the dream-power dances, and Annie remembered it very well. Such stories as these impressed the child
Annie, staying with her for a lifetime.

The Coos and Lower Umpqua Indians at Yachats also
came to fish at Sand Point on Yaquina Bay. Daloose Jackson,
who had recently taken Annie's older half-sister Fannie as
one of his wives, was fishing there in 1871 when Fannie gave
birth to their daughter Lottie. Lottie said later that her
father had been fishing for bluebacks and was getting
twenty-five cents each for them.[13]

Annie was present at Lottie's birth.[14] The delivery was
hard, and so the Indians called in a male doctor who was
reputed to have great power. He was a Lower Coquille Miluk
named Eli. Annie said that all he did was mark two close
lines on Fannie's abdomen with red and white paint. In
effect, he painted a road for the baby to exit. He then
mumbled a song, very low, and said, "Follow me, I am going
outside." Then he left the room. The idea, according to

Annie, was to induce the baby to follow him out, an idea
that in this case was successful. (According to Indian tradition, if a baby was hard to bear, this was because the father
had been with another woman while the mother was
pregnant.)

Whites coveted the harbor and the bay at Yaquina.
Among the first to take economic advantage of the area were
the oyster pirates. In 1862, when Matilda was at Yaquina,
oysters were discovered by speculators from San Francisco.
Several shiploads were harvested and sent to California.
Indian Agent Ben Simpson complained bitterly about the
matter to his superiors.

In 1864 the courts decided that such activity was
trespass and declared that the oyster pirates could be
evicted from the reservation, but the pirates countersued,
claiming that the oysters were in navigable waters. The
dispute came to an end on January 8, 1866, when the
federal government opened Yaquina Bay to white settlers
and forced the Indians to move out.[15] Matilda and her two
dependent children, Annie and Agnes, had already moved
back to Yachats.

Chief Daloose Jackson and his family: Daloose, standing; his wife (Annie's half-sister Fannie) seated, with basket; their daughter, Lottie, seated with child on either side of her. The two women standing are unidentified. The one on the left may be Jackson's "other wife"; the one on the right may be their daughter Kitty. Photo courtesy Iola Larson.

4

Childhood

The subagent in charge when Matilda and her family returned to Yachats was Amos Harvey. He had come to Oregon from Illinois in 1845 and served at Yachats from October 1, 1862, until July 1, 1864. Well into his sixties, he was a staunch Christian, a Republican, and a man of very little compassion toward the Indians.[1]

During Annie's early childhood at Yachats, conditions were not good. She remembered: "We lived poorly, we had nothing, we had no food, only just some Indian foods. That is how we lived at Yachats." She continued: "We had no clothes, we had to wear any old thing. That is how I grew up."[2]

The poor conditions during those early years drove many individuals and small bands to simply leave the reservation and return to Coos Bay. If a complaint was received from a white resident at Coos Bay, then the Indian agent was obliged to try to bring the Indians back to Yachats. On certain occasions corporal punishment was inflicted in the form of whippings with a rawhide lash. When Annie was young, she witnessed several of those whippings.[3]

Indians on the reservation could get passes for three to six months to work or fish off the reservation, but they had to return at the end of the specified time. Some of those who went to Coos Bay with passes failed to return. Some of the whites at Coos Bay were in-laws of those Indians and welcomed them. Other whites needed labor in the mills or farms and welcomed them for that reason. From time to time, however, a white would complain to the authorities about all of the "wild Indians" hanging around and would demand that the Indian agent do something.

In response to a complaint from a citizen at Coos Bay, Subagent Harvey went down to get some Indians who were to return during the fall of 1863. He failed because he was alone and he got very little support from the local citizens. Charlie Metcalf, who lived on the upper part of Big Creek, provides one example of the difficulties the agent encountered. He pulled a gun on old Amos Harvey and told the subagent to clear out.[4]

In May 1864 Harvey went back to Coos Bay, this time with a lieutenant and ten soldiers from Siletz. Tyee Jim went along as guide. When they arrived at Coos Bay they immediately ran into Jim's brother Daloose Jackson and a band of seventeen who had left the reservation the previous summer. These Indians returned to Yachats on their own. During the next few days the soldiers captured thirty-one others, some of whom had never been to the reservation in the first place.

As an example of the extremes to which Harvey would go to catch his quarry, he had the soldiers row the twenty-five miles from Empire to the forks of the Millicoma River (the present site of Allegany) to get Old Marlow and his wife. The couple lived about a mile beyond and so were not caught. The next day the men rowed another twenty-five

miles to the head of tidewater on the South Fork of the
Coos River where A. P. DeCuis, an original member of the
Coos Bay Commercial Company, had his homestead. Living
with him were his seven-year-old daughter, whose Indian
mother was apparently deceased, and the girl's grandmother, who was elderly and blind. One of the soldiers,
Corporal Royal A. Bensell, made the following entry in his
diary:

> May 1, 1864, Clear. Pike, Plunkett, Clark, Mr.
> Harvey, & Luce (Mill-man) go up Coos River 25
> miles to-day after some Indians. Find at the head
> of tide water a small ranch owned by one De-Cuys.
> He had a pretty little girl, some 8 years old. We got
> two Squaws and a Buck. After getting in the boat
> I was surprised to hear one of the Squaws (old and
> blind) aske me, "Nika tika nanage nika tenas Julia
> (Let me see my little Julia)." I complyed with this
> parental demand and was shocked to see this little
> girl throw her arms about old Amanda De-Cuys
> neck and cry, "clihime Ma Ma (dear mama)." De
> Cuys promised the Agent to school Julia. We
> started back with the tide. Got home at midnight.
> Good night.[5]

Bensell added that on the way around Cape Perpetua
heading back to Yachats, the blind Amanda "tore her feet
horribly over these ragged rock, leaving blood sufficient to
track her by."[6]

The fate of Amanda's granddaughter Julia may have
been happier. She is listed in the 1910 U.S. Census for the
Coos City Precinct as a fifty-four-year-old widow named
Julia Durrard. She had borne five children, three of whom
were still living. She had a daughter, a granddaughter, and
a grandson living with her. One of the questions asked of
Indians was, "What was the tribe of your mother?" Julia
answered, "Unknown."

Corporal Bensell wrote in his diary of the citizen resistance that Harvey and the soldiers encountered at Coos Bay. The opposition included encounters with Charlie Metcalf at Big Creek and with the "roughs" at Marshfield as well as a run-in with John Henderson on the north spit. Evidently, a significant portion of the white population were appalled at the forcible removal of the Indians from Coos Bay to Yachats. Corporal Bensell made the following observation on May 2:

> The lumbermen up these bayous and Sloughs are the roughest of men. Nearly all are married to Squaws or else have a written obligation that will marry rather than allow the Ind Agt to deprive them of their concubines. They conceal the Indians, warn them, and otherwise enhance the difficulties of catching the red devils. There are yet some 60 Indians on North Bend Slough, Kitchen Slough, and Coquille River. We arrive after a rough voyage across the Bay at camp by midnight. The fact of the business is, this rowing after Siwash is no part of a soldiers duty.[7]

One of the Indians who remained at Coos Bay was Marshfield Tom, a distant relative of Annie's. He lived at Marshfield during the entire reservation period and was still living there when the Indians returned after 1875. His place was on the northern side of a little gulch, which, when the town reached that far, became Alder Street.[8] He had built his shack from driftwood he had collected from the shores of the bay. He liked his whiskey and worked "pulling boat" for fishermen or working as a logger in the woods.[9] Annie remembered his dream-power song: "Timberman, that's my power. . . . That's what I had people with."[10]

The law, however, was against the Indians. Since they were not considered citizens, they did not enjoy the rights of citizenship. Shocked at the injustice being done, hotelier R. W. Cussans of Empire applied to the circuit court for a writ of habeas corpus. In it he attempted to force the army and the agent to return the Indians to Coos County and to "show cause why they were restrained of their liberty." At the June 1864 term of the Circuit Court of Coos County, the application for the writ was refused by Judge Riley E. Stratton.[11]

On their return to Yachats, some of the Indians were punished. One of the potato houses served as jail for Coquel Bill and his wife.[12] Several were tied to a post and whipped with the lash. Annie said that the agent would gather the other Indians together to see the whippings "to teach the lesson that they may not run away again from the agency without consent of the agent."[13]

Corporal Bensell had estimated that about sixty Indians remained in Coos County.[14] Some lived quite openly and were never caught. Others, to avoid capture and removal to Yachats, hid far in the hills, where resources were slight, at the head of the sloughs and rivers. They had been reduced to an animal existence and were poor beyond imagining. During 1868 a catastrophic forest fire in the Coos country burned almost ninety thousand acres of the old-growth Douglas fir forest. There were, very possibly, some unreported deaths among Indians who were still living hidden in those woods.

Whites who were living on the bay at the time of the fire passed on to their children stories of Indians who had shown up on shore, fleeing the flames. Mrs. Julius Larson, who with her family was escaping the fire, told of meeting "friendly Indians" who had escaped to Glascow Point. They helped Mrs. Larson with her baby and gave her some food.[15] Elwin Saling, repeating what he later heard from early settlers, told of Indians and animals together in the water near Cooston at Crawford Point.[16]

Norman Gould said that in 1885, when his great-grandfather, the pioneer George Gould, first went into the "Big Burn," as the area was known by that time, a family of

Indians was still living on the upper reaches of the West Fork of the Millicoma River. The head of the family, whose name was Joe, had evidently been there in 1868 when the great fire had swept through. He and his family had lain in the river, sustaining burns but surviving. When George Gould decided to establish what he called the "Elkhorn Ranch" at that location, Joe merely took his family two miles up the river to another creek, which to this day is shown on the maps as Joe's Creek.

In July 1864 Amos Harvey was replaced by George W. Collins as the $1,000-per-year subagent at Yachats. Collins had come out from Kentucky during the California gold rush, soon arriving in Oregon. He married an Indian woman and for several years conducted placer mining at the extremely low-grade black sands near the beach about four miles north of the Alsea River. He hired Indians to shovel the sand into the chute, he had a small grocery store, and he also worked part-time for the subagency before being named subagent.

The Indians at the subagency maintained many of their old traditions. When Annie was five years old, for example, she received her Indian name. Until they were five, the children went only by nicknames. Annie described the procedure: her mother and other relatives would have declared, "We will name our child." Relatives and friends were invited to a feast, and all sorts of foods were cooked. When they were finished eating, the shaman said, "We will give this name to the child." He then pronounced the name of a deceased person.[17] Most people had three names: the Indian given name, the Indian nickname(s), and the "modern" name.

The Indian given names were quite private and often not known even by close acquaintances. Annie's name was that of one of her deceased aunts: "He-T̓SMI•'XWN," a Hanis word that meant "She's tricky like coyote."[18] Annie's niece Lottie had at least two nicknames for her. One meant "to sneak (away from home)."[19] The other was *whentic*, the Hanis word for "snot-nose." Annie's granddaughter, Iola, remembered that Annie in later years had a problem with catarrh and that Lottie did call Annie by that name.[20] Annie's "modern" name was Annie Matilda Miner.

The U.S. government, then in the midst of the Civil War, was appropriating very little money in support of the obscure Alsea Subagency at Yachats. There were, however, some improvements being made. Collins's report for 1864 showed five hundred Indians total—including the Siuslaw to the south and the Alsea to the north. He reported: "The Coose and Umpqua tribes of Indians have at this place comfortable houses to live in. They have two barns and also two potato houses."[21]

According to Annie, in about 1867 Collins told her mother that Annie's father, James Miner, had died in a shipwreck. When Annie was told that her father had died, she did not even know what "father" meant. Her mother's next husband had been known as "uncle," or "father's brother." Annie, of course, had never seen her real father and knew very little about him.

Annie remembered that Collins told her mother that her father "had died where people ate people, in that place my father had been drowned."[22] The story, however, became embellished over the years. Later, Annie's niece Lottie told it as follows:

> Mr. Miner and others were heading for Australia to gold mining there, when the men got wrecked on a cannibal island. They cut the two men right away on the breast to see how fat. They ate Mr. Miner right away for he was fat, but they were fattening the other man, who was thin, and he walked on the beach where he saw a schooner and he took his shirt off and waved it and the schooner picked him up. But Mr. Miner got eaten.[23]

At about this time Annie came down with smallpox. She had collapsed while playing, and the other children took her home. She was sick for a long time, and she dreamed constantly. She dreamed that a man dressed in black carried her to a chopping block. He took a small ax from his pocket and split open her leg and took out a wriggling worm. Then he said: "Do you see the grass standing there? Tell your mother to cut your leg with glass, then she may wash your leg with that grass." He then asked: "Do you know me? I am the Father of the People. I came to help you." She said that he just stood there, and then he vanished.[24] Annie went through the rest of her life with faint pox marks on her face.[25]

The white man's God was only vaguely familiar to the Indians at Yachats during Annie's childhood. The immaculately conceived Father of the People, son of Coyote, bore some resemblance, but there was no schooling and no religious instruction at Yachats during most of those years. The shamanism and spirit power of Annie's ancestors appears to have prevailed.

Annie's dream in which the Father of the People appeared to her in black could have been inspired partly by visits in 1864 and 1865 by Father Adrian Croquet, the Belgian-born missionary priest stationed at Grande Ronde.[26] Father Croquet had baptized a number of the Coos at the Alsea Subagency during those visits, and Annie probably saw him. The subtleties of Christianity, however, seem to have been lost on her. She maintained a lifelong skepticism toward all religions—native, Christian, or otherwise.

Annie may also have maintained a skepticism toward the medical profession. In the 1860s the chance of survival after treatment by a medical doctor was a little less than if one had not seen the doctor at all. For many ailments the Indian shamans had every bit as good a success rate as the modern doctors.

To become a shaman, one needed a "power." The power was usually obtained at around the time of puberty as a result of a vivid, recurring dream. The power might be almost any natural phenomenon—most usually a plant or animal in the form of a person. Certain "powers" seemed to run in families. The elk and the eagle were most common with the family of Annie's Hanis grandfather Minkws. Stars were more common among the family of her Miluk grandmother.[27]

Annie told of a woman who had obtained fir tree power through dreaming. She dreamed she stepped over a fir log. The log was like a person with sore, red eyes. "Come," said the log, Fir, to her, "let us play a game." He merely poked a finger at her nipples. She awakened, and her breasts and her eyes were sore. Her eyes were just as red as Fir's eyes. When she dreamed again, Fir told her to gather certain kinds of weeds and to doctor her breasts with them and to gather a different kind of weed and to doctor her eyes with it. Then Fir became a log again. She tried the medicines, which healed her breasts and her eyes.[28] She had thus obtained a fir tree power and learned two medicines in the process.

Annie also told about a young man who obtained his power from the fir trees. While hunting, he sat down to rest. He evidently dozed off and heard singing. "He looked towards where he had been hearing it. Indeed people were having a dance there. But when he observed them again, indeed they had become just fir trees. No more did they dance." That is the way the fir tree became his power. From that time on he was a shaman.[29]

There were actually two kinds of shamans. One, the *ilaxqain*, was benevolent, and the other, the *mitadin*, possessed a "poison power" and thus tended to be more dangerous. Lottie explained that a *mitadin* was a doctor that had power to do harm. For example, if a lot of money was stolen from you, you paid a *mitadin* and he would find out who had stolen it.[30] The *mitadin*, according to Lottie, worked alone and wished ailments on people.

Lottie told of the time at Yachats when somebody stole some money from an Indian. It was known that old Coos

Bill's wife had stolen it, but a *mitadin* was consulted and prophesied, "The guilty one will take to the woods!" Coos Bill's wife was spotted taking to the woods, and she was forced to dig up the stolen money.[31]

Annie said that when people paid a *mitadin* he would say: "However you desire it, that is the way it will be done. If you wish him blind eyed, that is how it will be. If you want his legs to become no good, that is how it will be. If you want his feet to rot, that is how it will be. If his arms to be no good, that is how it will be. And if you want him to shoot himself, that is how it will be. If you want him to injure himself, that will be done also."[32]

The *ilaxquain* shaman, on the other hand, worked positively. Annie told of the time when Tinatsis, a *mitadin* shaman, was visiting a woman named Kwaisiya at suppertime. Kwaisiya was eating potatoes and did not offer any to Tinatsis. Kwaisiya got sick and called in an *ilaxquain* shaman named Tsilxan, an uncle of Annie's mother. Annie, who was present, said that Tsilxan began doctoring and said: "Humph! It is not a pain-power. He just looked at you. You were eating roasted potatoes and you were also eating elk meat but you offered nothing to Tinatsis. That is the reason he looked at you. You are not sick."[33] And so the shaman Tsilxan worked on her and extracted elk meat and roasted potatoes from her and cured her.

One time at Yachats a winter storm lasted much longer and was more intense than usual. There was a man named Ge'llh who was said to have "weather power." He was not a shaman, but he was supposed to be able to make good weather. A delegation visited him during the day and asked if he would go to work on the storm. He agreed, and that evening a large group assembled at his house to help him with the dance. Children were never taken to this sort of event because adults took these matters very seriously and were afraid that children might do something wrong and become poisoned or hurt. Annie, however, was able to go with her mother because she, being a "half-breed," was not considered a "person."[34] Whites and half-breeds seemed to have been immune to the possible ill effects of shamanism.

Ge'llh was barefoot, wearing pants but no shirt. On his head he had a handkerchief with yellowhammer feathers in it. He had one yellowhammer feather stuck through his nose. His hands were empty, and a skin drum was used to keep the rhythm. He danced and sang, then took a string of dried salmon eggs about a foot long and said, "Now I'll predict the weather." He stood the eggs on the floor, and they fell down. He repeated this five times, and then they stood. He said, "There will be rain five days more and then it will be clear." According to Annie, that is indeed the way it was. Always skeptical, Annie added, "They said he made good weather but this time he only *predicted* good weather."[35]

When a strong *ilaxquain* shaman worked on a tuberculosis victim, the shaman would reach into the person's body and remove the worm that was said to be causing the problem. The shaman would then show the worm to the assembled family. Shamans of both types were considered to be exceptionally powerful, much to be feared. They could be male or female and could come from any economic or social class.

Annie's two older half-sisters, Nellie and Fannie, both had a certain amount of power and dabbled in shamanistic healing, but neither actually became shamans. Nellie seems to have had a power strong enough to become a doctor, but her mother, Matilda, prevented her from using it. Annie was not sure the exact nature of Nellie's power, but it was evidently a sea-dwelling creature that looked like a dog.

Nellie predicted that because her mother prevented her from becoming a doctor, her life would be made short. Her power would turn against her if she did not use it. She told Annie that when she died, they would see a light or rainbow high up and they would see dogs leaving her. Annie was at

Alsea when Nellie died, and she did indeed see two dogs, as predicted. They were chasing over the beach rocks. Even with all her skepticism, Annie knew that those two dogs were Nellie's power leaving her because she could not use it. At the time she died, Nellie was about nineteen or twenty years old and was married to the nephew of an Alsea shaman called Old Lady Sam.[36]

According to general belief, Old Lady Sam had killed Nellie. Chief Joe Scott, a relative of Annie's family, took up the case. The two families sat a few hundred feet apart, outside in the daytime. Annie remembered the ceremonial "building [of] a fire" for the occasion. Each side had its own fire and two bilingual (Alsea and Coos) emissaries to do the negotiating. In the end, the Alsea family agreed to recompense Annie's family with a big money payment, divided between Annie's mother's and her stepfather's families. After the money was paid, they all made up and stayed for a feast that same night. But Annie said, "They were still sad and didn't dance." If there had been no settlement, a fight would surely have followed.[37]

The other sister, Fannie, was about fourteen or fifteen years older than Annie. When they were alone together, Fannie would secretly doctor Annie. If Annie had been hurt, Fannie would rub her hands on the hurt place, massaging it and singing in a low voice, but she never extracted the sickness as was done by the professional doctors. The Indians believed that if a person, such as Fannie, did not "come out" with her power and use it, she would lose her children.[38] This in fact happened to Fannie. She gave birth to thirteen children, but only Lottie, the first one, reached adulthood.

Annie's younger half-sister, Agnes, also had a certain amount of "power." Crows used to follow her. Once she ran into the house and said, "Crow said there are fish below." Her uncle and some others followed her, and sure enough the smelt were running on the smelt beach.[39] Another time

Agnes ran in and said: "Crow told me company is coming from the north. Clean the house!" Her family believed her, and sure enough, company came. Agnes never spoke of dreaming of Crow, but Annie assumed she did. The crow was a good power to have. If you had it, you would know a lot of things, and it could give wealth.[40]

The yellowhammer was a good power for doctoring. One time Annie and Agnes were wearing the tailfeathers from a dead yellowhammer they had found. Their aunt warned them to take off the feathers quickly before a doctor with yellowhammer power saw and poisoned them. They were told to give the feathers to a shaman named Gabriel, who was delighted with the gift. Annie assumed that Gabriel must have had yellowhammer power.[41]

Each of the differing kinds of powers had its characteristics. For example, Annie remembered that panther power would make you awfully mean. Fog power, she said, was no good. "They don't want you to have it. With it you can blind a person." But Annie admitted that some people secretly kept this power.[42] Chicken power was bad luck, and dog power made you fight all the time.[43] Water dog was the worst.* A person with that dream was a dangerous person to have around, since he wanted to kill people.[44]

Annie did not herself admit to having obtained a spirit power. With all her skepticism, however, she knew in her heart that there was something to all this. In later years she remembered the spirit-power songs of many of her relatives and friends. The songs she remembered included the dream-power songs of her sister Fannie, her niece Lottie Evanoff, her uncle Jesse, Carolyn Evans, Mrs. George Wasson, Ned, Cissy, Emily Taylor, Frank Drew's mother-in-

---

* The "water dog" is the western newt *Taricha torosa*, which contains the poison tetrodotoxin, one of the most powerful toxins known and one for which there is not antidote. See Frederick A. Fuhrman, "Tetrodotoxin," *Scientific American* 217, no. 2 (1967): 60–71.

law Maggie, his stepfather Old Cammon, Old Taylor, and Marshfield Tom, among others.[45] She knew a number of gambling songs and love songs of various people. She did have love songs of her own, a subject she was apparently more comfortable with than the more spiritual matters of shamanism.

One time while Annie was still fairly small, she went outside during a full moon and thought she saw a long-absent relative named Frank go into a canoe and disappear. She ran into the house and told her mother: "Mother! I saw Frank. Mother!" Everyone went outside and looked for him, but he wasn't there. They said: "Aha! It must have been his spirit double there."

The next day as she was playing, Annie said that she heard a baby bird. She looked and saw what she said was the head of a dead person rolling along, "just like the way a baby bird does it." She went back home and said: "Mother! A person's head was rolling along, chirping like a bird." Her mother responded: "Hmm! A person must have been killed, and another person is going to be killed. Maybe it will be one of our relatives."[46]

Sure enough, Frank had been killed. The story of why is revealing and involves the marriage of Annie's older half-sister Fannie to Daloose Jackson. Jackson was old enough to have had a wife and children before the whites arrived at Coos Bay.[47] Over the years he had several wives, both serially and concurrently.

After Annie's half-sister Fannie had her first menses, Jackson bought her "with his other wife's money," according to Annie.[48] She had evidently been given no sex information before the wedding night and was, in Annie's words, "an ignorant virgin." That night she cried out from her house: "Oh Grandma! Grandma! He's going to kill me."[49]

She ran away several times, but Jackson would find her and bring her back. Once he took after her with horses and caught her. On the way back she slipped off the horse and hung upside down from the saddle horn. Jackson set her upright, and after that she did not run away again.[50] Later, she became his principal wife and stayed with him through all of his long life.

In the meantime, however, Jackson's older wife became jealous of the increasing favor that the much younger Fannie was receiving. She resolved to bring Fannie down a peg or two. Her scheme was circuitous but, in the end, tragic. The older wife and Jackson had a daughter who was a little older than Fannie. This daughter, Kitty, had recently been married to Jack Rogers. The older wife told Kitty, "You should flirt with Frank." Frank was Jack Rogers's nephew and, as noted above, was also a relative of Fannie's. "You may merely pretend that he was bothering you." According to Annie, Kitty did as her mother had told her.

When Frank passed the house, Kitty asked him to come in and help her. He went inside, and she said, "Help me in the bedroom." He thought nothing of it, but while Kitty was flirting with him in the bedroom her own husband, Jack Rogers, came in. Kitty took her husband to the kitchen and said, "Frank has been bothering me." Her husband said nothing and went out.

He then went to his father-in-law, Daloose Jackson, and said: "What are you going to do about it? He was bothering your daughter. You kill him. It will be better if you kill him. Then Fannie will not think herself so big." According to Annie, that is indeed what happened.[51] Jack Rogers and others killed Frank. The murderers did not know that Kitty had lied about the sexual harassment.

Spencer Scott, an Umpqua Indian at Yachats, told the story differently. He said that Frank had had intercourse with Daloose Jackson's sister-in-law, Tyee Jim's wife. Scott said that Jim's family (possibly including Daloose) paid Old Pomli, a relative of theirs, to kill Frank. Scott said that later, at an Indian dance, Pomli danced at the front, carrying a gun. There were "lots of beads and many blankets to pay the relatives of the murdered Frank."[52] Probably both versions of the story are at least partly true.

Conditions improved slowly on the reservation as the population declined. About seventy acres of Yachats prairie were cleared for agriculture. A blacksmith shop, cattle sheds, and other structures were built, including a large barn made of logs.[53] By 1872 there were "35 acres of oats, 20 of potatoes, and 14 of wheat and some timothy and general garden of mostly carrots and turnips." Corn, potatoes, and oats were also grown on some cleared land farther up the Yachats River.[54] The government furnished the tools, seeds, and general supervision.

Lottie commented on the wood supply, noting that there was no timber, except spruce, at Yachats. The fir grew "way back," and spruce was poor for firewood. For that reason, the Indians got their wood from the beach. She remembered that her father, Daloose Jackson, used to drive an ox team down the cut from the prairie onto the beach to pick up driftwood on the beach.[55]

About ten board shacks served as the living quarters. The large ones were sixteen by twenty feet; the small ones were eight by twelve.[56] There were also a few log houses and several houses made of grass.[57] Annie grew up in one of those houses, probably one of the board shacks, with her mother and other relatives. In this environment, she absorbed the traditions of her people in the original languages. She was among the very last of her people to do so.

"The Smelt Fisher—Trinidad Yurok," a characteristic scene of an Indian fishing with a dip net on the Pacific coast. Photogravure print by E. S. Curtis, in the author's collection.

5

Yachats

Annie's mother was bilingual in Hanis and Miluk, but she nearly always spoke Hanis. Annie was also bilingual. She picked up Miluk from her grandmother, her other relatives, and her childhood companions.[1] She admitted that she did not use Miluk as often as she used Hanis, and she did not consider herself to be particularly fluent in the former.[2]

By her own account Annie enjoyed being with the adults, and she always went with her mother and the others when they were berry picking, root digging, and camping out. During those frequent outings the older people incessantly discussed and recounted the old folktales. Annie picked up much more of the culture of her ancestors than did most of the other children of her age at Yachats. The other children, most of whom were a little younger than her, stayed home more and were less interested in the stories and traditions of the older people. In the reservation period, the knowledge that the elders were able to impart on the young seemed increasingly irrelevant to most of the children.

But Annie was steeped in the traditions of the culture from a young age. An example is her account of the first berries she picked.[3] After she had picked her first basketful she thought, "I'll eat them for I have filled my basket." Her mother said: "Oh no. You must not eat them." She was supposed to give them away. Annie asked, "Why did you not want me to eat the berries?" Her mother, herself probably not knowing the reason, said, "Oh, you might have had a boil." The same custom applied to boys, who were not to eat any of the meat from their first kill.[4] If they did, according to Annie, they would not be able to kill anything again.

Annie always exhibited a certain skepticism toward many of the teachings of her elders. In the case of the berry picking, for example, she and two other half-breed girls her age told no one but did eat the strawberries that were forbidden to them at the time. As it turned out, no harm came to them.[5] By thus experimenting with some of the taboos of her people, Annie developed a sound basis for her skepticism. It may be significant that her name meant "she's tricky like coyote."[6]

Annie said that picking flowers and gathering shells and rocks were also prohibited. "It might start to rain or bring bad luck." She said, "Things were just to be there, not to be picked."[7] It was also bad luck to catch wild things.[8] The elders warned the children, but Annie was contrary and was constantly scolded for doing those things.

While the women and girls were picking berries and doing their other outdoor activities, they talked, gossiped, and joked continuously. Annie was wide-eyed, alert, and precocious. She hung on to every word, and she remembered everything. A sad and unsolved mystery occurred during one of the berry-picking sessions. One of the Miluk girls was a vibrant and vivacious teenager whom the soldiers had named "Minna Ha Ha." She had been brought to Yachats during the expedition to Coos Bay by the army detachment during May 1864. Corporal Royal Bensell had mentioned her in his diary. She was one of the girls who, along with Daloose Jackson's daughter Kitty, had been much noticed by the soldiers and had given them a good-natured hard time. On May 5 Bensell said: "At Ten Mile Creek (waist deep) the Indians wade. Miss Kitty and several of her stripe affected extreme modesty. I told them 'hyac (hurry)' and up they pulled their flounces displaying 'con-away squitch' to the great amusement of the Guard."[9] Sometime after they got to Yachats several women and girls were berry picking a little north of Yachats prairie. Minna Ha Ha got separated from the group. They searched for her for several days but found only a few torn bits of clothing in the brush.[10] No other trace of her was ever seen, and the mystery of her disappearance was never solved.

The children were not a part of the adult world and were generally kept away from strangers. At dances, children were almost always non grata. Dances were very much a part of a serious adult world in which no children were allowed.[11] Annie was privileged to have attended a few dances when she was small, however.

One was a hunting dance in which five or six men wearing ordinary clothes and artificial elk horns pantomimed a herd of elk feeding. Then, five or six men with headbands and bow and arrows pantomimed the stalking of the game. The elk, with much noise, tried to escape. Annie said that the old men did it best. The audience stood against the wall and sang and danced along with the performance, which lasted an hour or so.[12] Another dance was the "knife dance," which Annie and Martha Harney danced together when they were about fifteen.[13] In this dance the boys and girls were together, wearing two or three feathers in a headband. The girl would run and stab at the boy, then the boy would run and stab at the girl.

Life at the Alsea Subagency during the years of Annie's childhood began to fall into a routine. Food remained primarily the traditional food from the ocean and the river. Mussels and clams and other shellfish were staples. Attesting to the importance of shellfish as a major food source were the mountainous piles of clam and mussel shells at Yachats, which were eventually placed on the roads during the 1920s and 1930s.

There were salmon runs on the Yachats River, and a salmon dam was built of rocks near the river mouth. Flounder were so plentiful that they could often be caught by hand in shallow water. A smelt beach right at Yachats made for convenient outings every August during the smelt spawning season.[14] This smelt beach was so popular that after the Yachats part of the reservation was closed in 1875, the Indians continued to return annually during smelt season until the 1920s.

Sea lions were used only for their blubber by the Coos. The Alsea, however, sometimes ate the meat. Annie never tasted it.[15] Especially during the time that whaling was being conducted offshore, the Indians sometimes found a beached whale. Elk and deer were hunted, but they did not compare in importance with the seafood. The government provided very little because the treaty signed in 1855 with the Coos, Umpqua, and Siuslaw Indians had never been ratified by Congress.

Annie said of her childhood that she stayed inside the house only to sleep. She would be outside before it was fully light, missing meals to play in the water, the mud, and the woods. In the woods she would swing from one tree to another, sometimes falling. She would run along the bluff, often tripping and getting scratches all over her body. She said, "I had no clothes on, my poor rags of clothes just lay somewhere."[16] She was hardly ever at home, since it was the outdoors that she loved.

Annie learned early to enjoy hunting and fishing and camping. She became very good at these activities, which remained her favorite recreation for the rest of her life.[17] Elk hunting was a particular delight. With one or two packhorses to bring back the meat, she might be gone with several others into the mountains above Yachats for two or three days at a time in the early fall of each year.

Frank Drew, who was a little younger than Annie, told of one of those hunting trips. Annie did not go that time, but she had been on other trips. The party consisted of Frank and Annie's first husband, Henry Jackson, along with Henry's brother and his wife.[18] Frank said they had killed two elk the first day but that night there was a forest fire. Since "there was light like a town," they decided to get out of there. They slept that night on a bluff above the sea, and from there they saw a whale drifting north, not far offshore. When they got back to Yachats, no one was home because they were all butchering the whale. Frank said the whale was ninety or one hundred feet long and had been harpooned and lost by whites. He said: "My old daddy got on top of the whale and got hold of an iron harpoon wide as my four fingers and sharp. The wood part above that was about a foot long and broken off."[19] He added that the Coos Indians were happy that the whale had stranded so close to Yachats.

In addition to the hunting, fishing, and gathering was the farmwork. Potatoes, turnips, and other vegetables added some variety to the diet, but for the most part the Indians at Yachats maintained their traditional ways of life to a greater extent than did any of the other reservation Indians of western Oregon. They could get a pass for three to six months at a time to work, hunt, or fish off the reservation, and many of them took advantage of this opportunity.

The Indians were pretty much on their own at Yachats because there just were not very many whites around. Only at the mouth of the Alsea River, ten miles to the north, were there a few whites. The area between the Alsea and the Yaquina Rivers had been opened to white settlement on December 21, 1865. This split the Coast Reservation in two and deprived the Indians of the most productive part of it. In 1867 a farmer named Thomas Clark shot and killed an Indian. The agent at Siletz, cautious lest there be violence in reaction to the shooting, sent some soldiers to the coast.[20] Nothing came of the killing.

A fair amount of socializing existed between the Alsea who were living at Waldport and the Coos and Umpqua who were living at Yachats. The Coos considered the Alsea to be a bit strange because some of the Alsea customs were derived from the Salish and the Chinook Indians to the north. For example, the Alsea flattened the heads of their babies. None of the peoples to the south of them practiced that custom.

Lottie told of playing with the Alsea children at Yachats. The Alsea children called the Coos "seal-heads" because their heads were round. The Coos children called the Alsea children "bread-heads" because their heads were flattened, like a loaf of bread.[21] There was, however, a fair amount of intermarriage among them. Annie's second husband, William Jackson, was Alsea. Another Alsea, John Albert, married Annie's younger sister, Agnes.[22]

The Alsea would walk down the beach the twelve miles from Waldport to trade dried fish for clothes that the Coos might have. They had evidently not been around the whites very much and were not at all conscious of the white man's fashions. They would wear "underwear without pants. They would never put shirttails in their pants, and then they would put a coat on over their shirt."[23] The result was a white tail hanging below their coat. Daloose Jackson called them "fish-hawks" (osprey), which also have a white bottom.

The Alsea were equally unaware of the white man's table etiquette. Daloose Jackson's daughter Kitty once put on a feast for the visiting Alsea Indians. She set the table.

The Alsea "talked their language and decided to sit on the floor."[24] According to Lottie, they divided all the butter into pieces to apportion it, then they ate the butter. They drank the coffee and then apportioned the grounds; then they ate the grounds!

The game of shinny was a popular and raucous sport throughout North America for many centuries before Columbus arrived on the continent. It remained popular at Yachats, and the Coos and the Alsea sometimes played each other there or at Waldport. The spirit of the games was described by Frank Drew and Spencer Scott, who had played at Waldport: "Once at a shinny game at the Alsea shinny ground near Waldport, an Alsea bully knocked old Jesse Martin, a Coos Injun, down, and that started the fight. Alsea Jesse got his leg broken in that fight with a shinny stick. That was the nearest the Coos and the Alsea ever came to war."[25] Scott continued, "But that evening they had a big council meeting at Waldport and money was paid to damaged parties." He added: "The next morning I couldn't walk. An old Indian told me to bathe in cold water in the evening and again in the morning and all the soreness left. Cold water is a wonderful cure. The Indians used it quite a bit."[26]

Gambling was another recreation that brought the Alsea and the Coos together. The dice, or gambling sticks, were three or four inches long with marks that had been burned in.[27] Boys were taught how to gamble, and it was supposed that luck at gambling was a manifestation of the strength of one's spirit power.[28] If a man became unlucky, it was a sign that his "power" had left him. An unlucky gambler, after losing all his other possessions, might wager his wife and after losing her, would gamble away his daughters. Annie said, "They were terrible when they gambled." Annie noted that in early times women were not allowed to go to men's gambling games but that after the whites came, the women were present and sang for the men to help them with their luck. Women also gambled by themselves, with their own games.[29]

Some individuals appeared to have a very strong power. Annie's cousin Bob Burns was one of those. He had the reputation of being very lucky. Slender and good-looking, he was unsurpassed at shinny, gambling, singing, or dancing.[30] Annie did not know his power, but she remembered his gambling song: "Daylight is coming. . . ." He claimed it made him unbeatable.[31]

It was important to do everything possible to enhance one's gambling power. Frank Drew told about a time when he and Alec Jefferson, a boy about his age, saw a light in the graveyard. He said it was dead people gambling there. He explained, "They gamble and leave their gambling sticks and if you pick up a gambling stick and bathe and abstain for five days you get good luck forever after."[32]

Music always accompanied the gambling. The gambling songs, as well as the dream or spirit songs, had an extremely serious purpose. But there were also humorous and risqué social and love songs. Annie enjoyed all the songs very much and sang several of them in both Hanis and Miluk.

One of the love songs, her own, was in Hanis: "Come White man, to my house. . . ."[33] Another one was also inspired by the whites: "Adam has lots of money; Jimmy has no money but lots of potatoes!" When the Ghost Dance was introduced from northern California, a song came in with it: "I'd like to have one of those Coos Bay women!" Another stated, "If you want it that way it is all right with me!"[34] Annie's uncle had one that was probably risqué even in Hanis: "We wet the crack; she always wants to. She always wants the crack wet!"[35] This kind of earthy humor remained with Annie all her life.

The version of the Ghost Dance that showed up at Yachats in about 1872 was part of an Indian revivalist movement in which it was asserted that by doing these dances, the Indians would make the whites all disappear and would bring the dead back to life. Various types of these dances became immensely popular on the coast for a few years.

According to Annie, Cyrus Titchenor and Isaac Martin brought the dance to Yachats after a visit to the northern California coast. Titchenor was an Athapaskan from the Euchre Creek band of Curry County; his sister Ione later became Annie's mother-in-law. Martin was a Coos from Annie's mother's birthplace of Intesedge.[36] The two of them arranged a dance at Yachats the evening they got in from the south.[37]

Titchenor sang the spirit songs they had learned in California, the first of the revival to be heard at Yachats. Annie went to the dance, as did everyone else. Annie's niece Minnie Jackson, younger sister of Kitty, was a good dancer and asked Annie to accompany her in the center. Annie had not danced before and was a bit shy, but Minnie persisted. When they got into the middle Annie tried dancing but fell down. That broke the ice, and from then on she was confident to try any kind of dance. By all accounts, she loved it.

They danced in a circle, with men and women alternately in line. Two women might go into the center, then two men would follow. They called that kind of dance "dip netting." Other variants of the Ghost Dance became popular at Siletz, where the people from Yachats would go to join the dances. Entire families, men, women, and children, the old, the lame, and the blind, would all participate. Joel Palmer, at the time superintendent of the Siletz Reservation, observed, "Two-thirds who have engaged in these dances did so for mere amusement."[38]

One reason the Ghost Dance revival might have been accepted so easily at Siletz was that it bore similarities to the "dream dances" traditional among many of the peoples there. As Coquille Thompson said: "The Dream dance has been going on ever since there have been people in this world. Either a man or woman dreams something and he has to do it. He has to sing what he dreamed in front of all the people and they believe in him."[39]

In a few years the Ghost Dance and its immediate successors disappeared, but the dream dances, now infused with elements from the Ghost Dance, continued. They in turn merged with the Indian Shakers, a new messianic cult that had come originally from the Puget Sound area of Washington State. Many of the Shakers, in turn, were converted to evangelical Christianity. The similarities among these successive movements are more than superficial.[40]

Another of the traditional activities that persisted well into Annie's youth was the telling and retelling of the formal myths and tales. Before the days of writing, culture had to be transmitted by memory, and there could be no mistakes. It had to be transmitted efficiently because adulthood started at the age of thirteen or fourteen.[41] There was no time for an extended childhood.

During the various communal activities, the women talked incessantly about the characters in the myths that formed the oral literature of their people. They talked about Bluejay and Robin and Grizzly and Seal and Crow and Coyote and Kingfisher and Owl and Jack Rabbit and any number of ogres, tricksters, and others.

The formal myths were told by the men and women who knew them by heart. The storytellers recited the myths to their audiences in the evenings during the winter months. Some of the storytellers spoke Hanis, and some spoke Miluk. Annie listened to all of them. Among the Hanis were her brother-in-law Daloose Jackson, her uncle Dick, and her mother, Matilda. Among the Miluk were Cissy, Tar Heels, and Charlie Ned. Annie heard most of the stories in both languages.

The narrative tales fell into three groups, each corresponding to a period in the history of the people. First were stories from the Myth Age, the period before the world was fully formed, when animals had many of the characteristics of the people yet to come and when beings with super-natural power were establishing the way things would be forever. Second were quasi-historical tales set during the time after the people had arrived in the world. The third kind of narrative concerned customs of the people and events that had occurred in living memory.[42] Annie learned them all.

Some of the earliest stories that Annie learned were the Myth Age tales, cautionary tales meant to teach children a lesson of one kind or another. An example was a story the purpose of which was to teach children "not to laugh at things."[43] It seems that some boys went trapping and had killed a raccoon. That evening they roasted it on a spit and "when it became hot it began to shrivel." When the raccoon was all drawn and shrunk it looked so comical that the young men laughed at it. One of them did not laugh, but the rest could not stop, and they laughed until they died. Only the one boy who was serious did not die. Laughing at the raccoon had killed the rest of them, however, and they supposedly turned into raccoons as they died.

The elders told this story with great solemnity because it was supposed to instill in the children the importance of taking things seriously. The children at Yachats, however, took these cautionary tales with a grain of salt. They told this story to each other and laughed because they thought it was comical that the boys had turned into raccoons as they died. The tale seemed so funny that Annie and her friends would draw in their lips and make their hands like the claws of a raccoon and laugh some more.

Annie developed an ironic view of life from an early age. The earthy humor of her people had become a part of her being because, unlike in the societies of western civilization, adult jokes and quipping in the Indian culture were not withheld from the children. Some of the jokes, stories, and songs were a little off-color. Anatomical and scatological humor was very much in favor.

Among the songs Annie liked was the one about
Butterball Duck and his wife insulting each other. Whenever
the children saw a butterball duck, they would sing the song
and laugh.[44]

Butterball, butterball,
my husband is so ugly!
Haha!
Hu' short, short is my wife's thing on the upper side.
Hu' short, short is my wife's thing on the upper side.

Whenever they heard a bush pheasant (the ruffed
grouse, *Bonasa umbellus*), the children would laugh and talk
about the young trickster-person who had killed an elk,
which his grandmother volunteered to help him pack home.[45]
She complained about the weight of the load, however,
saying that she wanted to pack only the penis. She then fell
farther behind, and the young trickster-person heard a
peculiar and repetitious sound. He went back to look, and
"she was just doing it to herself with that elk's penis." He
said to himself: "You will not be a person any more, you will
become a pheasant. You are so nasty! The next people will
hear you making that sound." That is the reason people
hear the ruffed grouse make the "hm hm hm" accelerando
sound.

During a formal storytelling session the audience would
be assembled in a dimly lit shack, and the storyteller would
present the material as a little drama. He or she would take
on the voices and the roles of each of the characters and
would act out the material with gestures and actions. If there
were many children present, each line would be repeated by
the full audience. If there was an error, the storyteller would
repeat the line until everyone got it right.[46] Annie said,
"They did not want them to get it mixed up and 'lie' when
they told it."

For the younger generation the repetition was an irri-
tating and monotonous custom, but it helped them to learn

the stories verbatim. The custom extended even to everyday conversation. When a person came home with news, the person to whom it was told repeated it verbatim. The reason was to impress the news on the memory. Annie's niece Lottie would become impatient with Annie's mother, who maintained the old habit. Lottie would tell Annie's mother angrily, "Don't you be mocking me!"[47] Lottie was of a younger and faster generation.

Annie said that she used to doze off when she was listening to the stories as a child. She would be sleepy because she got up early in the mornings and usually returned home tired after playing all day. As a result she did not learn all of the stories verbatim.[48] The characters and incidents of the stories, however, were discussed continually throughout the year. She had ample opportunity to learn them.

In addition to learning the characters and incidents of the stories, Annie became familiar with the stylized plot devices common in the oral literature of the peoples of the Pacific Northwest. These devices included the use of a "five-pattern," following the five-base counting system of many of the Northwest peoples, including the Coos. Other devices involved stylized beginnings and endings and sometimes included revenge or spirit power. But probably most important were the plot devices that relieved the social tensions and frustrations resulting from certain customs or taboos.

One custom that must have created a large amount of tension and frustration was that of arranged marriage. Young women had very little say in the selection of their mates. Thus, in a myth motif that appears from time to time, a young woman goes forth and chooses her own husband. Stories of such tabooed customs have a romantic ring to them, especially if they are set in the Myth Age. One suspects that such Myth Age women acted as heroes and role models for Annie.

"Two Loose Women," a myth about two sisters, demonstrates several characteristic features of traditional stories of the Northwest.[49] In it the two women set out to get their own husbands; the younger sister turns out to be the more perceptive of the two. The story is set in familiar country inhabited by odd, dreamlike characters who can transform themselves. In a surprise but characteristic ending, we learn the reason for the beaver's large tail.

This story was told by both the Hanis and the Miluk Coos. Annie learned it from Charlie Ned, a Lower Coquille Miluk relative of hers. The tale begins: "They came from the Lower Coquille River country, they came canoeing up the creek, they portaged the canoe into Coos Bay. Now they went up North Slough, and they portaged from there over to Ten Mile Lake. Now they reached somebody's place there." The two women thought they had come to a wealthy headman's place. Inside was a boy whose penis was made of bone. They rejected him, then waited for his uncle, but the uncle was a short, fat, ugly man. Then they went away, saying, "He cannot be the husband we want."

They soon arrived at the Lower Umpqua and sought out the wealthy headman's house. He appeared ugly and was ill with diarrhea. The older sister was repelled, but the younger sister waited on him and washed away his feces. The older sister mocked the younger: "So that is the sort of thing you like!" The younger sister said, "What if I do like him?" They were there five days, and then one morning the sick person was gone. A handsome young man appeared after swimming, whipping the water out of his hair. He addressed the younger girl: "My wife! I like you. I merely wanted to learn if you did indeed want me. And you really wanted me. The one who did not like me, I will not want her."

Then the ugly fat man from Tenmile Lake appeared, coming to take the young women by force. The young man grabbed him, snatched his knife from him, and thrust it into the other man's anus. "Get away!" Then the young headman threw him out. "You will fall into the lake, and that knife of yours will be your tail. The next people [the Indians to come] will eat you. Your clothes they will have for their own garments. When you are frightened your tail will slap the water." Indeed that is the way it was. "The next people will eat that tail of yours. And you will be named beaver."

Myths such as "Two Loose Women" constituted the literary frame of reference of a "cultured" person of Annie's mother's generation. Annie absorbed as much as was possible, given the fact that she was living in a period of rapid and precipitous decay of that culture. She learned the oral literature, and she learned the techniques for producing food, clothing, and containers. "Motor memory" was instilled into her fingers and hands as she was taught the rapid, repetitious motions of twining the fine, flexible warp of spruce-root baskets, baskets so tightly twined that they could hold water.

Annie's basket-weaving teachers were among the finest basketmakers in western North America.[50] They were her mother's Miluk-speaking relatives. Their baskets are now considered to be as fine as any in the world, including those of the Tlingit and Haida of Alaska, which the Miluk baskets resemble in many respects. These baskets were distinctive in their decoration, with simple, horizontal, mud-dyed bands and triangles. In their elegant simplicity they were perfection itself. Annie mastered the basketry techniques of her teachers and stored them in her memory to be recalled later, along with the myths and other traditions she had absorbed during those early years.

By the time Annie had reached early adolescence, she had internalized most of the patterns of her culture, as had all of her Indian ancestors for thousands of years past. She knew the worldview of her people, especially as depicted in their stories and myths. She knew the etiquette and social graces. Her body and limb coordination for such acts as sitting, eating, and urinating had long been formed, and by the age of seven she most certainly had internalized the stylistic features of her people's music.

In any culture, the great majority of the people have limited and narrow interests and abilities. In contrast with the majority, a few are learned and skilled. Among those few is occasionally one who has very broad interests and participates fully in all aspects of the culture. This person is a "cultured" person.[51] At adolescence, Annie was well on her way toward becoming such a cultured person. The culture of which she was a part, however, soon disintegrated before her very eyes.

William B. Jackson as a member of the tribal police, Siletz Reservation. A full-blood Alsea, he was Annie's second husband (ca. 1875–1880) and the father of her daughter, Nellie. Photo courtesy of Iola Larson.

6

Womanhood

At the puberty rites of her first menses Annie became a woman. She was one of the very last of the Coos Indian girls to be initiated into adulthood by the observance of those ancient customs.[1] The year was probably 1873.

A shaman was needed to officiate over the ceremonies. Annie's half-sister Fannie wanted to get Gishgiu, an Upper Coquille Athapaskan who was reputed to be very good.[2] Gishgiu had returned to Coos Bay, however, and was living with her daughter, Adulsa, and her son-in-law, George Wasson, at South Slough. Annie's family had to settle for a male shaman who was resident at Yachats.

When her flow began, Annie was secluded for five days in a part of the house that had been partitioned by matting.[3] She remained naked and was not supposed to touch her head except with a scratcher, which hung around her neck.

For food, she was restricted to dried elk meat and water during the five days.

On the fifth day the older men came to sing humorous songs to her. She was not supposed to laugh or make any response to the songs, and her aunt was there to make sure she did not. After the songs, a shaman and four old women entered her secluded area and picked her up. They made light incisions with a knife all over her to draw a light flow of blood, which was smeared over her entire body. She then put on a light dress.

The shaman took her to the river and dipped her five times into the water. Each time she was dunked into the water, someone else passed a toy canoe over her while the shaman chanted something to the effect that if she believed, she would grow old. The canoe, about two feet long, was filled with sand and had a little fire burning in it.

The shaman then took her back to the house, where four women, hired by her family, acted as waitresses. They put beads around her neck, tied bells onto the ends of her braids, and applied facial and body paint. She was then seated on a fine mat and was told not to look at the fire. If she did, her eyes would become filmy, which was considered undesirable. The shaman then gave her some dried elk meat and said a little prayer.

The women assistants and the shaman were then fed and paid by the family. That night Annie and Lena, a Chetco girlfriend about five months younger, spent the night on the beach.[4] Lena's mother was married to Old Taylor, one of the Coos who had signed the treaty of 1855.

A little before dawn they went back to the house and slept as much as they wanted. They repeated this for five nights. They could not eat or drink while they were out of the house, and they could not look at the fire while they were in the house. They were to avoid all fresh food.

At the tenth day after her menses the shaman brought her to the fire in the house and called for the tattoo women.

He gave her new, wooden fire tongs and had her stir the charcoal in the fire. This symbolized that from now on she was to do her own cooking. The tattoo women took the charcoal, mixed it with elk tallow, and dipped a thread into the blackened mixture. With it they made a row of eleven light dots about a quarter-inch apart across the back of Annie's hand. A month later, they returned and tattooed similar dots on her other hand. This was repeated for several months, producing light tattoo marks on the backs of both hands.[5] Some sixty-five years later, the dots on Annie's hands were still clearly visible.

All of the friends and relatives assembled while the shaman made the following statement: "I am glad this day you are becoming a woman. Take good care of yourself. Look on, be sure to look on the good things of this world for your own good. Think of things as good and clean as the sky above, which is so nice to look upon that your life may be a long one. Don't do anything that is mean."[6] The shaman then took a drink of water, gave some to Annie, and blew a little water on her face. After he dried her face, six of her male friends and relatives, three on each side, each with a hand on her head, sang a song and congratulated her on becoming a woman. She then walked to the other end of the house, sat down, and watched the feast. She was not allowed to eat salmon for another five days, however.

A little later the audience began individually singing their own dream-power songs, then stood for the "dream dance." The dance and the singing lasted for about an hour. At the end of the ceremony the guests took whatever food was left over and went home. That was the end of the period of seclusion for Annie, but for the next several months she had to dress up before eating. She had to cook outside and eat inside; she could not eat any fresh foods; she could pick berries but could not eat them. There were probably other restrictions as well.

About a year later, in another ceremony, Annie was painted and dressed in her very best. The guests sang again, and this time the shaman could give her any kind of food. At the end of this feast she removed her special clothes, and as of that moment she was considered ready for marriage.

Annie was attractive to the boys, and the boys were attractive to her. She remained a good-looking woman well into old age, and she must have been a knockout when she was in her prime. She learned early that with her large, bright eyes she could get the attention of the opposite sex quite easily. In fact, she no doubt got the attention of the opposite sex whether she wanted it or not.

According to her niece Lottie, Annie enjoyed playing around. She said that Annie's older half-sister Fannie (Lottie's mother) "had an awful time with her—fighting around in the brush with the boys!"[7] Annie might indeed have been a bit wild as a teenager. Lottie said that Annie had run away from home at Yachats. "She would never say anything but would just disappear from home and be gone at Siletz or somewhere for several days." Lottie said that at that time her mother, Fannie, gave Annie the nickname that meant "to sneak away from home!"[8]

Annie herself admitted that she was quite wild for a long time, even after she had grown up. She said: "I started in to run horses. No matter if a race horse, I would take it anyway. . . . I was not any good. I was just a wild little wanderer. But still they all wanted me in marriage."[9]

Annie told of the type of wife that was most desirable. The desirable wife was not a downcast woman who never looked at people and never smiled. The desirable wife, she said, was "not bashful." Annie added: "She jokes, she speaks forth when you address her. She speaks and jokes, she looks you right in the face, not with downcast head. That is the kind you should get. She will be a good wife."[10] In her later years Annie exhibited those very qualities, which she probably also displayed when she was young.

At Yachats was a Hanis Coos *mitadin* named Old
Lyman. He was the first man to seriously want Annie for a
wife. Annie's mother and her aunt were both opposed to
him. Annie was angry at the very idea. They all agreed that
"the long legged fellow was pretty horrible." But there was
a danger. Lyman was a *mitadin*, the type of shaman who has
power to cause ill to people. The danger was that Annie
might die if she did not accept him. They took what Annie
called "the chance of her life" and turned him down.[11] Either
Lyman did not use his poison power, or it had no effect on
Annie, since she did not die.

According to Lottie, and this may or may not be true,
Lottie's own father, Daloose Jackson, first had intercourse
with Annie after her first menses.[12] Afterward, Daloose
helped his brother to buy Annie in marriage for Daloose's
nephew Henry Jackson.

Henry was about thirty-five years old and already had
a wife. His Indian name was Tlapta, which meant "flapping
arms," as a baby flaps his arms.[13] He was the son of one of
Daloose's brothers, a man who was called Thick Mouth and
whose white name was Cammon.[14] Evidently Daloose and
Cammon jointly paid the marriage price for Annie.

It is interesting to note the manner in which the
relatives of Daloose all took the family name of Jackson. His
daughter Lottie explained this when she told about her
uncle Jim: "He began calling himself 'Chief Jim' or 'Tyee
Jim.' He had no surname. He was my father's brother. He
was way younger than my father, by an Umpqua mother. So
his modern name must have been 'Jim Jackson.'"[15] Cammon
no doubt came about the Jackson name the same way, and
his son Henry was called Henry Jackson. Thus Annie's name
during her first marriage was Annie Jackson. By coincidence
her second husband, an Alsea, was also named Jackson,
though he was no relation at all to the Coos Jacksons.

Annie's mother gave her premarital advice. Annie
probably knew it all, but she listened anyhow. Her mother

said: "Whatever your husband will want of you, that is the way you are to do it. When he will want to get on top of you, and he wants intercourse of you, you accede to that, because everybody does it. It will hurt a person the first time only. After that there is no pain any more."[16] Annie did just as her mother had told her.

Annie was also given advice on the hazards associated with excessive sexuality, which would cause a loss of strength and beauty. Her mother told her: "If you want your husband constantly on top of you, it will not be long before you will be ugly and lose your red-headed-woodpecker-scalp-feathers. And that is why your breasts too will not stand erect, they will hang down. Your body will be good no more, if you have wanted too much of that all the time."[17] Annie said, "That was the reason why they did not do it all the time, because that was what they feared."

In the days before the reservation period the sanctions against adultery were severe. A girl who fooled around too much before marriage could be killed by her father. A boy who fooled around too much and would not marry the girl could be killed by the girl's father. If the boy's parents were too poor to purchase the girl, the girl's father might cut off the boy's nose and ears. According to Annie: "That is what the people did. That is why they were afraid of that."[18] One needed to be careful in a culture in which morality was so strictly enforced.

Annie's husband Henry Jackson was abusive. She said: "He beat me all the time, though I did nothing wrong. Nevertheless he beat me." In characteristic fashion, Annie left. She said, "I would not go back there again to him. That is the way I was. But the relatives of my husband found out why I had left him, so they bought me again, and so I had to go back there to him once more."[19] Annie said that he not only beat her but chased other women as well. It was not a happy marriage.

On June 7, 1873, a little before Annie's marriage to Henry Jackson, George P. Litchfield was assigned as the last subagent of the Alsea Subagency.[20] While Litchfield was there, according to Annie, the Indians received some clothing and food from the government for the first time. A school was started, and the first teacher, Frank, was a young nephew of the subagent's.

Annie, about fourteen years old and married, started school. A young, fully developed, attractive, and bright-eyed girl like Annie was more than Frank could stand. Right away he decided that it would be a good idea to have her sit on his lap. She did, and he caressed her. Because she was already married, she decided that this was inappropriate behavior, and so after three or four days, she felt obliged to quit school.[21] She never learned to read or write. Years later Frank saw Lottie at Coos Bay. He said, "Lottie Jackson my dear girl. Is Annie Miner still living? She was my sweetheart!" Lottie said later, "He was really mash on the biggest girls. They fired him."[22]

Later, Litchfield's cousin James Watts was religious director and teacher for six weeks, and there were other teachers, but the subagency would be closed in another year.[23] Education was not one of the benefits conferred on the Indians at the Alsea Subagency.

Annie, back with her husband and his other wife, got pregnant for the first time and had a baby boy. According to Coos belief, if a boy's father played too hard in a shinny game, the baby's feet would puff and swell up. Sure enough, Henry Jackson played too hard in a shinny game when the baby was only two days old, and as expected, the baby's feet swelled up.[24] The family was able to reduce the swelling by using heated leaves.

The birth of a boy called for more of a feast than did the birth of a girl. Annie suggested this was because a girl cost the family more, at least in the short run. The short-run expenses that a family might expect for a girl but not for a boy included the entertainment expenses for a prospective groom's parents during prolonged marriage negotiations.[25] The costs of elaborate puberty rite ceremonies, as described at the beginning of this chapter, were certainly an expense for girls only. In addition, the costs of clothing and personal adornment may be expected to be greater for a girl than for a boy. The investment in a girl was returned when she married and the bride-price was paid by the groom's family.[26]

According to Annie, Henry continued to beat her even after she had the baby, and so she left him again. She took the baby, who was about one year old, with her. The custom of the people was that if a wife wanted to leave, she could do so if she left her children with her husband. That was the way the wife paid for herself. Henry Jackson's family wanted the baby, and so Annie finally gave her son to them so that she would not have to go back there again.[27] The baby died in a few years.

Annie's mother, Matilda, was not getting any younger. Her Coquille husband had died, and she had teamed up with an Alsea Indian named Kinv. They were both hard workers, and they were both survivors. They worked for Joel Winkler shoveling black sand onto the chute at what was then called Winkler Creek, a poorly paying placer mine near Big Stump Beach.[28] Matilda and Kinv together were paid one dollar per day.

Big Stump was on the beach about three miles south of the mouth of the Alsea River. It was a huge redwood stump that had drifted in from California hundreds of years earlier; the Alsea Indians considered it to be the center of their world. It was about halfway between the northern and the southern limits of Alsea territory and was actually within about forty miles of the forty-fifth parallel, halfway between the equator and the North Pole.[29] The intersection of the Pacific Coast with the forty-fifth parallel was not a bad analogy for the center of the world, if you happened to live on the Oregon Coast. This was, in any case, where Annie married into the Alsea tribe.

After Annie had left her first husband, she went up to Winkler's placer mine, where her mother and Kinv were working. Before long, arrangements were made for Annie to marry a full-blood Alsea her own age. His Indian name was Qualipcali; his white name was William Jackson. He and his eight brothers and sisters, who lived at Waldport, had grown up knowing the Coos, Coquille, and Umpqua Indians who were living at Yachats. His relatives made the arrangements for the marriage, which evidently began as one of young love.

Annie and her new husband worked at the placer mine with Annie's mother and others, shoveling the black sand onto the chute. The mine was almost worthless, and the pay was small. Even while engaged in the hard manual labor of the mine, Annie quickly became pregnant again. This time the baby was a girl, and they named her Nellie Agnes, after Annie's oldest and youngest half-sisters.

The connection with the Alsea continued. Before Annie's youngest half-sister, Agnes, had come of age, she married an Alsea, John Albert. Agnes was the first of many wives John had during the course of a long life. He lived long enough that when he died in 1950, he was the last of the Alsea full-bloods.

Shortly after Annie's marriage to William Jackson, a new version of the Ghost Dance was introduced from northern California by Coquille Thompson and Chetco Charlie. Annie attended the first of those dances at Alsea. Later, at Siletz, two sweathouses were built for the dance, and Annie attended the dances there along with most of the Alsea people.[30] Thompson and Charlie eventually took the dance on down the coast, and Annie was at Siuslaw when it was presented there.

The social life among the Alsea, the Lower Coquille, the Lower Umpqua, and the Coos who were living in the area was lively. Annie's husband William used to play a lot of cards, along with his brothers—Tom, Fred, and Joe Jackson—and Alsea Grant. Spencer Scott, a Lower Umpqua, sometimes played with them and once said, "That was how I caught on to understanding the Alsea language."[31] Spencer later married one of William Jackson's sisters, thus becoming Annie's brother-in-law.

A little after Nellie Agnes was born, the government decided to close the Alsea Subagency at Yachats and move the Indians from there to Siletz. The decision was promoted by pressure from commercial interests in the Willamette Valley to open all of the Coast Range to timber and other speculators. The low birth rate and the high death rate among the Indians had reduced their population by half during the fifteen years they had been there, and the government justified its action on economic grounds.

The cost of maintaining the Alsea Subagency at Yachats was not much more than the $1,000 annual salary of the subagent.[32] The government apparently appropriated $10,000 to facilitate the removal.[33] The economic justification for the removal was obviously a pretext for opening the land to speculation.

During their years at Yachats the surviving Coos and Lower Umpqua had found a home. Most of the elderly who had moved to Yachats had died there. Their children had grown up there and had come to know the fishing, hunting, and gathering grounds. Above all, they were left alone. The whites did not bother them because there were virtually no whites around. Yachats was home, the only home they had been secure in since the white settlers had arrived on the coast a generation earlier.

Ben Simpson, previously the agent at Siletz, was now the surveyor general for Oregon. He strongly supported closing the Yachats Subagency, even though he fully understood the injustice of the action.[34] In an earlier letter, he had eloquently stated the predicament of the Indians: "For

sixteen years they have been fed on promises that were
made only to be broken, and their hearts have sickened with
'hope deferred.' For sixteen years they have seen the White
man gathering his golden harvests from the lands they have
surrendered. And for all those long, weary years, they have
waited, and waited in vain for the fulfillment of the solemn
pledges with which the White man bought these lands."[35]
Amazingly, the same official who could describe the situation in such poignant terms was also an active party to the
cruel policy that was now being carried out.

The Indians within the Alsea Subagency were given a
choice: they could move to what remained of the reservation at either Siletz or the Salmon River, or they could move
out into the white culture and become assimilated. It was a
hard choice. The Coos, the Lower Umpqua, and some of
the Lower Coquille met in conference for four days at
Yachats to decide which alternative they would take.[36] At the
heartrending and soul-searching meeting, everyone had
their chance to speak. Some merely bewailed their fate. "If
the White man could take the water from us, he would,"[37]
said some of the older men who had been through a move
before.

Some of the Alsea came down from Waldport to take
part in the conference. The men sat in a row and passed a
single, straight-tubed stone pipe from one to another around
the circle, each taking a draw or two.[38] Last of all to speak
was an old Alsea Indian whose name has been forgotten. He
said in the Chinook jargon, "Nika mam'ook ill'ahee. Nika
muck'a muck nika." Lottie Evanoff, who heard the story
from her father, Daloose, commented that it sounded as if
he said (in translation), "I'm going to eat my land." But what
he really meant, she explained, was that he would put a fish
dam at his place and eat salmon, not imposing on the
whites.[39] In the end, the Alsea moved a few at a time from
Waldport to Siletz over the next three years.[40] The Coos and
the Umpqua decided to try to go back to their homes to the

south, homes that they had been forced to give up fifteen years earlier. This was the last major trauma in the diaspora of those peoples.

Soon after the council meetings at Yachats in 1875, the Indians began to move out. By going south at that time, about 360 persons ceased to be wards of the government.[41] Those few, such as Annie, who had marriage or other ties to Siletz moved there. Some of the others had relatives or other connections at the Umpqua and at Coos Bay, and they moved to those locations. The greatest number moved the twenty miles south to the Siuslaw.

The subagency was not officially closed until September 1876. Subagent Litchfield turned over all government property and records to Agent William Bagely at Siletz at that time.[42] All of the Indians had been gone for months. The land was then opened for filing by white settlers, at least one of whom obtained the Yachats prairie with its seventy acres of cleared farmland and other improvements made during the fifteen years of Indian residency.

Since Annie was married to an Alsea, she and the baby went to Siletz with her husband. He was part of a large family, which included Old (Alsea) Jackson and his four sons and some daughters-in-law and his four daughters and some sons-in-law. Most of them settled at Lower Farm on the Siletz Reservation.

Conditions at Siletz were much different from those at the coast. In 1876 there were about 650 Indians, plus the agency staff and a few soldiers.[43] A bewildering number of languages were spoken, with remnants of the tribes of the Willamette Valley, the Upper Umpqua, the Coquille, the Chetco, and the entire length of the Rogue River and its tributaries. The lingua franca among the older generation was the Chinook jargon; among the younger generation the preferred language was rapidly becoming English. Annie spoke only Miluk and Hanis Coos and was married into an

Alsea family. She could not talk to many people in her own languages.

The various cultures of all the peoples at Siletz had rapidly decayed into a confused and undifferentiated mélange. The younger people were being schooled in English and the practical trades. Tribal and family ties were maintained only loosely among a gloss of religion from Methodists, Catholics, and others. An infusion of Plains Indian culture and periodic revival movements such as the Ghost Dance added to the mix.

White intruders and resident soldiers, as well as the Indians themselves, found that they could take advantage of the differing sexual mores among the peoples on the reservation. As a result, the number of babies of mixed parentage and unknown paternity increased. Venereal disease, especially gonorrhea, was common. The situation at Siletz at that time could be considered classically decadent.

The temptations within this environment were too much for Annie's husband. He began consorting with Annie's best friend, an Alsea woman named Mary who was also his uncle's wife. Annie said, "As for my husband, his mother's brother was married to my very own chum and he was having an affair with her."[44] It has been alleged by Lottie, Spencer Scott, and others that Annie also began having an affair at about this time, with another Alsea named Alsea Grant.[45]

Several Alsea brothers were named Grant, just as several brothers were named Jackson. One of the Grants was Jesse, also called U. S. Grant. He had become an influential preacher of the Ghost Dance movement at Siletz and was considered to be a "very smart man." The family was of some importance at Siletz. Interestingly, in 1910 Alsea Grant's brother Jesse and William Jackson's brother Tom were the principal Alsea informants to the anthropologist Leo Frachtenberg. They provided the bulk of what is

known of the Alsea language and ethnology, just as Annie
later provided most of what is known of the Miluk Coos
language and ethnology.

Annie had been at Siletz for about two years when, in
1877, Matilda arrived from the Siuslaw, where she had been
living since leaving Yachats. Quickly realizing what was
going on with Annie and her husband, Matilda told Annie,
"Do not live in this place."[46] Annie, who by then was seventeen years old, was still obedient to her mother. She later
said that whatever her mother told her, that is what she did.
She told her mother: "Very well then. When you return to
Siuslaw I will go with you." She then told her husband:
"When my mother goes back, I will go with her. You can
come and get me." He replied: "All right. I will come and
get you."

William Jackson's mother did not want Annie to take
the baby, Nellie, with her. Annie did not even bother to
reply to this demand. She had already given up one baby,
who had died. She had made up her mind to take Nellie,
and take Nellie she did. William Jackson never did go down
to the Siuslaw to get Annie back, however, and so that was
the end of that marriage.

When Annie arrived at Siuslaw with her mother and her
baby daughter, most of her relatives and friends were already
there. Her grandmother and her grandfather, Minkws, lived
there, as did her half-sisters Fannie and Agnes. Fannie's
husband, Daloose Jackson, and their daughter Lottie were
there, along with Daloose's other daughters, Kate and
Minnie. In fact, most of the Indians who had been living at
Yachats in 1875 had moved in with the Siuslaw Indians on
the North Fork of the Siuslaw River a few miles from the
present town of Florence. Among the other relatives living
there were Annie's maternal uncles. Annie and her daughter
moved into the household of one of them, her mother's
brother Jesse.[47] This remained their home during their three
years at Siuslaw.

The Siuslaw River is only about twenty miles, by the beach route, south of Yachats, past Cape Perpetua, Heceta Head, and Sea Lion Point. The trail had been used often since the Coos and Umpqua Indians had first moved to Yachats in 1860. Visits, intermarriage, and other communication between Yachats and Siuslaw had been continuous, and so this next move was not to a completely unknown place. It was, however, a move from a place where they had security and a land base to a place where they had neither.

The town that later became Florence had only a general store and two saloons at that time. Frank Drew, who was then a young man, said that the Indians lived very well by hunting, fishing, and trapping.[48] "In ten minutes," he said, "I could dig a mess of clams." There was an abundance of flounder and other fish.

At that time there was only canoe travel on the Siuslaw River. Frank Drew said that there were only "deer and bear and elk trails through the woods up there for a man to go on." He had once gone up the main river with his uncle Michel to get eels at a place above Swisshome. His uncle Michel was brother-in-law to old Jean Gagnier of the Hudson's Bay Company. Frank remembered, "That evening in June you could hear the otters and beavers playing in the creek water."[49] It was memories such as these that the old-timers most relished in later years.

Frank added that elk were "as tame as cows, and numerous!"[50] He told of the time that Jean Gagnier's son John came on a band of three hundred elk at Maple Creek. He killed three and took merely the hindquarters of one. Frank said, "He shot them just to see them fall."[51]

Whites were killing whales offshore during those years, and occasionally one that had been killed and lost would drift onto the beach. This was always an event of importance to the Indians, who would butcher the carcass for the blubber. Sawmills in those days were lubricated with whale oil, so there was a ready market. The beached whales were considered communal property and not the property of any individual.

Lottie told of a female whale that had drifted ashore on the beach a little north of the mouth of the Siuslaw River. Both the whale and its dead baby were found there. Ike and Jesse Martin found them, cut off one-half of the female whale, and hid it for themselves. They then reported that they had found a half a whale! When Daloose and the Siuslaw people went there and saw that the cut was fresh, they knew what had happened and were determined that Ike and Jesse would not get away with the deception.

The Siuslaw *mitadin* doctors, in a rage, danced in their houses all night. This action ostensibly created a storm, which carried to sea the whale half that had been hidden by Ike and Jesse.[52] The Siuslaw got their share of the whale, and Ike and Jesse were thereby taught a lesson.

The Indian doctors at Siuslaw had a reputation for holding considerable power. John Gagnier's wife, a doctor, took Lottie's younger brother as a patient when he was dying of tuberculosis. According to Lottie, she worked very hard to get a "pain" out of a person. The "pain" she pulled from the side of Lottie's brother's chest "looked like wood-worms." Lottie added, "The worms were wriggling in the water."[53] Daloose and the family then went to Coos Bay to earn some money, but the boy got worse. They returned to Siuslaw to see the doctor again. Lottie said: "The doctor always finger-flips cold water quickly on the patient and if the patient jumps, there is hope. But if he does not jump, you are too far gone."[54] The doctor said that Lottie's brother was too far gone. She refused the case, and the boy died soon thereafter.

In the culture of these peoples, nothing of this nature happened by chance. Somebody caused it. Annie told the story that Melsin, a man whose ears and nose had been cut off by Tyee Jim, was accused of putting poison power into Lottie's brother, who had died as a result. Two women of the family then asked Melsin to go with them in a canoe. As they went downstream, they tipped the canoe over in the shallow water of the mud flats. They clubbed Melsin over the head, held him under the water, and drowned him.[55] The two women then went to the gold-mining camp north of Bandon and lived there.

At about the time that Annie arrived at Siuslaw there was a revival of the Warm House Dance. This was a Siletz variation of the California Earth Lodge Cult, which in turn was a version of the original Ghost Dance of 1870. Coquille Thompson and Chetco Charlie had come down from Siletz to introduce it to the Indians on the coast. They first tried it for one night only at Alsea (Waldport), evidently in April. Annie was there, and she said that Thompson was performing the dance to make money. She said that he charged people to see it. He told the Indians that if they danced, their dead ancestors would come back, and that if they did not join in, they would turn into rock.[56]

Thompson and Charlie were in their prime and were very persuasive. At Siuslaw it took them only three days to talk the Indians on the North Fork into building a large ceremonial dance house on the west shore near the mouth of that stream. The Indians built it in three weeks, following a design that had originally come from the Shasta or the Wintu Indians of central California.

They dug a rectangular pit sixty feet long by twenty-four feet wide by four feet deep. Then they set three ten-foot posts down the center with eight-foot supporting posts on the sides. Ridge poles were set on top of the center posts, and horizontal cedar siding was lapped to keep out the wind. A fire pit was placed in about the center of the building, and a cedar-board partition about seven feet high was placed at one end. This area was used to store costumes and props and to give a place for the shamans and dancers to make their entrances and exits. There was only a single narrow outside entrance at the side of the building, opposite the center post.[57]

The major props were clappers specially made of eighteen-inch-long elderberry stalks. The dancing was done by ten or twelve men, barefooted and barechested. They wore modern trousers and a feathered headband. They held hands as they danced around the fire, singing the prescribed songs with no drumming. They continued for half the night, three nights in a row. Frank Drew remembered that even though they did this twice during 1878, the dead did not return. The lodge was never used again, and it eventually rotted down.[58] Dream dances continued at Siuslaw, however, until 1894, when most of the Indians remaining there were converted to evangelical Christianity.[59]

Coquille Thompson and Chetco Charlie, both of whom were receiving the attentions of some of the women, were treated well and paid with guns, horses, blankets, and clothing. They then went on to Gardner to try the dance with the Umpqua Indians; they rented a hall and charged fifty cents for admission. According to Frank Drew, who was there, whiskey was plentiful, and many whites came to see the dance. A fight broke up the event, however.[60]

Later, Thompson and Charlie went to Coos Bay and set up a big dance at Empire. This lasted about a month, with dances three times a week. At the end of the month, Thompson and Charlie divided the money: Thompson took the "white man's money," and Charlie took "all the beads and clothing."[61] Frank Drew and Alsea Jefferson attended one of the dances at Empire. Frank said there were forty or more Indians dancing there. Daloose Jackson was present.[62] Old Taylor, a Coos Indian, fell dead indoors at that dance.

Annie's skepticism toward spiritual matters is revealed in her observations of the Warm House Dance. She noted that if you did not give Thompson and Charlie clothes and other objects, they threatened to turn you into rock. "They made money on it," she said.[63] However, she did occasionally have an experience that seemed to her to have a spiritual origin. For instance, the day after one of the dances at Siuslaw, Annie and some others were sitting outside the building. One of the women went inside while Annie stayed outside alone. As Annie told it, another woman, a Siuslaw woman, went around the building and into some huckleberry bushes. Annie watched her and then went inside the single door of the building and there was the same woman, seated inside![64] "She did not live long after," Annie said.[65] This was considered a case of seeing a person's spirit double and was the second time in her life that Annie had experienced such a phenomenon. She laughingly told Melville Jacobs, "That was my eyes deceiving me." But Jacobs strongly suspected that Annie at least partly believed she had seen a spirit.

The year that Annie arrived at the Siuslaw also saw the first beginnings of commerce on that river. In July 1877 the three-hundred-ton steamer *Alexander Duncan* crossed the bar, the first ship ever to do so, and delivered machinery for a salmon cannery and a sawmill. The ship was owned by R. D. Hume, the "pygmy monopolist" from San Francisco who was establishing salmon canneries at the mouths of some of the rivers on the Oregon Coast.

Later that same year the cannery began operation near the beach on the northern side of the river. The following year the sawmill, which was set up next to the cannery, began cutting lumber for local use.[66] It is more than likely that both Annie and her mother worked in the cannery. All of the employees of the cannery at that time were Indian women, and all of the fishing was done by Indian men.[67] According to Lottie, there were no Chinese working there.

Annie was probably still living at Siuslaw when the settlement got its new name. In 1880 an Indian found a plank of driftwood that turned out to be the nameboard from the three-masted bark *Florence*, which had sunk offshore in a storm in November 1875.[68] Someone leaned the ten-foot board against the general store, then nailed it above the door of a "hotel," which was later designated as the post office. Thus the settlement was conveniently named "Florence" because there was a sign available with the name already on it.[69] At about that time, Annie and her daughter moved down to Coos Bay.

Near the head of Haynes Slough, Coos Bay. Annie lived near this site for several years during the 1880s. Photo by the author.

Return to Coos Bay

The beach route from the Siuslaw River to Coos Bay had not changed in centuries: forty miles of sand on one side and the sea on the other, punctuated by the Umpqua River and a few creeks. The only change was in the means of transportation. Twenty years earlier, when Annie had gone from Coos Bay to Yachats, her mother had carried her while walking the entire distance. Now a stage line made the trip irregularly, and passengers could ride in comparative comfort with a canvas sheet blocking the wind from the seaward side. At Umpqua River there was now a ferry service.

Annie's half-sister Fannie was already living at Coos Bay and was well acquainted with the area and the people there. Her husband, Daloose Jackson, was still a chief of the Coos Indians. All through the reservation period he had regularly gotten a pass from the subagent at Yachats and had spent a part of each year at Coos Bay along with Fannie, their daughter Lottie, and his other wives and daughters.

Lottie remembered the trips on horseback to Coos Bay with some affection. She told of a horse they had named "Wild Charley" who would swim fast across the Umpqua River towing their canoe behind him—"North or South," Lottie said.[1] When they went around Cape Perpetua, she said, they would wait for low tide and then her father would put her on the horse and whisk her around the rock between waves.[2] She said that the women of the party went on the trail over the hill.

At Empire, Daloose's family was well-known. Lottie remembers one time while they were there when she and her half-sisters were spoken to by Bill Luse, son of Henry Luse, the sawmill man. He said, in Miluk, "Whose girls are you?" Lottie later told her mother, "A Whiteman talked Indian to me!"[3] The Luse sawmill at Empire hired primarily Indian men, and Bill was probably the only white ever to have learned the Miluk language.[4] His wife at that time was a South Slough Miluk.

Daloose once told his daughter Lottie about the time when the Luse sawmill closed down for a day because a whale had gotten stranded at the mouth of Pony Slough. Usually any whale that came into the bay would swim out again, but this one had become stuck on the mud flats when the tide went out. The entire crew went over to Pony Slough to kill and butcher the whale to get oil for the sawmill. Daloose said that where the whale swung its tail there was a deep hole.[5] Quite a crowd of Indians and whites had gathered, with probably one hundred men there.

Daloose was quite a colorful character who knew how to get what he wanted from the whites. They in turn liked nothing more than to be acquainted with "The Chief." Frank Drew once commented, "Old Jackson and those old fellows were fond of whiskey."[6] The Indians also provided a mild sort of amusement to the whites and gave them something to talk about to each other.

Daloose and his family moved into a float house at Dewey's Rock, where they lived for many years. Dewey's Rock was at the edge of the upper bay at the southern end of what is now the downtown part of the city of North Bend. Evidently, several of the old Coos Indians lived there. The 1880 census showed Mrs. Marlow, age sixty, and three other Indians in the "North Bend Precinct." Her husband, Old Marlow, does not show up in the census at all. The sawmill and the shipyard of Simpson Lumber Company were just a little to the north of Dewey's Rock, near the location of the old Upper Hanis Indian village of Kolokaytch.[7]

The well-known Daloose was well thought of around the sawmill and could get anything he wanted there. In the early days of the mill, Superintendent Alfred Butler would tell visiting Indians to go into the cookhouse. He would then order the head cook, Bill Walker, to feed them.[8] This was a tradition continued for many years. Daloose was very much at home at Dewey's Rock and at the Simpson mill.

Daloose always wore a plug hat and carried a cane; for years he was seen every day along the roads around North Bend. He addressed his white friends as "Boss," and most of them would slip into his hand a silver dollar, gratefully received. He was known to have a "friendly disposition, absolute honesty and fidelity towards those whom he cherished as friends." He was considered by the whites as "a truly loveable character."[9] Of course, his white friends knew about Daloose only that which he wanted them to know. His other side was known only to the Indians.

The stage from the Umpqua terminated at Jarvis Landing on the north spit of Coos Bay. A one-mile boat ride across the bay brought the passengers to Empire. In 1880 Empire was a lively little town, serving as the county seat of Coos County and as the site of the U.S. Customs House.

With a population of about 600, its economy was dominated by the Luse sawmill, which had been operating since before the Indians had been removed north.

It was as though there were two towns of Empire at that time, one Indian and one white. The business section was on the narrow, flat beach area, a few feet above high tide, and on the wharfs. The Indian quarter was at the southern end of that beach. The homes of the white families were for the most part on the plateau some forty or fifty feet above the sawmill and business section. One of the whites who grew up in Empire stated, "No generation ever had a better childhood than the children of Empire in the 1880's."[10] Such an idyllic childhood may have been reserved for the white children, however.

Lottie remembered that there were thirteen saloons in the little town at that time.[11] Orvil Dodge enumerated some of them: "Of the saloons, which were numerous, when business was lively, the pioneers will remember Hopkins, John Nasburg, Dick Cussens, A. C. Rogers, James Jordan, Hank Barrot, Billy Buckhorn, Kiley, Knowls and Floyd, and so many others whose names occur to the writer, that we forbear further record, except Henry Shafenburg, who catered to the wants of a thirsty public for a number of years."[12] The 1880 census for Empire listed John Flanagan, age fifty-two, as a "liquor dealer." John was a younger brother of Patrick and James Flanagan, who had arrived at the Umpqua River in 1850. He was a very early and permanent fixture at Empire and had been long and well acquainted with Annie's half-sister Fannie, Daloose, and the rest of the family. Being in the liquor business, he was also well aware of the fate that awaited good-looking young Indian women if they stayed in the Indian quarter of town.

Annie said in her autobiography: "At the time I came there the moving people were bad. They bothered the Indian girls at Empire."[13] When Annie and her daughter, Nellie, arrived at Empire in 1880, one of the first people they ran into was John Flanagan. He advised Annie not to live in the Indian part of town because of the alcohol, venereal disease, and abusive men.

Much to their credit, John and his wife, Mary Flanagan, insisted that Annie and her daughter stay with them until she could find a job and other accommodations. Annie said later, "Indeed from that time on I did not live any more with the Indians."[14] And it was from this time, at the age of twenty, that she began to learn the English language.

Although Annie had not been to Coos Bay since infancy, she had many relatives there. Her aunt Mary, whose Indian name was Ticeket, had married "Dutch Henry" Miller and lived on Haynes Slough. Mary had lived on Coos Bay during the entire reservation period. She told Annie: "Do not stay at the village of the white people, because they are no good. People from the 'Island Land' [false analogy for Ireland land] live close to where I live. You go there to live. They will show you how white women labor."[15] She wanted Annie to learn the ways of the whites because she was certain that the Indian ways Annie had lived up until that time would do her niece no good from now on.

The people from Ireland were the family of William Weir. Actually, only William was from Ireland. His wife, Eliza, and their six-year-old daughter had been born in Canada. The two younger daughters were born in Oregon. Mrs. Weir needed help with the housework. Annie's aunt Mary arranged for Annie to go to work there for room and board while she learned the ways of white women. Annie's half-sister Fannie agreed to take care of Annie's daughter, Nellie, while Annie was boarding out at the Weirs. She said, "I will take your child, while you live with the moving people."[16]

The 1880 census shows that William Weir, thirty-three, was a coal miner working at the Newport mine on Coalbank Slough. The Newport mine had been established by John Flanagan's brother Patrick. Like William Weir, the Flanagan brothers had originally come from Ireland. William Weir worked part of the time in the mine and lived the rest of the time at his farm on Haynes Slough. His clothes, filthy from working in the mine all week, had to be boiled and scrubbed. There were the three young children and a hired man, besides Annie and Mrs. Weir. In addition to the cooking, baking, cleaning, and general chores, the bedding and clothing for all of them had to be washed each week. The washing meant getting the wood for enough fire to heat the fifteen gallons of water needed to boil the clothes, which were then taken out of the boiler with a stick and scrubbed by hand on a washboard in a washtub.[17] The job of washerwoman in those days was one of hard manual labor. Mrs. Weir was fortunate to have Annie as a live-in housekeeper to help with this work.

During the twenty years since Annie and her mother had gone from Coos Bay to Yachats, white settlers had moved into all of the locations that had formerly been occupied by the Indians. Most of the homesites selected by the white settlers were the same sites that had previously been selected by the earlier inhabitants. A homesite is a homesite, Indian or white. However, nearly all of these sites had been abandoned for many years by the time the wave of white setters moved in during the 1880s. The whites were often surprised to find, while digging in the garden or plowing the fields, that they would uncover bones, shells, stone implements, and occasionally trade beads and other items. On Haynes Slough there were such locations on both shores, and at least one settler had a "nail keg full" of these items, nearly all of which were subsequently lost.* They were given away, thrown away, scattered, and forgotten.

---

* The author lived on Haynes Slough during the 1940s and remembers Emil Peterson—among others—telling of the "nail keg" full of Indian artifacts that his family had collected from a site adjacent to his house.

Annie in later years often talked about the way the whites would dig up the graves and village sites of the Indians.[18] One of the worst offenders was later a neighbor of hers at Big Creek, a "Dr. Cook," who in the 1880 census for Empire was listed as a thirty-eight-year-old boot maker. Lottie told how he rose from that modest profession through the study of anatomy: "Clear over to Umpqua, Siuslaw, and clear over to Yachats that George Barrett and others dug the dead people up, Doctor Cook helping him. Digging those dead people Doctor Cook got to be a doctor. First he was a shoemaker."[19] All of the sloughs and inlets had been renamed, most of them after the settlers who moved onto them. Only Willanch, the slough at the village where Annie was born, retained its original Indian name.

Lottie remembered one time when they were living at Dewey's Rock: a white man named Glen Aiken asked her for the Indian name for South Marshfield. He was evidently doing some subdividing and wanted to name either the town or a lodge after the Indian name. Lottie could not remember the name until five days later! The name, as Lottie later remembered it, was something like "hal-tch," but it was never used.[20]

Annie must have worked for Mrs. Weir for two or three years at least. During one winter she went with them to the Newport coal mines on Coalbank Slough, returning to Haynes Slough in the spring.[21] She washed the clothes, she cleaned the house, and she did all the domestic chores. During this time she was quickly learning enough of the English language and the ways of the white people so that she could get by in this new world.

While Annie worked for Mrs. Weir she became acquainted with a young woman who did taxidermy. This may have been Mrs. Weir herself or a neighbor. In any case, Annie became interested in the craft and learned to mount small animals and birds. One night she dreamed that she heard the birds and animals say: "Oh, I'm so cold. They

have my clothes." After that she gave up taxidermy, having
"sort of lost heart in doing that to things."[22]

There seems to have been a social or class difference
between those Indians who had remained at Coos Bay
during the reservation period and those who had been
forced to go north to Yachats. At Yachats the Indians had
kept their own languages, and some of the customs had
been passed on to the young. There was very little influence
from the whites because there were very few whites around.
At Coos Bay, by contrast, the Indians experienced powerful
social and economic pressures to adapt to the ways of the
whites, to learn English, and to play down their Indian roots
as much as possible.

Almost all of the Indians who had remained at Coos
Bay during the reservation period were women who were
married to white men. Their children grew up knowing very
little of the language and culture of their mothers. Any
children who happened to have predominantly Caucasian
features found it very much to their advantage to deempha-
size the Indian part of themselves. As Annie's granddaughter,
Iola Larson, told the author, "If you could pass for white,
you did."[23]

The Indians who returned from the reservation at
Yachats had no chance to "pass for white." They had not
learned English, they did not have white spouses, and they
had learned very little of what it took to enter into the white
economy. They became the lowest economic and social
class on the bay.

Of the approximately 360 Indians who went south from
the reservation at Yachats in 1875, there are very few
descendants today. The 1900 census entry for Annie's half-
sister Fannie gives a poignant statistic that tells the story:
Fannie reported that in her lifetime, she had been the
mother of thirteen children, only one of whom was living.
That one was Lottie, and Lottie had no children.

With all of his wives and all of his children, the blood-
line of Chief Daloose Jackson ended in 1944 when his last
offspring, his daughter Lottie, died. Low fertility and high
mortality are said to be common wherever a group of people
of one race is being displaced by a numerically superior
group of people of another race. That was certainly the case
among the Coos.

There was, however, fairly high fertility among the
descendants of the mixed marriages of Indian women and
white pioneers. One of these families was that of James
Jordan, a hunter from Kentucky, and his Hanis wife, Jane.
They raised a large family at Haynes Slough. Their oldest
son, George, was born in 1861. George took quite a liking
to Annie. In fact, he seems to have made himself into
something of a pest because Annie was not interested in
him.[24] In the 1880 census George was listed twice: once at
home at Haynes Slough and once at the bunkhouse of the
sawmill where he worked in Marshfield. At home on weekends, he continued to try to win the favor of Annie, who was
reluctant to get involved.

More and more of Annie's relatives and acquaintances
were arriving from Florence to live at Coos Bay. Her mother,
Matilda, and her grandmother, Miluk-w'mae (Susan), moved
from Florence to Haynes Slough. They moved in with
Annie's aunt Mary and "Dutch Henry" Miller. The Millers
had a shed built especially for the grandmother to live in,
and she lived there for the rest of her life. One day she
was sitting in her canoe at the Millers' place when she fell
asleep and died. She did not have the straight black hair
that predominated among the Indians of the Northwest.
Hers was a wavy dark brown, considered to be very beautiful. At the time she died, she was said to have been about
one hundred years old and did not have a single gray hair.[25]
Her husband, Minkws, had preceded her in death some
years earlier.

Annie's niece Lottie often stayed either with Annie or with Mary during those years on Haynes Slough.[26] She remembered Annie and herself being told that there were rattlesnakes on the hill between the mouths of Haynes and Larson Sloughs.[27] This seemed unlikely, however, because there were said to be no rattlesnakes on Coos Bay. It is, however, a tribute to the reliability of oral history to note that, in 1989, over one hundred years later, rattlesnakes were found in that precise location. This was a matter of such local interest that it made the front page of *The World* newspaper.

One matter that is not clear is the source of the animosity that later emerged between Annie and Lottie. In later years Lottie would not visit Annie and was quoted as saying vicious and hateful things about her.[28] Both Annie and Lottie were known to have been exceptionally strong-willed individuals, and during the 1880s both were single. The beginnings of the problem might have been over a man. When one is considering friction among relatives, however, there is seldom a single cause.

Lottie's half-sister Kate, or Kitty Hayes as she was sometimes known, also came to Coos Bay. She is the one who at Yachats had lied to her husband, Jack Rogers, saying that his nephew Frank had sexually harassed her. That lie resulted in Frank's murder.

According to Annie, Kate was a jealous woman. A few years into her marriage to Chief Jack Rogers she had reason to be jealous because, it was said, Rogers began frequently to consort with other women. Whenever Kate found Rogers with another woman, "she would nearly kill that woman." Once, according to Annie, she thrust a burning brand into a woman's crotch. "That is how she was jealous," continued Annie.[29]

After they returned to Coos Bay, Kate admitted to Rogers that she had lied to him about Frank, that there had been no sexual harassment after all. Rogers flew into a rage

because Frank had been his own nephew and he had caused
Frank to be killed because of the accusation. He beat Kate
almost to death and would probably have killed her had it
not been for the intervention of their daughter. Not long
afterward, Jack Rogers became ill and died. The common
gossip was that Kitty had poisoned him.

Kitty thereafter began to stay drunk much of the time.
She moved in with "Joe, a Port Orford Indian."[30] According
to Annie, she began to prostitute herself for drink. George
Jordan showed up at Kitty's place one night, having himself
been under the influence of liquor. Joe was in bed, crippled,
according to Lottie. Evidently, as George made out with
Kitty, Joe, from his bed, shot and killed George. Incidentally,
this got Annie off the hook. As she said, "I did not marry
because he had been killed."[31] According to Annie, Kitty
then "was just completely drunken all the time. Then she
died poor."[32] This was not an uncommon fate for the
Indians who had returned to Coos Bay from Yachats.

Annie was exceptionally strong-willed. This one characteristic stands out in all accounts of her, from early childhood until her old age. The story of how she ended her
employment with Eliza Weir is representative.

> I was washing clothes. That woman said, "Leave
> your washing! You will paint the house here!" That
> is what she said to me. "Not until I have finished
> my washing. Then I will paint." "No, leave your
> washing here anyway. Come! paint the house!"
> "I don't do such painting. Even if my mother
> wanted me to paint her house, I would not paint
> it." Then I was angry. I threw down the washing,
> I went inside, I went up above. My old trunk or
> thing, I put my poor clothes into it there. She
> came up to there. "Don't go away! Do stay here!"
> "Get away! rich-person's child! I might strike you.
> Don't bother with me! don't talk to me! you evil
> smelling person! I have labored for you for nothing,

and then you want to boss me. Child of a dog! Get
away! don't talk to me!"[33]

Annie then went directly to work for Mrs. Weir's sister, who
lived nearby. She later worked in various places up and down
Haynes Slough. She had become conversant in the English
language, and as a bright, attractive young woman, she was
becoming well-known. She began to socialize. She said:
"Then about that time I began to learn the moving people's
dances. I went wherever they had a dance somewhere."[34]

Annie's first experience with dance had been the Native
American revivalist Ghost Dance at Yachats in 1872.[35] The
Moving People's dances were quite different. There were
the round dances and the square dances, the Virginia reel
and the waltz, the schottische and the Paul Jones. These
dances were held in the barns and other outbuildings up and
down Haynes Slough, North Slough, Kentuck Slough, and
all around the bay. Annie went to all of them that she could.

Almost anyone would like to excel at something, and
almost anyone would also like to have the fellowship of a
group. The dance is said to provide satisfaction on both
counts. Annie loved dancing and was good at it. She danced
in groups, and she danced alone. She even danced at the
masquerades. She was popular.

In 1885 Charles McFarlin, a cranberry farmer from
South Carver, Massachusetts, bought George Beale's farm
near the head of tidewater on North Slough.[36] The Beale
farm was little more than a bog of insectivorous plants
known as darlingtonia, the French flytrap. This place was a
bog, and McFarlin was looking for a bog, since that is where
cranberries grow. His cranberry enterprise, as it turned out,
was one of the most innovative agricultural experiments on
the West Coast. Through the 1920s it was also the most
significant social and cultural institution for the Indians of
Coos Bay. The local importance of McFarlin's cranberry
bogs cannot be overestimated.

The location of the McFarlin cranberry bogs near the head of tidewater on North Slough had been the site of an Indian settlement for two or three thousand years. At one time it was part of the ocean beach, but as the sand dunes developed, a bog was created and the darlingtonia plant took over.[37] At the time the whites arrived, the Indians called the place by their name for the darlingtonia.

McFarlin needed seasonal workers for his cranberry harvests, and for generations at his home in Massachusetts, Indians had been hired to pick cranberries. The cranberry is in fact a native American berry, introduced to the whites by the Indians. McFarlin found the Indians of the Coos Bay area to be a perfect source of labor for picking. He treated them well, and he went to the trouble of building a large hall with bunks upstairs and a dance area downstairs.

Annie lived at Haynes Slough, only a two-mile walk over a low hill. She was almost certainly among those who took advantage of McFarlin's enterprise when the first crop was picked in September 1887.[38] She continued to look forward to those annual harvests for more than thirty years.

Lottie said that the pickers used to have dances every night during the cranberry harvests. She said that the farmer girls would come in from the surrounding country. "They would have an exclusively white people dance, and then the next one would be for mixed halfbreeds and whites."[39] The music for the dances would usually be provided by a two- or three-piece band composed of a piano and a fiddle with sometimes a harmonica, an accordion, or another fiddle.

Annie commented in her autobiography that she had become acquainted with one of the fiddlers. "After that at the moving people's dances," she said, "whenever there was a dance of the (white) people, there I myself mingled with them too."[40] She did not mention the name of the fiddler or the nature of their relationship.

In fact, not much is known of these years during which Annie was a nubile young woman. Other than mentioning the dances and the fiddler, she chose not to talk about this time in her autobiography. It may be fair to say that what she did was nobody's business but her own. As far as is known, she bore no children after Nellie. If she married anyone during this period, we know nothing of it. A record at the Coos County Courthouse indicates a marriage in 1892 between an Ed Livingston and an Annie Minor, but there is no substantiating evidence to prove that this was our Annie. The first hard documentation of her activities is her marriage to Eli Metcalf in 1898, when she was thirty-eight years old.

The cranberry season soon became an important social event for the Indians all along the coast. Meetings were sometimes held during the harvest to plan ways in which the Indians might convince the government that they were due some compensation for the lands that had been taken from them.

George Bundy Wasson was nine years old when he attended the first harvest of the cranberries with his mother in 1887. George and his several brothers and sisters were raised on South Slough, where the elder George Wasson was a lumberman. His mother was Adulsa, the child of a Coos father and an Athapaskan Upper Coquille mother.[41] Adulsa's mother, Gishgiu, was the shaman that Annie's half-sister Fannie had wanted as the officiating shaman for Annie's puberty rites years earlier.

Young George Wasson went to the harvest each fall until he left for Chemawa Indian School in 1892. Throughout the rest of his school years he continued to go to the cranberry harvests during the last week or two before leaving for school each September.[42] It was at the cranberry harvests that he became acquainted with many of the older Indians, including a number who had signed the unratified treaty of 1855.

The Wasson family was one of the few families of Indian descent in Coos County to have taken advantage of the higher education opportunities that the government was making available during those years. George went on from Chemawa to the Carlisle Indian Institute and ultimately became an attorney. After becoming a lawyer, he devoted eleven years of his life to attempts to get a settlement for the Indians of Coos County for the lands taken from them.[43] These efforts failed, but they established the groundwork for the successes that were to come many years later. Neither George nor any of his generation lived long enough to reap the benefits.

The same year that George Bundy Wasson left for Chemawa Indian School, C. H. Holden, a land attorney, came to Coos Bay from Florence with Frank Drew and some of the other Coos who were still living on the Siuslaw River.* They held a meeting at the Pioneer Hotel in Empire. Frank Drew and others spoke; the thrust of the meeting was an attempt to get financial support from the Indians around Coos Bay so that a suit could be filed against the government.

Probably most of the people of Indian descent who were living on the bay at the time—including Annie, her half-sister Fannie, and her niece Lottie—attended the meeting. Lottie's new husband, Alex Evanoff, a young Russian-Aleut from Alaska, was present and remembered that Fannie contributed $5.00 and Lottie donated $1.50 to the cause.[44] The "Chief" of the group, until he died in 1907, was Daloose Jackson.[45] This was the first of many "Indian Nights Meetings" held in Empire.

Over the years Annie became a fixture at these meetings, strongly supporting the effort. Her granddaughter, Iola,

* Colonel C. H. Holden was an appointed land commissioner for Oregon, which authorized him to process hamestead applications in the Siuslaw area. His field of law related to land titles, making him an obvious choice to help the coastal Indians pursue their land claims, I am grateful to the volunteers at the Siuslaw Pioneer Museum in Florence, Oregon, for providing me with information about Holden.

remembered that at the meetings later called by George Bundy Wasson, Annie would wear a beautiful white buckskin dress.[46] It was a magnificent dress, its style inspired by the Plains Indian culture that had by then caught the imagination of many other Native Americans, as well as the American public at large.

Chief Daloose Jackson (Annie's brother-in-law), dressed up on the docks at North Bend, 1890s. Photo courtesy of Iola Larson.

"The Cranberry Pickers," North Slough, 1910. Families from Big Creek and South Slough are well represented in this photograph. Standing, third from left: Nellie Aasen; fourth: Ione Baker; fifth: Annie (in checkered blouse); sixth: Ellen Metcalf; seventh: Nancy Palmer; eighth: Susan Wasson (in dark clothes); ninth: (behind, with black hat) George Baker; tenth: Jim Elliott; eleventh: Wentworth Baker (with beard); twelfth: Milton Elliott; thirteenth: Francis Elliott. Most of the children in front and the men in back are unidentified. Postcard photo courtesy Iola Larson.

8

Big Creek

During the late 1880s, federal legislation was enacted to break up the land base of the Indians on the reservations so that they would more quickly assimilate into the mainstream of American society. The legislation, incidentally, opened surplus reservation lands to white speculators. Legislators in the East felt that this was the most humane and civilized policy; legislators in the West saw it as an opportunity to open the reservation lands to private ownership. The legislation was known as the General Allotment Act, or the Dawes Severalty Act, of 1887. Basically, it permitted reservation lands to be allotted to individual Indian families in lots of 160 acres. The unallotted lands could be sold by the government.

The Dawes Act was quite popular among many Indians as well as whites. It permitted qualified nonreservation Indians, such as many of the Coos, to file for allotments on marginal federal lands. As a practical matter, however, the Indians at Coos Bay who had returned from the reservation at Yachats were not the ones who filed for allotments. More than likely, they did not understand the system. The ones who filed for and were granted allotments were the families of mixed blood with white fathers and Indian mothers, most of whom had not been removed to the reservation in the first place. Annie never filed, but she lived on and around the allotments that were made on Big Creek, near Sunset Bay.

Big Creek is the small stream that runs into Sunset Bay, a large ocean cove that lies about two miles southwest of the entrance to Coos Bay. "Big Creek" was coincidentally the translation of the Miluk name for the stream. The creek is "big" only in the sense of being long, not wide.[1] About four miles long, it is small enough to be jumped across at its mouth. Several hundred acres of grazing land lie along the course of its length. The sandy soil of this land was also excellent for raising potatoes.

At least five Indian allotments under the Dawes Act were granted on the drainage of Big Creek, which was also the location of several other farms in private ownership. The first family to live there was the family of Charlie Metcalf. His oldest boy was born in 1865 and the youngest in 1878. Eli, born in 1873, was in the middle. Charlie Metcalf, an old Vermont Yankee, was the frontiersman who had run off the Indian agent in 1863 and who had tried to run off the army in 1864. That same year he had married the young Miluk woman named Susan who, according to Lottie, had been brutalized as a twelve-year-old by two white boys from Empire.[2]

The 1880 census for Coos County showed Charlie Metcalf and his six young sons living at home on Big Creek. The family lived part of the time at Big Creek and part of the time on Haynes Slough at a place called Goose Point—a bench area on the western shore of the slough that had once been the location of a large Indian village.[3] Whether Annie got acquainted with the Metcalfs at Haynes Slough or at Big Creek is unknown, but she did get to know Eli.

Eli, like most of the other men of mixed parentage who lived around the bay, became a logger. Before the turn of the century, several logging operations were on South Slough, which is probably where Eli was working. The logging was done with oxen, or bull teams as they were called in the Northwest.

Other important activity at and around South Slough involved the building and maintenance of the north jetty to the Coos Bay harbor entrance. This was a very large project by local standards, federally funded at some $725,000 between 1892 and 1902.[4] During all this economic bustle the community at the mouth of South Slough became known as Charleston. Among those who gravitated toward Charleston and the South Slough area during that period was Annie Miner.

The largest concentration of people of Indian descent in Coos County were living at South Slough and Big Creek at that time. There were still a few individuals with whom Annie could converse in her native languages of Miluk and Hanis. Hunting and fishing and clam digging and the other traditional activities she liked so much were very good there. Annie had found a place where she felt at home.

Eli was twenty-five years old and Annie was thirty-eight when they were married at the house of Edward Mecum on September 6, 1898. The affidavit for the marriage, signed by Edward Mecum, had been sworn nine days earlier. In her autobiography, Annie neglected to mention this marriage, her first "legal" marriage. Her two previous ones—to (Coos) Henry Jackson and to (Alsea) William Jackson—were Indian marriages. Thus, before 1898, she went by the name of either Annie Jackson or Annie Miner; after 1898, she became Annie Metcalf.

One thing we know about Annie is that she was exceptionally independent and strong-willed. Her granddaughter,

Sunset Bay and the mouth of Big Creek (lower right), two miles west-southwest of the entrance to Coos Bay. The valley of Big Creek, where Annie lived from 1898 to 1916, is shown at upper left. Annie's grand-daughter, Iola, was born in a tent on the beach at Sunset Bay. Aerial photo by the author.

Chief Daloose Jackson, standing. Lottie (in sailor outfit) and her mother, Annie's half-sister Fannie (with necklaces), are seated. The woman at right is unidentified. Photo courtesy Coos County Historical Museum, neg. #R39-687.

Iola, said: "She didn't care what the men were doing. She did what she wanted to do!"[5] During the years following the birth of Nellie, we know that Annie was at the bottom of the economic scale and that she worked as a washerwoman to support herself and to raise her daughter. From the evidence, we can conclude that she did a good job of raising her daughter, since Nellie emerged as quite a capable young woman. Annie sent her to the Chemawa Indian School for six or seven years.[6] The program at Chemawa was designed to make the students self-sufficient after graduating. The girls learned the practical homemaking skills; they could specialize in such fields as nursing, bookkeeping, sewing, waitressing, or other jobs in which women of the period might be expected to find employment. The education that Nellie received at Chemawa held her in good stead for a lifetime. Her English was very good, and she had the education of a high school graduate. She was always able to hold a job to support herself and her children.

Annie almost certainly looked ten years younger than her chronological age. Eli probably thought he was getting a much younger woman. The two of them no doubt got along well enough for a while. Annie had grown up on the Coast Reservation, and Eli had grown up at Coos Bay, but they shared many of the common beliefs and assumptions of their respective maternal ancestors.

Discussing one of these beliefs, Annie told of the time when she and Eli had heard a dead person cry near one of several pioneer graveyards at the places on Big Creek.[7] When the two of them told old Daloose Jackson about what they had heard, he said, "Oh, the smallpox is going to go through again." And, according to Annie, the smallpox did indeed strike again. According to Daloose, the cries had also been heard in the graveyards in earlier times when smallpox had occurred.[8] The Coos name for smallpox meant "visitor," meaning that it came from afar to visit the Coos.

Two years after the marriage of Annie and Eli, when the census-taker came around in June 1900, there was no Eli Metcalf to be found in Coos County. Annie Metcalf was listed as the head of a single-person household at South Slough. Her occupation was listed as "washerwoman." Interestingly, on the separate enumeration of the "Indian Population," she was listed as Annie Miner. Yet she legally carried the Metcalf name until 1910.

After the turn of the century there was plenty of work in logging the timberlands of the former Siletz Reservation. Eli moved north, spending most of the rest of his life as a logger around Siletz. But he was at Coos Bay part of the time. In 1912 his older brother Harvey had been found drowned in the lower bay under suspicious circumstances. A few months later a neighbor, Jacob Evans, was found murdered in his home.[9] Eli and his brother Ira attempted to get the county district attorney to investigate whether or not the two deaths were connected, but nothing came of their efforts.

After Eli left her, Annie continued living at Big Creek. The things she enjoyed most were there. She liked to dig clams and gather mussels and collect barnacles from the rocks. She liked to hunt and to fish. She liked to socialize with others who spoke her language. South Slough and Big Creek were the best places in the Coos area to do those things.

Not far from the Metcalf place on Big Creek was George and Adulsa Wasson's place on South Slough. Adulsa's mother, Gishgiu, was still living.[10] Annie remembered her from Yachats and had been with her many times at the cranberry harvests. Sometimes Annie visited her at South Slough. Gishgiu, a *mitadin* shaman of the Upper Coquille Athapaskans, was blind during her later years. Annie thought that she was uncanny in her ability to accurately predict events.

One time while Annie was at the Wassons', Gishgiu predicted that Ira Metcalf's uncle and his wife would be coming up with the tide. Sure enough, they came up with the tide. Another time she predicted that Old Ned would be coming at noon. Sure enough, he came at noon. Another time she said: "Oh children. Poor old Itcgine. Her bird is going to die." A few minutes later Itcgine, a Miluk who was an aunt of Ira Metcalf's, came in and said that her bird had just fluttered around and died.

When Gishgiu was very old and sick, on her deathbed, Annie was staying with the Wassons. One day Gishgiu died, but in an hour or so she came back to life. She said: "They wouldn't let me go by. The bridge was down. People were there fixing the bridge and they held me. I could not cross. It will be a week from today." A week later she said: "My two dead grandchildren are coming for me. Don't worry about me. I'm old. I'm going to die now."[11] And so she died.

Living at Big Creek with its access to Sunset Bay and the Pacific Ocean was unique. The valley of Big Creek was over a ridge to the west of South Slough and was quite isolated. Sunset Bay is the largest of all the coves of its kind on the Oregon Coast and has since become the major recreational beach for the Coos Bay area. During the time that Annie lived there, it was in effect a private little harbor. Fishing boats could get in and out, placing them an hour or more closer to the fishing grounds than boats that had to cross the Coos Bay bar.

There were other advantages to living so near the ocean. Immediately to the north of Sunset Bay was a long reef called Yoakam Point, which had a seemingly unlimited quantity of mussels, barnacles, and limpets and was later named Mussel Reef. These were easily collected and were favorites of the families of Indian descent who lived in the area.[12] When whites discovered the tasty mussels, however, they had big picnics at which hundreds of pounds were collected and eaten, until the rocks at Mussel Reef were bare.

A bog of the darlingtonia flycatcher was located just a little inland from Mussel Reef. These strange plants were in demand by people who liked to have them in their homes as potted conversation pieces. Transplanted into cans, they brought fifty cents each in Portland until they were rendered practically extinct.[13]

Between 1901 and 1910 Annie and her daughter, Nellie, shared similar circumstances regarding their love lives. Both were awaiting divorces from short marriages that had not worked out. Both had found new men. Both were to be married again, within two years of each other.

In 1901 Nellie married Andrew Winkler. His father was said to have been old Joel Winkler, who had a poorly paying placer mine on the beach below the Alsea River at about the time that Nellie was born. He later worked a mine on the beach near Bandon.[14] Andrew's mother was a woman of the Lower Coquille named Cissy, a good friend of Annie's.

The marriage of Andrew Winkler and Nellie was childless and did not work out. They were together for about five years. After divorcing Andrew, Nellie met and married a Norwegian immigrant named Alfred Aasen. Alfred worked in logging camps, and he sometimes engaged in deep-sea fishing with Annie's next husband, Charlie Baker. Their fishing boat was berthed at Sunset Bay, which at that time had not yet silted up and could accommodate fishing vessels. Nellie and Alfred had a tent at the northern end of Sunset Bay, and Nellie's daughter, Iola, was born there in 1911.

Annie continued to go to the cranberry harvest on North Slough each September, along with most of the old-timers who were left among the Coos Indians. These harvests were true family occasions. Everyone went—babies, children, the elderly, and all. The families from Big Creek were exceptionally well represented and included the Talbots, the Metcalfs, and the Bakers, few of whom ever missed a chance to be there. It was the Baker family from whom Annie was to choose her next husband: her son-in-law's fishing partner, Charlie Baker.

During one season Annie's second husband, (Alsea) William Jackson, came down to pick cranberries. According to Lottie, this was at Annie's invitation. While he was there she casually suggested that they go down to look at a rock near Fossil Point, the site of a gruesome Coos myth that Annie had heard from Old Tar Heels, among others.[15] Annie evidently did not believe that the rock actually contained the bones of the many children killed by the ogres of the myth. After they looked it over, Lottie said, Jackson "went back to Siletz and soon afterward died."[16]

The people of the generation that had been at Coos Bay when the whites had first arrived were fast disappearing. In January 1907, Daloose Jackson died. The newspaper gave his age as 107, which was certainly an exaggeration.[17] He was likely born in 1827, which would have made him eighty years old. He had become a fixture at North Bend and was the subject of anecdotes and conversation for another fifty years. When he died, there was nobody to take his place. His death was symbolic of the ending of one era and the beginning of another.

In 1907 the economy and social life of the Coos Bay area changed irrevocably. This had nothing to do with Daloose or with those few Coos Indians who were still living but was due to a millionaire lumberman from Minnesota who had obtained control of tens of thousands of acres of Coos County timberland and was building the largest, most modern lumber mill in the world just to the south of the town of Marshfield.[18] Construction of the C. A. Smith Lumber Company sawmill more than doubled lumber production on the bay. For the first time there would be reliable, year-round sawmill and logging jobs. Logs to supply the largest sawmill in the world came initially from seven logging camps of the Smith-Powers Logging Company at different locations around the bay. One of them, Camp 4, was on South Slough. The young men of mixed parentage who lived nearby could at last find steady work if they wanted it.

Chief Daloose Jackson and his daughter Lottie, probably not long before Jackson died in 1907. Photo courtesy Iola Larson.

As the area became industrialized, evidence of the earlier native inhabitants became nearly invisible. Interested whites scrambled to gather artifacts, photographs, information—in short, anything they could get—from any Indians who were still around. Annie became involved in this search for traces of the "vanishing American" when she was asked to pose for postcard photos taken by a local photographer. Picture postcards of Native Americans would always sell.

A number of photographers worked in the area, and they did a good job of recording the progress of the county. The period from about 1900 until the First World War is very well covered photographically, and Annie appears in some of those pictures. In September 1910 one of the photographers happened to be at the McFarlin cranberry bogs during the harvest, where he had the pickers pose for a picture. They were of all ages including the elderly and the children. Quite a number of the people from Big Creek were there.

Annie and Nellie are in this picture. Nellie was soon to be married to Alfred Aasen. Annie had recently married Charlie Baker, whose mother was the last living survivor of the Euchre Creek band of the Athapaskan-speaking Tututni Indians of Curry County. Charlie is not in the picture, but his foster brother George and his mother and father, Wentworth and Ione Baker, are. Wentworth, who was always known as "Mr. Baker," is resplendent with his flowing white beard. The census of 1910 indicated that Mr. Baker was seventy-nine and Ione was sixty-three years old. They had been married forty-two years.

Mr. Baker, originally from the state of Maine, was a pensioned veteran of the Indian wars. During the Civil War he had enlisted in Company D, Fourth Infantry Regiment, California Volunteers, and had been assigned to the Coast Indian Reservation at Fort Yamhill and the Siletz Blockhouse.[19] One of the young Indian women he met there was Ione Tichenor of the Curry County Tututni Athapaskans.

Most of the Indians from Curry County had been transported by ship from Port Orford to Portland in June 1856. The remainder had been forced to travel along the beach. As a young girl, Ione had been with the group that went up the beach. According to Coquille Thompson: "Many Indians were brought along the beach, bringing 10 head of cattle. They swam the cattle across all the rivers, and they killed one bossie every day to feed the Indians."[20]

We know very little of Ione's trip north, except for an incident she once described to Lottie. Ione said that one of the places they had camped on the way north was at the large flat just to the south of Yachats Creek. They had stopped there to gather and dry mussels. There were no Alsea Indians at Yachats, since nearly all of them had succumbed to smallpox in 1853. It would be another four years before the Coos and the Umpqua would be settled there. Ione said that while they were camping at Yachats, several old women were gathering mussels and some young boys were playing around when the boys spied a buckskin thing hanging high in a tree. The boys were "going to eat elk meat" but on climbing the tree found that the "elk" was a dead person in a tree burial. The women, who did not want to see the dead person, kept on gathering mussels.[21] The Indians south of the Alsea buried their dead in the ground; the Alsea and those to the north buried theirs above ground, sometimes in trees.

Ione came of age at the reservation at Siletz. She and Private Wentworth Baker were married "until death do us part" in 1868, when she was twenty-one and he was thirty-seven. Ione, whose Indian name was See-Nee-Nis ("Long-hair"), later became eligible for an Indian allotment under the Dawes Act of 1887. The allotment that she received was on the lower end of Big Creek in Coos County.

Ione had a brother, Cyrus Tichenor, who also lived on the allotment. Back in 1872 Cyrus had brought the Ghost Dance from northern California to the reservation at

Yachats.[22] He was also probably the last person to know how to make a canoe in the "Rogue River" style. One time, after a big redwood log had drifted ashore at Sunset Bay, Cyrus made a "Rogue River" canoe from the log. When he finished it, he brought it around Coos Head and across the Coos Bay bar and on up into the bay.[23] By that time, dugout canoes were very rare on the bay, and this one was evidently used by a variety of people over a number of years. According to a folklorized tradition within the family of George Wasson, the redwood canoe was considered unlucky.[24] The canoe may have ended up being the last dugout canoe in use on Coos Bay.

Ione had another brother, Oregon George. He had never gone to the Siletz River but spent most of his life on the Chetco River near the California line.[25] He was possibly the father of George Baker, born of a white woman at Ione's house in about 1880. George Baker had been raised from birth by Ione and was now Annie's "brother-in-law."[26] He became a well-known head sawyer in the various smaller sawmills of Coos County up until the late 1940s, when he retired.

By 1911 Annie had been married into the Coos, the Alsea, and now the Tututni tribes. She had also been related by marriage to people of the Siuslaw and the Umpqua. She had, perhaps more than any other person, become intimately acquainted with representatives of the major language groups for the 350 miles of Oregon Coast between the California line and the Yaquina River.

Charlie Baker and Annie Miner Metcalf were married at the office of Justice of the Peace E. G. D. Holden in Empire on April 6, 1910. Their affidavit for the marriage license, taken out the same day, stated, "Each of said parties are of over half Indian blood." In 1886 Oregon had passed a law that whites could not marry anyone having "Negro, Chinese, Kanaka, or Indian blood." The law was seldom enforced, but the disclaimer on Charlie and Annie's marriage license was likely in compliance with that law.

Annie's daughter, Nellie Winkler, and Nellie's soon-to-be husband, Alfred Aasen, were the witnesses. The census for 1910, taken about two months later, indicated that Annie and Charlie had been married for two years. The marriage, of course, could not have been official until after a divorce from Eli had become final.

Charlie Baker had an Indian allotment of his own, adjacent to Charlie Metcalf's property on Big Creek. While Annie had been married to Eli Metcalf, they had lived on the Metcalf property. It is not known whether Charlie Baker had become interested in Annie while Eli was still around or whether this happened after Eli had left for the Siletz.

Charlie was a deep-sea fisherman. He fished salmon from up and down the coast. Clayton Barrett remembered a time on the Umpqua River when Charlie Baker was boat puller and they pulled in more than one hundred salmon in one night.[27] The tide was going out, and they were so engrossed in pulling salmon that they were almost carried out to sea, over the bar of the Umpqua River. The salmon were worth from twenty-five to fifty cents each at the cannery at Reedsport.

Annie was able to enjoy the abundant fish and shellfish at the ocean near where she was living on Big Creek. She was able to add to her collection of baskets and other Indian artifacts. She even had the leisure to revive the skills she had learned as a girl, and she began making baskets again herself.

The actual twining of the basket is only the last and smallest part of the process. The hardest part is gathering and preparing the materials. Big Creek had an abundance of large, old-growth Sitka spruce. Spruce root, properly split and soaked, is the most superb of all basketmaking materials and was used by nearly all of the coastal Indians from southeastern Alaska down to northwestern California. Annie was a master at making spruce-root baskets, and she was an artist in their design.

Annie preserved for posterity as much as she could of the culture of her Indian ancestors. She kept their memory alive in the names of her grandchildren; she remembered the myths, songs, and stories that she had learned as a child at Yachats; during her life she helped keep alive the two languages of the Coos. Probably most revealing, however, was the superb collection of baskets and artifacts that she had assembled over the years.

She said that among themselves, basketmakers almost never bought or sold their baskets; they nearly always traded.[28] It was through trade with her friends who were also basketmakers that Annie was able to build up her enviable collection. In about 1912 she was photographed in Empire surrounded by her baskets, including ones from Siletz and other parts of western Oregon as well as some of her own Coos baskets.

Some of Annie's collection almost certainly became a part of the collections of Native American art at the University of Oregon Museum of Natural History and the University of California Lowie Museum and possibly others. Annie's granddaughter, Iola, remembered, "A man who interviewed Annie from the University of Oregon bought most of her collection."[29] The Coos baskets at the University of Oregon are a part of the Weatherbee Collection and are credited as having been collected "on South Slough of Coos Bay."[30] The Coos baskets at the Lowie Museum at the University of California were donated by Agnes Ruth Sengstacken, formerly of Coos Bay, and there is every reason to believe that she had obtained at least some of them from Annie. The Coos County Historical Museum has a poorly preserved basket collection that includes one gem of a closely twined, flexible bowl with zig-zag bands. Attached to it is a tag that reads, "Annie Baker."

Beginning at about the turn of the century, professional anthropologists were obtaining some of the first detailed information about the Hanis Coos myths and language.

They assumed that Miluk was already extinct. The anthropologist who was doing most of the work on the Penutian languages of the Oregon Coast was Leo J. Franchtenberg. He was living at Siletz and had worked on Hanis Coos with Jim Buchanan and Frank Drew at Florence in 1909. In 1910 he was working with Annie's former brother-in-law Tom Jackson and others among the Alsea at Siletz.

According to an interesting legend circulated among later anthropologists, Annie had been Frachtenberg's cook during those years. Melville Jacobs told the story as an example of the manner in which the rapidly disappearing languages and oral literatures of Oregon had slipped away before the very eyes of the scientists. Of Frachtenberg he said, "Unfortunately he presumed the extinction of Miluk Coos—although his cook, Annie, spoke it perfectly even twenty years later."[31]*

Of course Annie did speak Miluk perfectly twenty years later, but it is almost certain that she was *not* Frachtenberg's cook, since Annie was at Coos Bay during those years, living on Big Creek. Frachtenberg's cook might instead have been the sister of his Alsea informant, Tom Jackson. Her name was also Annie—Annie Jackson. Annie Jackson had at one time been our Annie's sister-in-law, but she spoke Alsea, not Miluk. Jacobs had probably confused the two Annies, but it made for a good story and it made the point that the anthropologists really did not know very well the people with whom they were working.

All did not go well with Annie's marriage to Charlie Baker. She lived on his Indian allotment on the upper part of Big Creek and did what she could to survive while Charlie succumbed for a time to alcohol. Alcohol was a notable curse to many individuals on lower Coos Bay but seemed to be particularly harsh to those of Indian ancestry.

---

* I am grateful to William R. Seaburg of the University of Washington American Indian Studies Center for bringing this item to my attention.

The suffering borne by the afflicted individuals and their family members is incalculable.

Annie described her life with Charlie while she was living on his Indian allotment at Big Creek:

My husband just ate hot water (imbibed liquor) all the time. I lived there alone almost all the time. My husband never stayed there. He worked, then he was continually drunk. He had other women for companions, he was always there at North Bend at the dance hall. He just threw his money away. And I lived alone. When I lacked food I would sell various farm things, and then I would get food for them. Then I became ill. I had to spend all my savings there. Now he sold the ranch place, he just drank it all up. We were without a place, we were without savings. He just kept on drinking.[32]

Charlie Baker's ranch on Big Creek was his Indian allotment. It was Indian trust land and belonged to the government. He could not sell the land, but he could give up his rights to it, something he probably did in return for a small dollar amount. The Simpson Lumber Company became the new owners after obtaining it from the U.S. government. Annie had to move out.

Fortunately for Annie, her in-laws, Wentworth and Ione Baker, had already given up Ione's Indian allotment on Big Creek and had moved to Empire in their retirement. According to Lottie, Ione had given her rights to her 160-acre allotment to Ralph Barker for twenty dollars.[33] Mr. Baker, then very elderly, paid Annie's rent in Empire so that she could move to town. Annie said: "Had it not been for his [Charlie's] father who paid my house rent at Empire, I should have become destitute. That is how I lived there with my house paid for. If it had not been for his father who paid for it I should have been destitute. Even my very own father could not have taken better care of me. Then his father died."[34]

After Mr. Baker died, Annie became destitute indeed. She was forced to move in with her mother-in-law, Ione, who was becoming a bit senile. Charlie, increasingly alcoholic, also lived there. Annie described her situation:

> He began to hit me when he came home extremely intoxicated, and he tried to injure me. If I had not taken care he would have injured me. And then also when in bed he would wet it there. That is how worthless he was. One time he came home and he was going to throw a burning lamp at me where I was in bed. Then I was furiously angry. But he just laughed at me when I said to him, "You will never want to injure me again. You are worthless, you child of an unpurchased woman! And you make fun of me!"[35]

Meanwhile, Annie's daughter, Nellie, was getting on with her life. On May 4, 1911, she was due with her first child. She was in her tent at the northern end of Sunset Bay, and Annie was in attendance as midwife. There were difficulties, and Nellie's husband, Alfred, went all the way to Marshfield, about fifteen miles, to get Dr. William Horsefall. The birth was hard, but Dr. Horsefall fortunately arrived in time to deliver Iola with forceps.[36] Iola, Annie's first grandchild, would be greatly loved.

Annie's ancestors had customarily given their children the names of deceased relatives. Annie had continued the custom in naming her daughter Nellie, after Annie's deceased half-sister, and Nellie in turn carried on the tradition in the naming of her own children. It was a way to ensure family remembrance and continuity.

Sixteen months after Iola arrived, Oscar Marlow was born. He was named for Old Marlow, who had been a relative of some degree. Marlow Creek, a tributary to the Millicoma River, is named for him. Nellie Annie, named for her mother and her grandmother, was next but died in infancy. Last born was Alfred Minkws, named for his father and his great-grandfather.

Continuity was also maintained at the annual cranberry harvests. As a child, Iola attended those September outings on North Slough with her mother and her grandmother. Iola remembered that the two women spoke Hanis to each other, "especially when they didn't want the children to know what they were saying!" Iola never learned to speak the language, but she "knew some of what they were saying."[37]

The adults would pick the cranberries with the large, heavy scoops, but some of the cranberries would drop off into the vines. The kids would go along behind and pick up the dropped berries. Their fingers would get sore from reaching into the thin, wiry vines, but they were paid something for their efforts. Those outings were looked forward to with great anticipation and were the high point of the year for the children who were there.

Iola remembered Annie at the harvests trying to tell the children some of the stories from her own childhood. Iola remembered that her grandmother sometimes talked of a flood and of a fire and of a raven. Robin carried embers for the fire, and that is why his breast is red. Iola hardly listened. The stories were unimportant to her, and she thought that they sounded something like the fairy tales and Aesop's fables that she had already heard.[38] The elders had very little to tell that the young could find relevant.

Annie might also have had something to teach the young concerning the modern world, but Nellie did not think the children were ready. Iola remembered one time when Annie broke into a bawdy song about "Two-dollar Lue." Nellie said: "Mama! Not in front of the children!" Annie stopped abruptly. Iola remembered that the children were all ears, wondering what it was that they were not supposed to hear. She never did hear the rest of "Two-dollar Lue."

Alfred went to work in the logging camps, a much steadier source of income than fishing. In 1913 or 1914 the

Simpson Lumber Co. began logging the old-growth spruce on Big Creek. Edgar Simpson arrived from California to supervise the operation and brought oxen to provide the motive power. The Chinese cook from Edgar's ranch in California was brought in to run the cookhouse.[39] Alfred may have worked for a time at that camp. This was possibly the last bull-team logging operation in the county, the oxen having been superseded by the steam donkey at all the other camps. Alfred Aasen appears in a photo of a large steam donkey being unloaded from a barge onto the mud flats of South Slough at about that time. Except at Big Creek, steam had taken over the woods.

In 1916 most of the Simpson timber interests were purchased by Philip Buehner, an important Portland lumberman.[40] One of the logging camps that was included in the purchase was a large railroad camp at the head of Marlow Creek, above the head of tidewater at Allegany. Thirty-three-year-old Alfred moved into that camp and rafted the logs dumped from railroad cars into the river at Allegany. One cold winter day in early spring 1916, he slipped and fell in the river. That evening, soaking wet, he rode the ten miles back to camp on an empty log car, exposed to the elements. As a result he caught pneumonia and died, leaving Nellie a pregnant widow with two small children. She received a few hundred dollars in insurance money and nothing more. She was on her own. The baby, Alfred, was born four months after his father had died. Nellie then went to work in a veneer plant, and she continued to work in veneer plants for the rest of her life.

With Iola, six, Oscar, four, and the baby, Alfred, Nellie had her work cut out for her. The family moved into a rented house on the hill on the upper bay at about the site of the old Centerville Saloon, where Annie's biological father had tended bar fifty-five years earlier. Annie's niece Lottie and her husband, Alex, lived in a float house in the bay just below the hill.

Nellie had not seen the last of her misfortunes, however. One day Iola was watching her brothers. Oscar was asleep at the house. Iola went down to the float house to visit with her baby brother, Alfred, who was with Aunt Lottie. While Iola was there, Oscar woke up. Pouring some coal-oil into a lamp, he spilled some. He lit it and set fire to the house. Iola saw the fire and was able to pull Oscar from it, but the house and all its contents were burned to the ground. Among the personal effects that were lost were the names and addresses of Alfred Aasen's relatives in Norway. All contact with his side of the family ended with that fire.

Friends collected scrap lumber, some of it driftwood on the bay, and built a two-room shack on the marsh near Lottie and Alex's float house. Lottie and Alex later moved their float house to the mouth of Catching Slough. Alfred, by that time four years old, moved with them—against his will.

Empire, ca. 1913. Left to right: Alfred Aasen, Nellie Aasen, Cissy Winkler, Ione Baker. Annie's grandchildren Oscar and Iola in front. The photo original is from a postcard that read in part: "Grandma is doing fine. They are going to start to pick cranberries today." Courtesy Iola Larson.

Annie with a part of her collection of baskets, beads, dentalium, and other artifacts at Empire, 1914. Some of these baskets were made by her, but most were obtained through trade with other basketmakers. The baby cradle at Annie's left is currently in the possession of her great-granddauther. Photo courtesy Iola Larson.

9

Portland

Coos Bay had been fairly inaccessible until 1916. The easiest way in and out by land remained the same beach route that Annie had used and that her ancestors had been using for centuries. By sea, regular steamship transportation could be taken to either San Francisco or Portland. But before the railroad came in from Eugene, no one could go in or out of Coos Bay without seriously planning the trip. All of that changed on July 24, 1916, when rail service began.[1] From then on, all one needed to do was buy a ticket on the train and, after riding for ten or twelve hours, get off in Portland. The change was revolutionary.

Life was moving fast. Automobiles were becoming common in Coos County. Some parts of town had electric lights and telephones. Lumber production increased, and new logging camps utilized larger and faster steam equipment. Everybody was working.

Annie was not benefiting from any of these great changes, however. She had had an operation and was only slowly recovering. She owed her doctor bill, and she had no income. She was stuck with a drunken and abusive husband and a mother-in-law who was slipping into senility. She was fifty-eight years old. It was time for her to enter into a new phase of her life.

Annie had some close friends, among them a Klamath woman named Ida Wasson. Ida had become a widow when her husband, James Wasson, had been killed in what might have been the first fatal automobile accident in the county. Ida was a few years younger than Annie, and she too was ready to move on.

Annie confided in Ida and asked her advice. Ida already knew the situation and said: "I know. I will help you. We will leave here." Annie was ready. She said, "Very well, if you will help me."[2] Their plan was to go to Portland, the greatest metropolis in the state, and on June 13, 1917, they got on the train in Coos Bay and headed out.

Annie had so far in her life lived only in small Indian communities and isolated farmsteads. The largest population center she had lived in, and then only briefly, was the town of Empire, which at that time had a population of about 150. Annie said: "Then we did leave, we went to the Columbia. There we lived. I had no possessions, I had no money."[3] At fifty-eight years of age, with her friend's help, she was finally ready to tackle the world of the big city.

In 1917 Portland was the world's most bustling lumber town. It had 258,000 people, which was a full one-third of the population of the state. Its sawmills were turning out a billion board feet of lumber each year. The lumber left the docks for ports all over the world. Sailing schooners and square-riggers could be seen alongside the most modern steam-powered ships. Press gangs were still working the skid road, shanghaiing drunk loggers to complete the crews for the worst of those sailing ships. The old and the new were conspicuously mixed.

Portland was at the heart of the largest and most valuable stand of commercial timber in the world. The timber stood on both sides of the Columbia River and its tributaries for all of the 350 miles from The Dalles to the Pacific Ocean. Title to the best of it had been granted by the U.S. government to the railroads, which could turn it into cash only through cooperative arrangements with lumber companies. The logging camps of those lumber companies along the Columbia River were railroad camps. The logging operations used large, fast, and expensive steam machines operated by large, highly specialized crews. There was work for any man tough enough to take it.

Hundreds of men came to Portland every weekend. They came by train from the camps, and they stayed in hotels and rooming houses until they went back to camp again. If they wanted to change jobs, practically all of the saloons on Burnside Street, from First Avenue up to at least Sixth, displayed "hiring boards." There were always jobs for loggers. For a dollar or two a man could hire out for just about any place he wanted to go.

The ratio of men to women in Portland was quite high. On the weekends the ratio soared. Portland was still something of a frontier town, and like most frontier towns, Portland definitely did not have enough women to go around. Annie and her friend Ida, two middle-aged Indian women, one of whom was not even in good health, went to a rooming house and immediately picked up work for room and board. It was as easy as that.

Annie and Ida seemed to be off to a good start, but Annie was not getting any younger, she was not in good health, and she owed a doctor bill that she could not pay. Working in a rooming house for room and board would pay no bills, and it would not help to prepare for an old age that would soon be coming.

One of the weekend tenants at the rooming house was a forty-seven-year-old logger named Carl Peterson. He worked at one of the big camps out of Kelso, Washington. He would come into Portland with hundreds of others on Friday night and leave for camp Sunday evening. He arrived in town tired and would rest up on the weekend so that he could work another week in camp.

It is often forgotten that with all of the large, modern steam equipment used in the woods for yarding, loading, and transporting the logs, every one of those trees were felled by hand. They were bucked into logs by hand, with crosscut saws. The manpower that pulled those large cross-cut saws was, as often as not on the Columbia River, the manpower of Swedish immigrants. Carl Peterson was one of those Swedish immigrants.

Carl had arrived in the States from his native Sweden in 1894, when he was twenty-two.[4] In those days bull teams were still being used for logging in the Northwest, but the felling and bucking of the timber was done by hand. This work continued to be done by hand until the late 1940s, when the chain saw came into general use. It took a lot of powerful Swedes to do that work, and there were a lot of powerful Swedes along the Columbia River in those days.

Carl became a naturalized citizen of the United States in 1900.[5] We know nothing more of his early life except that he was a logger and that he was a sober and thrifty one. Logging was hard and dangerous work, but it paid well by the standards of the day. Carl had saved up a bit of a stake, and he was ready for a companion to be with him through the rest of his life.

He could not have avoided noticing Annie, the new washerwoman at the rooming house. She still had the youthful bright eyes, girlish energy, and robust sense of humor that had carried her through fifty-eight years of life. She got along very well with Carl and appreciated his gentle sense of humor and love of fun. They no doubt kidded and joked until Carl finally decided he would take a chance on this very special and remarkable woman.

Annie described her situation: "I had no money. I did not know how I would get along, I was not strong, I was ill all the time, because I had been cut by a white doctor, and I had to be paying him for it. But that one white (Peterson) wanted me."[6] Annie pointed out to Carl, "I cannot marry you, because I have not wiped off my paper." In other words, she needed a divorce from Charlie Baker. Carl said, "I will pay for it if you wish." Annie was worried that she would not be able to support herself by her own labor as she had been doing up until that time. She was also afraid that if she married, she would not be able to retain her independence. But then she thought: "I am not strong. I will do it anyhow." She told Carl that she would go ahead with the divorce.[7]

Carl gave her enough money to go back to Coos Bay and get the divorce. She obtained an attorney, George Watkins of Marshfield, and filed the papers. Then she waited. Charlie asked her to come back to him, but Annie said she "did not want to return." She had had enough of Charlie.

At the Circuit Court of the State of Oregon for Coos County at Marshfield on January 2, 1918, Annie appeared with her attorney, and Charlie Baker appeared with his. Annie's attorney presented her case and rested. Charlie waived the introduction of testimony. The court found the following facts duly proven (Divorce Decree No. 4833, dated January 2, 1918, Coos County Courthouse):

> That since the marriage of plaintiff and defendant, the defendant on many different occasions, without good cause, seriously wounded, beat and bruised plaintiff with his hands and feet and habitually swore at her and called her many vile and apprebious [sic] names and threatened to kill plaintiff and to do her great harm, substantially as in her complaint alleged. That all allegations of plaintiff's complaint are true and have been duly proven.

That the plaintiff cannot longer live with defendant without danger that defendant will kill her or do her some great bodily harm.

Therefore the court concludes that the life of plaintiff has been and is rendered burdensome and intolerable by the cruel and inhuman acts and conduct of the defendant toward her and that she is entitled 1st,

To a decree of this court forever annulling and dissolving the marriage contract now existing between them and for an absolute divorce from defendant.

2nd. That plaintiff is further entitled to have her name changed from Annie Matilda Baker to Annie Matilda Miner.

3rd. That she is entitled to recover her costs and disbursements herein from the defendant.

Dated the 2nd day of January, 1918.

Annie said: "I waited a long time for it. Then I got my wiped off paper. It was a long long time until the day they wanted, before I could be married again (but he waited for me). Then I went back to the Columbia, and I had him for my husband."[8]

From all accounts this was a good relationship, the marriage of Annie and Carl Peterson. Annie had never had a husband like him before. Her granddaughter, Iola, said that Carl was a very nice man. "They certainly got along well together," she said.[9] After they were married, Annie apparently made a good recovery from her operation, and she remained in good health until near the end of her life.

Carl made a down payment on a modest house at 92 E. 74th Street, in the Montavilla area of Portland. He continued to work in the camp out of Kelso, Washington, and came home on the weekends. During the week Annie was by herself. Her natural curiosity led her to explore the city of Portland. The trolley came not too far from her house, and she soon learned how to get around. It was a brand-new world for her, exciting and stimulating.

Her daughter, Nellie, was still working in the veneer plant at Marshfield. She and Annie decided to send Iola to Portland to stay with Annie. In 1921 Iola arrived and stayed for two years. It is from her that we get some idea of Annie's new life in the big city. These two years turned out to be a very important time in Iola's life as well.

Iola corresponded regularly with Annie and Carl both before and after her two years in Portland. Deciphering her grandmother's letters was quite a challenge. Annie's English was limited, and she could not write. Carl wrote the letters, but he was not very good in English either. He spelled the words phonetically, but being Swedish, he interpreted the sounds a bit differently. One can imagine the results.

Although Annie could not read, she could get around the streets of Portland very well, to the amazement of her young granddaughter. She knew which streetcars to take and when to make changes, and she could always get to where she wanted to go. And she was always going someplace, anyplace. She was a person on the go.

Among the special attractions in Portland for both Annie and her granddaughter was the vaudeville matinee. They would take the trolley downtown to the Pantages Theater or the Orpheum Theater; the two were near each other. For a very modest admission charge they would be drawn into the magic and splendor of the colorful sets and the music and the dance and the slapstick antics of the best talent of its kind on the Pacific Coast. The entertainment value of the vaudeville was universal. It amused and delighted everyone, regardless of cultural or linguistic background. When the curtain went up on the magnificently painted backdrops, Iola's eyes would grow large with wonder. Her grandmother beside her was no less enthralled.

There was a movie theater in the Montavilla area, near their house. They loved to go to the movies, especially on Saturday night. As the titles appeared on the silent screen, Iola could read them and whisper them into her grandmother's ear.

And Iola would read the newspapers to her grandmother. Annie insisted that Iola read the newspaper to her every day. She wanted the entire newspaper read, regardless of the subject of the stories. Iola credits her good reading skills to her constant reading aloud to her grandmother when she was ten or twelve years old.

Annie always dressed neatly and well in modern clothing, and she liked to stay in style. She had a treadle sewing machine, and Iola remembers one black satin dress that Annie made over several times as the fashions changed. She had one unusual sewing accessory, a "sewing bird," which Iola still owns. This is a bronze bird whose mouth is on a strong spring. The bird is clamped to a table, and the loose end of the material to be stitched is held in the bird's mouth. It is a very practical item that Iola uses to this day.

Annie did not sew with her machine as much as she did hand stitching and crocheting. She tried to teach Iola how to crochet, but Iola could not get the hang of it. Annie would stand over her and tell her every mistake as she made it. Iola was too nervous, and so Annie finally said, "Oh, let's quit!" Later, Iola practiced by herself and learned how to do it. She embroidered a scarf and put lace on it and gave it to Annie for Christmas. It was a wonderful gift because Annie was so surprised and delighted at what Iola had learned by herself.

Iola's first Christmas tree was in Portland with Annie and Carl. Annie was an inveterate collector of things and had accumulated a big collection of ornaments, candleholders, birds, and china dolls made in Germany. She had a Santa Claus about eleven inches high and other items.

Annie took one of the German china dolls and made a beaded carry-basket for it out of deerskin. She could crochet and bead and follow pictures perfectly. She made a beaded bag with a picture of a deer, a bag that Iola's daughter still has, along with the deerskin china-doll basket. Thus, a few of Annie's things remain in the family.

The house on 74th Street was at the eastern edge of Portland in those days. A little beyond was Sullivan's Gulch, where people threw their trash. Annie and Iola would go there to scavenge things and to pick serviceberries, which grew in abundance during the summer. In the early spring Annie would gather the fresh shoots of blackberry, salmonberry, and other plants, which she would peel and serve fresh. In the spring she also boiled nettles, both the stinging and the nonstinging types. At other times of the year she cooked various wild tubers, which Iola never learned to identify and use. Above all, Annie loved fish and other seafood. Portland was a long way from the sea, but there was a fresh seafood market not far from the house. Annie shopped there and also at the Yamhill Market downtown. From the description of Annie's time in Portland as given by Iola, she lived a contented and interesting life there.

Annie appreciated the freedom she had, and she did what she could to make Carl's life comfortable when he came home from camp. He was usually happy to stay around the house when he was home on the weekends. He needed some rest. But he liked to go to the movies sometimes on Saturday night. He had a car, and occasionally they would go for a ride. These were pleasant times.

Even though Annie was adapting to the fast, cosmopolitan life of the big city, she always remained true to her roots. When Iola got a thick crop of warts on two fingers of her right hand, Annie used a traditional cure. She took chitum (cascara) bark and steeped it in water. Iola soaked her hand in this every day, and the warts disappeared. When Iola caught a cold, Annie cooked fir needles and bathed her in the broth. The odor cleared her head and may have helped the cold. No one would dispute Annie. She always knew best.

Once while Iola was staying with Annie and Carl they received a surprise visitor. It was Eli Metcalf, Annie's former husband from twenty years earlier.[10] They had a pleasant visit, and it appeared that Eli was doing well. At about this time, in 1925, testimony was being taken on an Indian claims hearing at Florence. It is more than likely that Eli's visit to Annie was in connection with that hearing. Eli was well acquainted with the older Indians of Coos descent and during the hearings had been photographed at the Siuslaw along with Frank Drew and Jim Buchanan.[11] Drew and Buchanan had been the linguistic and ethnologic informants for Leo Frachtenberg when he had collected some of the first data on the Coos in 1909.

Eli undoubtedly brought Annie up to date on the latest scandals at Siletz, where he was living and working in a logging camp. It seems that Annie's ex-husband Charlie Baker was now living at Coos Bay with Mrs. Ida Bensell, the undivorced wife of Jim Bensell of Siletz. Both the Bensells and the Bakers were descendants of the Curry County Tututni. It was said that Charlie and Ida were living at Coos Bay rather than at Siletz "to avoid trouble."[12]

Eli might also have told Annie about the new Shaker Church that had recently been built at Lower Farm, a few miles downriver from Siletz. The Shaker Church was a messianic cult that had started several decades earlier among the Indians of Puget Sound. It soon appeared in northern California, and by 1923 many of the Indians at Siletz had become converts.[13] The new church at Siletz was the only one in western Oregon, although there were adherents among a number of the Tututni descendants of Curry County. One of its most fervent converts was Mrs. Ida Bensell, Charlie Baker's new woman.[14] She may have introduced the new religion to Charlie's mother, Ione Baker, and others at Coos Bay.

Annie was not a religious person. She had not attended a church service, as far as Iola knows, until they were invited by their neighbors. Most of the neighbors were white, but two families quite friendly with the Petersons were black. Annie and Iola dressed up and went to church with them one Sunday morning. Iola characterized it as a "Holy Roller" church, "all Negroes who rolled in the aisle and got quite excited" during the service. This was probably Annie's first and only direct experience with Christian religion. She never went back.

Annie later told Melville Jacobs of a dream she once had. Jacobs commented that it was a nice dream, showing Annie's ambivalence about sin and sinful ways of life. In her dream she went to heaven but was refused admittance. She went down below, and men in red with two horns coming out of their heads met her. She was so frightened that she woke up.[15] She felt deep in her thoughts that she could not be admitted to heaven and was meant to go to hell, and she feared the latter. Some of the concepts of the nominally Christian culture in which she lived could not have failed to rub off on her.

One summer Iola's mother, Nellie, stayed with them. She went to work at one of the veneer plants in Portland while she was there. Nellie and Annie could talk to each other in Hanis, which must have been pleasant for Annie. The big event of that summer was the Rose Parade, and they all attended.

Nellie went back to Coos Bay, but she could barely get by financially. One way out would have been marriage, and she had received offers. She seriously considered at least two of them but in the end turned them down. These two offers were from prominent local businessmen. According to Iola, Nellie was afraid that she was wanted mostly to be a housekeeper, and she did not want that. Her marriage to Alfred Aasen had been a good one, and he had treated her so well that she did not want to take a chance on someone else and spoil her good memories.

On the morning of April 30, 1923, there was a tragedy in the family. Nellie was working in the veneer plant, and

six-year-old Alfred was staying with Lottie and Alex at their
float house on Catching Slough. At about nine o'clock that
morning Alfred was playing on the fishing boat owned by
Alex. He fell overboard, his shoelaces got caught in the
limbs of a submerged log, and he drowned. It is possible
that this unfortunate incident broadened the gulf between
Annie and her niece Lottie.

Alfred's great-great-grandfather Minkws had been a
headman of the village of Intesedge; his great-grandmother
had once been married to the last headman of the village of
Takimiya. Takimiya had been located just a few hundred
yards upstream and across the river from where the boy
died.

In 1925 the Chemawa Indian School was trying to
increase its enrollment and was recruiting among descendants of the Indians along the coast. The government-run
school provided a good vocational education free of cost to
students of Indian ancestry. As Iola remembered it, they
would not take anyone with less than one-fourth Indian
blood. Iola and her brother Oscar got in with their three-
eighths. Their father had been a full-blooded Norwegian,
but their mother, Nellie, was three-fourths Indian: one-half
Alsea and one-fourth Coos.

Iola remembered that a whole trainload of students left
from Marshfield that September. The recruiting program
was so successful that although the school was built to
accommodate about six hundred students, one year that
Iola was there the school enrolled nine hundred. Many of
the students' parents had attended Chemawa a generation
earlier.   .

When she got to Chemawa, Iola was surprised to find
that some of the students did not look Indian at all. There
were Swedes with brown eyes, and a girl from Alaska had
black hair and blue eyes. They all lived in a dormitory, and
Chemawa was run like a military school. The students
marched everywhere. They learned the facing movements,

the oblique, and so on. The girls used wands, not guns, but they learned the manual of arms. The boys used guns.

The school day was divided into the mornings, which were academic, and the afternoons, which were vocational. The boys worked in the dairy and did carpentry and kitchen work. The girls worked in the hospital as aids to nurses, but Iola did not like that. The first time she was on hospital duty, one of the students died of tuberculosis.

The girls learned other skills, including bookkeeping, and they worked as waitresses and seamstresses. They made their own uniforms, which were gingham dresses or duck skirts. They made the shirts for the boys. All in all they learned the skills that would make them self-supporting when they graduated. The program was quite successful for those who completed it. The school ran for nine months, with the summers free. That first summer Iola went back to Portland and stayed with her grandmother.

The biggest event to occur in that summer of 1926 was the opening of the Bridge of the Gods, which spanned the Columbia River gorge at Cascade Locks, permitting land travel between that part of Oregon and Washington for the first time since the Myth Age. Indeed, the myths of the Indians along the Columbia River had included several traditions of a rock bridge that had once connected the two sides. This Myth Age bridge, according to some versions, was destroyed in a cosmic battle between Mount Hood and Mount Saint Helens, and the debris created the cascades of the river.*

The Bridge of the Gods was owned by a private company, whose profits depended on the tolls to be charged.

* For two typical examples of the myth, see Clark, *Indian Legends of the Pacific Northwest* (Berkeley: University of California Press, 1953), 20–23, "The Bridge of the Gods," and 88, "How Coyote Made the Columbia River." The myth is discussed further in Clark, "The Bridge of the Gods in Fact and Fancy," *Oregon Historical Quarterly* 53 (March 1952): 29–38.

The tolls in turn would be a function of how much traffic could be generated. A huge publicity campaign promoted the use of the bridge. Several bowdlerized versions of the Indian legend of the Bridge of the Gods were published amid considerable hype.

Carl drove Annie and Iola the thirty-five miles through the Columbia River Gorge to attend the celebration. Indians held a powwow and various other activities. There were speeches and fireworks and a lot of people. Annie did not take part in the Indian ceremonies, but she could not have failed to notice the attention given to the American Indians in this important dedication to the joining of the two sides of the river.

The following year, Iola was sixteen and old enough to work with her mother at the Evans veneer plant in Marshfield, where she continued to work until she was twenty. At about that time, the Evans company expanded its capacity to manufacture battery separators made from white cedar. The company employed primarily women, and Nellie stayed there until her health failed in about 1945.

Carl and Annie Miner Peterson, 1929. Photo Courtesy Iola Larson.

Carl and Annie Peterson, with Annie's daughter, Nellie, behind them, ca. 1929. This is the little beached float house in which Annie and Carl lived at Charleston from 1929 until they died in 1939. Note the float log (left and under Carl) that is used as the foundation for the one-room shack. Photo courtesy Iola Larson.

10

The 1931 Court of Claims

Carl continued to work in the big camps on the Columbia River through the 1920s. He could not get home every weekend, and Annie had a lot of time to herself. She crocheted and did beadwork and basketry. She loved flowers and raised them. Then she began raising canaries, mostly as a hobby but she sold them when she could. Still, she began to miss Coos Bay and the clams and mussels and barnacles and limpets and the smell of the mud flats and the salt air of the ocean.

She and Carl began spending vacations at Charleston, and eventually they bought a lot and a beached float house along the mud flats there. In those days the logging camps usually had two or three weeks off over the Fourth of July, and Annie and Carl looked forward each year to spending that time at South Slough. Carl fit in very well with the people there. He was a Swede, and at that place Swedish

was still spoken by some. Even the Indians of the new
generation at Charleston tended to be half Swedish. And
Carl was very well liked. He was just an old Swede logger,
by now pushing sixty, and he was among his own kind. He
and Annie were eager for the time when they might be able
to retire there.

That time came shortly after the stock market crashed
in 1929. Orders for lumber were sharply curtailed, and the
camps began laying off men, then shutting down operations
altogether. At the time of the crash, Annie was sixty-nine
years old and Carl was too old to continue working in the
woods for much longer. When his income stopped, they
could no longer afford to live in Portland.[1] He sold his equity
in the house at a considerable loss, and they moved into
their little beached float house along the mud flats in
Charleston. They could live there without much money.

At Charleston Annie could walk out behind their house
at any low tide, and in a few minutes she would have enough
clams for a meal. She used all kinds of clams and mixed
them with limpets and barnacles, which were perhaps her
favorite food. A mess of crabs could be caught just as
quickly, using a basket crab-pot with some crushed crab as
bait.[2] She took seaweed and dried it into black cakes, and
she prepared eels, both fresh and dried. She was in her
element. Carl too fell right in with life at Charleston. In a
short time he was going out over the bar and "pulling boat"
for commercial fishermen. He could pick up a few dollars
that way. Deep-sea fishing thus became his second career.

Annie began stocking their little shack with knick-
knacks. Her coffee table was covered with seashells, sea
urchins, and other small items she had found on the beach.
On the kitchen table Annie had a huge barnacle that had
come off a whale. She used it as a toothpick holder.[3] She had
an impressive collection of beads, bows and arrows, baskets,
and other items of the coastal Indians.[4] By this time her
granddaughter, Iola, had married and had a daughter of her

own. When they visited Grandma, Iola would tell her daughter, "Don't touch!"[5]

Possibly as a result of the economic depression, efforts were renewed to get a money settlement from the U.S. government for the Indians of Coos County. On November 4, 1931, more than one hundred members and descendants of the Coos, Siuslaw, and Umpqua tribes met in North Bend to prepare for the arrival of Attorney Daniel B. Henderson of Washington, D.C.

Henderson would be the attorney for their case against the U.S. government.[6] Altogether, more than two hundred Indians and descendants were interviewed and took part in various aspects of the procedures.[7] George Bundy Wasson had organized a number of meetings in Empire before the hearings.

Wasson had worked since 1916 trying to get compensation for the lands taken from the Indians during the 1850s. In 1929 Congress had finally passed a measure allowing the matter to be taken up by the U.S. Court of Claims.[8] It was at this time that the Coos, Siuslaw, and Lower Umpqua Indians had filed their formal petition for compensation for their confiscated lands.

Nearly all the Indians were related to some degree, but as is the case in many families, there was friction among some of the individuals. For example, Lottie refused to shake hands with Frank Drew because she believed Frank had killed Old Ned by giving him poisoned whiskey.[9] She would not speak to Annie either, for whatever reason.

At the meetings in Empire, Wasson had tried to get together with everyone who could testify as to the original boundaries of the lands and the circumstances of their confiscation. How far back one could remember was crucial. Frank Drew deferred to Annie, saying that she was older than he was. According to Lottie, Annie was offended because Frank had betrayed her age![10]

The court of claims set the date for taking depositions in the "Plaintiff's request for Special Findings of Fact" at North Bend for November 11, 1931. The major problem for the Indians was that the only one of them who had actually been present at the 1855 treaty with Joel Palmer and who was still living was the aging Jim Buchanan. He was living at Florence but was quite sickly. Buchanan had been about ten years old at the time of the treaty. Annie was now the second- or third-oldest Coos Indian, and she had not even been born at that time. Most of the rest of them were several years younger than Annie.

On the ninth, Henderson and the rest of the attorneys finally arrived.[11] The depositions were taken on the eleventh.[12] Seventeen tribal members gave sworn testimony, but some of the material was probably not too helpful. For example, George Barrett, who had carried mail from Haynes Slough to Fort Umpqua in the early days, did not think there had been any Coos villages. He explained his opinion: it was because "they had removed the Indians away from here, except a few that had escaped and came back again."[13] This is the type of fuzzy logic that had prevailed and had become the "common knowledge" of the citizens of Coos County.

Old Jim Buchanan, frail and sickly, was brought in from Florence because his testimony was crucial. He was able to testify that he had been present at Winchester Bay when General Joel Palmer had told them that the government would pay for their lands.[14] He said that they were treated well at Fort Umpqua after they had been removed there but that conditions were hard at Yachats. After his testimony, Buchanan was taken back to his home, where he died in June 1933, the last living witness to the treaty of 1855.[15]

Mrs. Irene Waters was a little older than Annie. She said that she was about nine years old when she saw Indians taken across the bay in big rowboats.[16] This was probably during one of the times they had been rounded up to be returned to Yachats. Mrs. Waters had a white father and had lived at Coos Bay during the entire reservation period.

Laura Metcalf also had a white father and had lived at Coos Bay during the reservation period. She was questioned about Indians who had been whipped at Yachats. She knew that her mother's uncle, whose white name was George, was one of those who had been whipped for leaving the reservation.[17]

Lottie Evanoff testified that she was about ten years old when the Yachats Reservation was closed. The Indians then moved to Siuslaw for about a year before returning permanently to Coos Bay.[18] Lottie was exceptionally well informed and had learned much from her father, Daloose, about the old limits of the territory of the Indians of Coos County.

George Bundy Wasson himself gave lengthy testimony on the history of the treaty and the subsequent diaspora of the Coos Indians. He had made an intense study of the subject from documents he had uncovered in the archives in Washington, D.C. He also testified about his acquaintance with the older Indians he had known during the cranberry harvests at North Slough and about his mother Adulsa, the daughter of a Coos chief. He had done his homework well.[19]

Part of the strategy was to have as much of the testimony as possible be taken in the original languages. Annie testified in Hanis, and her interpreter was Agnes Johnson, the daughter of her longtime, dear friend Alice.[20] Agnes was the same age as Annie's daughter, Nellie; Alice had been about the same age as Annie. Alice's mother and Annie's mother had both come from the village of Intesedge.

Henderson asked Annie on direct examination the name of the tribe of her mother. Annie answered, "Intesedge." Henderson asked her to tell whether or not she had learned from her mother or other old Indians the history of the Coos tribe. Annie said, again in Hanis, "Yes, I know what my old

peoples tells me." Henderson then asked her to tell whether
she remembered from her mother or other old Indians what
country had belonged to and had been occupied by the
Coos tribe in the early days before her birth. She said, "The
Coos Bay country, in general, it belong to the Coos Bay
tribe."

One of the crucial issues was establishing the boundaries of the old tribal territory. Henderson asked Annie to
tell, if she knew, where the eastern boundary of the Coos
Indian country was before the time of the removal of the
Indians. The government attorney, W. C. Shoup, objected
on the grounds that the question called for hearsay. The
objection was overruled, and Annie answered, "The only
way I know is from what they told me, from my old people,
that the Summit Range would be the east boundary line of
our country." Henderson asked about the northern boundary line. Annie, using the Hanis name for the place, said,
"Skayedge." Henderson asked if it had an English name
and, if so, what that was. Annie said, "Tenmile."

When Henderson asked Annie how far south the Coos
Indian country ran, Annie said in Hanis, "There is a canal
cut from the lake out in the ocean, that name I don't
know, would be the south boundary line of the Coos Bay
country." She was no doubt talking about Flores Lake
in Curry County. The outlet to Flores Lake is through
New River, which in turn joins Fourmile Creek near its
entrance to the ocean. Fourmile Creek was usually considered the southern boundary of the Gwisya, or Lower
Coquille Miluk.

There was often ambiguity in the term "Coos" when
applied to the Indians of Coos County. Annie no doubt
took the boundary question of "the Coos Bay country" to
mean the Indians of Coos County, which included the
Indians of both the Coos and the Coquille watersheds. The
Flores Lake answer makes sense in that context. But
Henderson next asked Annie what tribe of Indians lived just

south of the Coos country. Annie answered, "Quisseah."*
Henderson asked what the white people called that tribe,
and Annie answered, "Coquille Indians."

The questioning then went to establishing the conditions of the Indians during the reservation period. Henderson
asked Annie to tell who provided a living, if anyone, for the
Indians at Yachats while she lived there. Annie replied, "No
one provided food for us only what we secured for our-
selves." Henderson then asked what she knew about the
Indians running away from Yachats and being brought back
by government authority. Annie said, "The reason why they
do run away from Yachats because of them being on the
point of starvation." Henderson asked her to tell about
punishment being administered to those who ran away and
were brought back. Annie, becoming visibly emotional,
answered: "They have posts and to these posts they would
tie them and flog them. That might seem unreasonable but
that is just what they did." Henderson asked her to give
instances that she remembered of punishment being administered by the government officials to the Indians who ran
away and were brought back. She broke down in tears and
said, "I don't care to dwell any longer on the treatment that
was given to them."

It must be understood that these hearings were very
important and emotional to all of the older Indians. They
had been helping to support the legal efforts of George
Bundy Wasson since 1916 and had supported previous
efforts going back to 1892. They had nothing to show for

---

* Melville Jacobs noted that "Gwsi'ya" was the name applied to the Lower
Coquille Miluk-speaking villages; "Baldiyasa," or "Beach Shore People,"
was the name applied to the Miluk-speaking people who lived twenty
miles to the north, around South Slough of Coos Bay. Melville Jacobs,
Coos Narrative and Ethnologic Texts, University of Washington Pulbica-
tions in Anthropology, vol. 8, no. 1 (Seattle: University of Washington,
1939), 4.

it, and this was their one chance to get the matter to trial. Those who remembered were getting very old. Annie was seventy-two, and the memory of those hard times at the reservation when she was small were too much for her.[21] She broke down and cried on the stand.

When she regained her composure, Henderson resumed the questioning. He asked her if, when the Indians left Yachats, the government had given them any land or any money or any provisions. Annie said: "No, never gave us no provisions or no money. . . . The Government don't restore no land to us." In response to more questions she said: "The Siuslaw Indians have given us provisions after we left Yachats. . . . the Government did not give us anything." Henderson asked how the Indians made their living. Annie said, "Fishing." He asked whether they worked for the white people. Annie said, "Yes, they worked out for the white people to earn money to buy provisions and clothing."

On cross-examination the government attorney, Shoup, went back to the question of punishment of the Indians at Yachats. He said: "I don't like to distress the witness with questions concerning the punishment that she says occurred at Yachats, but I want to ask just one or two questions. How many persons did you yourself see who were tied to a post and flogged?" The translation might have been vague because it appears that Annie thought Henderson was asking how many people had witnessed the punishment. She answered, "It is several of them who have been an eye witness."

Shoup, beginning to get a little testy, said, "I ask you how many you yourself had seen." Annie responded evenly: "I don't remember but there was many of them who the agent would gather them together to see the performance carried on. The object of the spectators at this place is to teach the lesson to the other Indians that they may not run away again from the agency without consent of the agent." Shoup, a little impatiently, said, "I must ask you again: What is your best recollection of the number of persons whom *you saw* tied to a post and flogged?" To the interpreter he said, "Put the question exactly." Annie replied simply, "At that time I could not tell 'cause I did not count them, but I saw the performance."

Henderson was able to get Annie to make the issue very clear on redirect examination. He asked her to give the names of Indians who had been punished in the way she had mentioned. She said, "I know the names of their villages. Their names go by the villages that they belong to. Those who were punished were: Milokwitch, Hanasitch— would be about two or three from Hanasitch, and about the same amount from Intesedge. That is as much as I remember."

At the end of the questioning Henderson said: "Now Mrs. Peterson, there is one question that comes at the end. By the rules of the court you are allowed to state anything more in regard to the merits of this case that you wish to tell and at this time you are permitted to do so." Annie gave a final statement to the court: "Long years ago my parents were living happy in their own homes. They have abundance of food of all kinds such as fish and game from the forest of the Coos Bay country. Immediately after the whites came to our country we then right away experience hardships and we have no way of remedying conditions that we once enjoyed. That is all." Henderson said, "That is all Mrs. Peterson." Agnes Johnson translated the transcript of the testimony from English into Hanis for Annie and certified that to the best of her knowledge and belief, Annie "fully understood the purport thereof." The transcript was signed by Agnes Johnson, with Annie's thumbprint added on each page.

The 1931 court of claims hearing at North Bend was the most important gathering of the descendants of the Indians of Coos County during that generation. But there were other concerns. The younger generation was preoc- cupied with making a living in the most seriously depressed economy the nation had ever encountered. A cash settle-

ment would have been very nice at that time. The case,
however, dragged out through the next seven years and was
finally dismissed in 1938 on the grounds that the Indian
testimony was hearsay and the Treaty of 1855 had not been
ratified. Neither the testimony nor the treaty could be used
to establish prior title to the land.[22]

After the hearings were finished, life returned to normal
for Annie and Carl. Then, in July 1933 Annie received an
unexpected visitor. Frank Drew arrived at her home in
Charleston with a professor who wanted to talk to her. The
professor was Melville Jacobs from the University of Washington. He had recently received his Ph.D. at Columbia
University under Franz Boas, the father of American anthropology, and he was searching for the last surviving speakers
of the native languages of Oregon.

Jacobs had worked at Florence the previous summer
with Frank Drew and Jim Buchanan. He was "rehearing" the
Hanis Coos linguistic work that Dr. Leo Frachtenberg had
done with them back in 1911. Among other things, Jacobs
was recording some of their speech and songs on the
Ediphone wax recording cylinders. When he returned to
finish his work in July 1933, he found that Jim Buchanan
had died in June.

Jacobs had already met nearly all of the surviving
speakers of Hanis Coos and had not found anyone who
would be suitable as a linguistic informant. Probably the
most knowledgeable among them was Annie's niece Lottie,
but for whatever reason, Jacobs found that it was impossible
for him to work with her. On the other hand, Jacobs hit it
off perfectly with Annie from the beginning. Annie was
witty, forthright, and knowledgeable, and as Jacobs said, "A
great deal is owing to her for her delightful cooperativeness,
humor, intelligence, and for her considerable sensitivity of
language."[23]

Jacobs, for his part, was already well experienced in
collecting linguistic and ethnologic information. He was to

devote his career to seeking out the last speakers of the then-surviving languages of western Oregon. He is credited with saving, for future science, important aspects of the languages and cultures of Klikitat Sahaptin (1926–31), Clackamas Chinook (1929–30), Molala (1929–30), Hanis and Miluk Coos (1932–34), Tillamook (1933), Alsea (1935), and Tualatin Kalapuyan (1936). He also worked with Cayuse and several southwestern Oregon Athapaskan languages, and he recorded "precise notes on the Indian use of the Chinook Jargon."[24] His work with Annie was probably one of the more satisfying projects of his distinguished career.

Jacobs's technique was to devote the first few days to transcribing the informant's pronunciation. In the case of Annie, the pronunciation was of Hanis words. He sat with his lined notebook on the closed top of her treadle sewing machine (probably a Singer) and asked for the Hanis word for this or that. He copied the answer in his notebook, using transcriptional symbols for each of about thirty sounds that do not appear in English. He then repeated the word. Annie corrected his pronunciation, and Jacobs made corrections in the transcription, then read the word again. Since he was quite experienced in this procedure, it took him only a few days to be perfectly proficient in the sounds and accents of the language.

During those first few days with Annie, Jacobs learned what to him was an astonishing fact. Annie was fluent not only in Hanis but also in the Miluk language. The scientific community had thought that the last speaker of Miluk had died ten or fifteen years earlier. This was a breakthrough of enormous importance: Annie carried within her head the remains of an entire language thought to have been extinct.

Annie Miner Peterson and Melville Jacobs at Charleston, Oregon, summer 1934. Jacobs is recording Annie's Miluk language songs and connected speech on an RCA Victor recording device adapted to run from the car battery. Melville Jacobs Collection, University of Washington Archives, Seattle, Photo Negative No. NA 4080. Reproduced with permission of the Whatcom Museum of History and Art, Bellingham, Washington, and the Trustees of the Melville Jacobs Collection.

11

The Anthropologists

A newspaper clipping in the possession of Iola Larson, Annie's granddaughter, reads as follows:
Oregon Squaw Only Living Person Who Knows Old Tongue

Seattle, Oct. 7.—An aged Indian woman—Mrs. Annie Peterson of North Bend, Ore.—was believed today to be the only living person to speak Miluk, a near-extinct tribal language.

Melville Jacobs, University of Washington anthropologist, said he discovered Mrs. Peterson speaking the language when he talked with 10 Indians who spoke Hanis, another near-extinct language.

She sang several Miluk folk songs she had learned about campfires of her people. Scientists had believed the language was dead.

McGee's Auto Camp in Empire is where Jacobs was staying. Each day after lunch he drove the five miles to Charleston and worked with Annie through the afternoon. When the vast extent of her repertoire became obvious, he decided that this would be a summer-long affair and that he would need help. He returned to Seattle and brought his wife, Elizabeth Derr Jacobs, back with him.[1] She was becoming a quite competent field-worker in her own right and was of inestimable help.

Jacobs enjoyed working with Annie. In the kitchen of her little beached float house at Charleston with his notebook on the closed top of her sewing machine, he would sit where he could closely watch her mouth as she dictated in a language that had not been heard on this earth for the better part of a generation.[2]

The languages of the Northwest were extremely difficult for outsiders to learn. Jacobs took great pleasure in the difficulty. In Hanis and Miluk, as in many other languages of the Northwest, there was a marked tendency to cluster two or three or more consonants together without an intervening vowel.[3] This might sound to the uninitiated, Jacobs sometimes said, like small hammers operating on tacks![4]

The hours and days of patient and accurate listening and questioning paid off in saving the essentials of another language. Jacobs transcribed Annie's dictation in "careful, neat, and consistently high-quality phonetic notation."[5] One might question whether the achievement was worth the effort, but Jacobs certainly thought it was. He had once said that every language that is still remembered may be of commanding importance for some "now unanticipated element of scientific theory." This is true, he said, even if the language is remembered by only "one or two elderly and quite toothless American Indian survivors."[6]

Jacobs believed that every food gatherer's language is as important to science as English, Hittite, Greek, Korean, Sanskrit, or Scotch Gaelic. This is true, he said, whether the language is remembered by only one survivor or by twenty or twenty thousand.[7] He thought that it was important to find out everything possible about the world's languages because only then could science understand the many ways in which a "linguistic bedrock" had been laid. For Jacobs, finding out the multitudinous ways in which adults use the tool of language was immensely important.[8] Only then, he said, could the whole of human nature be depicted.

Because Jacobs was already familiar with Hanis and a variety of other Northwest languages, he almost immediately began to elicit sentences and short phrases from Annie. They worked together through July, August, and September of 1933. After the first few weeks, he gradually and carefully began recording myths, narratives, and ethnologic texts. Using the techniques he had developed over several years of working with elderly speakers of almost-lost languages, he at first encouraged her to dictate slowly to him while he copied into his lined notebooks. By the end of the summer he could write out Annie's texts in dictation about as rapidly and accurately as he could write in English.[9] The first notebook with Annie's connected speech in it is dated July 14, 1933. It was Jacobs's notebook number 93.

At the end of each dictation he would read the material back and Annie would correct his pronunciation if necessary and translate each word or phrase. Jacobs would make corrections, and immediately under the word he would write its translation. He placed these recordings of connected speech on the right-hand pages of his notebooks; on the facing, left-hand pages he wrote other comments that Annie might have made, or he sometimes noted his own observations. When he filled one of the 180-page notebooks, he would start a new one. By the end of the summer he had filled eight of those notebooks with Annie's dictated material.

As the work progressed during the summer, Jacobs broke out the Ediphone recording device that the university had furnished. Annie sang into it the songs that accompanied the myths. The wax cylinders of the songs still exist and provide a surprisingly faithful copy of Annie's voice. Playing them back today is an eerie experience. At seventy-three, Annie sang with energy, enthusiasm, and humor. She remembered almost all of the songs that accompanied the myths.

Field-workers nowadays tend to rely exclusively on the tape recorder. Jacobs, however, was a firm believer that for recording myth and other memorized speech, it was better to record the material by hand into a notebook. Translation was easier, faster, and more accurate using that old-fashioned method. He believed that electronic recording was most useful only for a sample of the material and was important only to yield accurate data on junctures, melody contours, and the like.[10] For preserving music and song, however, the recording devices were essential.

It was Jacobs's teacher Franz Boas who had developed the techniques used in recording the unwritten Native American languages. Boas had found that in order to document an unwritten language, one needed to collect a body of texts in that language. Traditional myths and folktales were the most convenient sources of text because they could be recited verbatim or nearly so and had the additional value of preserving a sample of the oral literature of the culture.

Boas said that no one "would advocate the study of antique civilizations or . . . of the Turks or the Russians, without a thorough knowledge of their languages and the literary documents in these languages; and contributions not based on such material would not be considered as adequate."[11] He pointed out that in regard to the American Indians, no such literary material was available. He believed that one of the essential tasks for anthropology was to collect such material and to make it available for future research.

In addition to the myth texts, Jacobs copied a large number of other narrative and ethnologic texts from Annie.

Some of these were taken in Hanis and some in Miluk, and some were recorded in both languages. Jacobs was most interested in collecting a large body of Miluk text because Frachtenberg had previously collected text in Hanis and because it was less likely that Hanis would suffer an early extinction. At least ten competent speakers of Hanis were still living, but if Annie should unexpectedly die, the Miluk language would be gone.

Annie impressed Jacobs with her fluent dictation of both the Hanis and the Miluk texts. He commented that her Miluk was not as rich in vocabulary and idioms as her Hanis but that she gave a satisfactory sampling of the Miluk dialect. He added that after having worked with both Jim Buchanan and Frank Drew, he believed that "for linguistic research Mrs. Peterson is a better person to employ in either Coos dialect." He thought that Annie was "largely responsible" for his sharp delineation of Hanis phonetics, a delineation sharper than what Frachtenberg had been able to secure from Jim Buchanan twenty-five years earlier. Jacobs said that Annie's translations were rapid "though hampered by broken and infelicitous crudity of English vocabulary and idiom."[12] She had not learned English until after she was twenty years old, and she never spoke it with fluency.

At the end of the summer of 1933 Jacobs had to break off his work with Annie and return to his teaching job at the University of Washington. He asked if she would consider coming to Seattle the following summer to work with him at the university. She declined the offer. The expenses of the fieldwork at Charleston with Annie had been paid for from a research grant provided by Franz Boas and Columbia University. The University of Washington had provided the automobile and the Ediphone recording device.[13]

Jacobs returned to the university with quite a coup. He had discovered what was very likely the last person to speak one of the little-known languages of the Oregon Coast. And it turned out that his informant was knowledgeable and cooperative and pleasant to work with. And he had not yet exhausted her exceptional repertoire of myth. He planned to return the following summer and finish his work with her.

The quality of the material that Jacobs was able to gather from Annie during the summer of 1933 was impressive. Most significant, she was able to give the myths in an unexpurgated form. He had found that most of the Indians he had worked with in the Northwest had been influenced by the Christian or the Indian Shaker religions. As a result, some of the more important aspects of Indian cultures were not accurately reported by them.[14] Annie was uninhibited in that regard and had resisted, with a sense of humor, accepting the "new taboos" of the white culture.

Jacobs immediately began to prepare for his 1934 summer fieldwork with Annie. He carefully and methodically placed on index cards each of the concepts and cultural features that Annie had referred to during their sessions together. He noted on the cards all that had been discussed, and he left room for the answers to questions that he intended to ask during the next summer.

Annie's reputation had evidently spread among anthropologists working on the cultures of the Northwest states. Jacobs arrived at Charleston to continue his work with her in June 1934, but by that time Annie had already been visited by three of Jacobs's colleagues from other universities. In November 1933 the almost legendary Smithsonian ethnologist John Peabody Harrington had been at Coos Bay. He was on his way to the Medford area of southern Oregon to check on place-names with Molly Orton, one of the last speakers of Takelma, and with others.[15] While at Coos Bay he stayed overnight at Black's Auto Camp in Empire. In the morning he drove to Charleston looking for Annie.[16] She was not home, but he talked briefly to Carl, who told him that Annie was staying temporarily in Marshfield, helping Dora Lambert, an Indian woman whose husband was paralyzed. Harrington located Mrs. Lambert and her daughter in Marshfield, but as it turned out, Annie was in North Bend at the time visiting her good friend Agnes Johnson.[17] John Peabody Harrington and Annie Miner Peterson were thus fated never to meet. The next time he was at Coos Bay was in 1942, and by then Annie had passed away.

On May 27, 1934, Homer Barnett of the University of Oregon interviewed Annie and her friend Agnes Johnson. He was working up material for a paper on culture element distributions on the Oregon Coast. On May 30 and 31 Philip Drucker from the University of California interviewed Annie.[18] The field notes of Barnett and Drucker reveal information that complements and sometimes duplicates the material that Jacobs had been collecting in more systematic detail.

Also during early 1934 Annie was interviewed by Cora Du Bois of the University of California. Du Bois was researching the exceptionally complex series of interacting sects and cults that had developed in northern California and western Oregon as an outgrowth of the 1870 Ghost Dance. Such messianic and revivalist movements arise from time to time, sporadically throughout the world, as a reaction to the crushing and overwhelming impact of European culture. The specific case of the 1870 Ghost Dance provided a unique vehicle, Du Bois thought, for tracing the struggle of the Oregon and California Indians "to integrate their cultural life to the unavoidable demands of European invasion."[19]

Annie was one of approximately 140 informants interviewed by Du Bois during the course of her research. She found Annie to be pleasant, willing, and moderately well informed about the movement.[20] Annie had been present at the first of the Ghost Dances at Yachats in 1872. She had later attended the Ghost Dance and the Warm House Dances at Siletz. She had evidently attended Coquille Thompson's Warm House Dances both at Alsea and at Siuslaw during 1878.

Du Bois interviewed eleven Oregon informants. Only Coquille Thompson provided more and better firsthand information than Annie. Frank Drew was also interviewed and was described by Du Bois as "pious, pompous, verbose." She noted that he tended to interpolate his own religious speculations, probably the result of the influence of evangelical Christianity among the Indians at Siuslaw following their conversion in 1894. Of Lottie Evanoff, Du Bois said: "Moderately informed but not very interested. Slovenly."[21] This last remark may partially explain Jacobs's inability to work with Lottie.

Jacobs and his wife, Elizabeth, turned over to Du Bois the Ghost Dance material that they had previously obtained from Annie and others. This information was most gratefully received.[22] Du Bois noted that for Annie, "the affair had no religious connotations."[23] This observation is well in line with Annie's known skepticism.

Meanwhile, Jacobs had obtained a small grant-in-aid from the National Research Council and received further support from the Department of Anthropology at the University of Washington. Because the Miluk language would never be heard again as spoken by a native speaker after Annie was gone, Jacobs was interested in using the most modern electronic recording techniques. Two engineers at the University of Washington Department of General Engineering constructed for him a portable electric phonograph recorder that would operate from a six-volt car battery.[24] The recorder used RCA Victor pregrooved home recording blanks. One can understand Jacobs's interest in using the very latest technology to preserve this material. Ironically, however, in a comparison of the recordings on the old Ediphone wax cylinders and those on the new RCA pregrooved records, Annie's voice is much clearer and of a better fidelity on the old Ediphone!

The recording machine was not quite ready when Jacobs departed from Seattle for Charleston. It was delivered to

him a little later in the summer while he was interviewing
Annie with the aid of the index cards. He was eager to get
started with the electronic recording right away. He began
by running a couple of practice disks so that sound levels
and general quality could be set. Annie started speaking
clearly into the microphone in the Hanis language. Jacobs
interrupted her, and she laughed and said: "Oh, you want
the South Slough language. I forgot!"[25] She then talked for
a few minutes in Miluk while Jacobs fiddled with the con-
trols, adjusted her distance from the microphone, and
satisfied himself that this was going to work.

He then put her through a marathon recording session.
She started with the "Song of Matluc," the slave of the
Chinook whom she had known as a child at Yaquina. Then
she sang the wolf power doctoring song of an old Coos man,
"You came for the timber . . . ," and the dream song of
another Coos. She remembered Marshfield Tom's dream-
power song, "Timberman, that's my power. . . . That's what
I had people with." She then recorded two sides of Miluk
text and some children's games.

At that point Jacobs had her rerecord the myth songs
that she had recorded the previous summer on the Ediphone
cylinders. It is a testament to her memory and to the
accuracy of her work that she sang them all exactly as she
had the year before. These traditional materials, most of
which had been imprinted upon her during preadolescent
years, were still with her to be recalled and recited in her old
age so that future generations could carry them on. This was
the manner in which the traditions of her people had been
transmitted for thousands of years, but now not even her
own children and grandchildren were interested in them. As
a result, they were recorded on the sterile disks of the RCA
Victor recording machine, with the idea that someone might
someday gain something important from them.

It is amazing how many of the songs of her friends and
acquaintances she remembered: Coquille Mary's doctoring

song, Bob Burns's gambling song, dream songs of Gishgiu, Emily Taylor, Frank Drew's mother-in-law, Old Taylor, Old Ned, Old Cammon, and her own uncle Jesse and her half-sisters. All of these were remembered from her childhood.

She then sang a number of the round dance songs from the Ghost Dance revival of the 1870s. Finally, she became too hoarse to continue. She coughed and said, "Too much for my sore throat!"[26] After a rest she started again with love songs, some more text in Miluk and the same text in Hanis, for comparison, and a Ghost Dance dream-power song in which it was said that all the dead people would return in a white ship.

Annie's good friend Ida Wasson, who had accompanied her to Portland in 1917, was now remarried and living at Charleston. She was of Klamath parentage, and Jacobs recorded her recitation of the text of "The Bears" in the Klamath language. In August, Annie recorded a few more dance songs, as well as a myth in Miluk, repeated in Hanis for comparison.

One morning Annie told Jacobs of a dream she had had the night before. She was amused by the fact that she had dreamed in Miluk—something she had probably not done since childhood. She said, "My dream was funny." She was playing with two girls, who spoke in Miluk. Annie asked one of them, also in Miluk, "Whose child are you?" The girl replied, "My mother's name is 'One-Eyed!'" Annie said, "Oh! I have never known a person named 'One-Eyed!'"[27]

Jacobs was interested in the Freudian view of culture and personality, a view in which the interpretation of dreams plays an important part.[28] Jacobs asked her whom she had known who was one-eyed. Annie replied that she had known Old Lizy and her son Pike, both Miluk and both lacking the use of one eye. Pike, in fact, was called 'One-Eyed' in Miluk.[29] He had lost his eye in an accident and did not like the nickname.[30] Jacobs tried to give a hypothetical analysis of Annie's dream, but he admitted that he was not well enough acquainted with her to do so.

Jacobs did not think there was any close association between the content of the dream and the "easily elicited recollection of one-eyed natives."[31] There is, however, some indication that having one bad eye was not all that uncommon among the Miluk. Even among the elders of the present Coquille Indian Tribe, who are themselves descendants of the Miluk, several have only one good eye.* It is possible that the content of the dream was associated with nothing more than that.

Among other things, Jacobs was interested in checking, through Annie, some of the work that Leo Frachtenberg had done with Jim Buchanan in 1909. The results of one scientist's research should always be subject to the scrutiny of other scientists. If the experiment cannot be replicated, then there was something wrong with it. In 1909 Leo Frachtenberg, one of the early Ph.D.'s of Franz Boas from Columbia, had collected nineteen myths in Hanis from Jim Buchanan, who at the time was living a few miles east of Florence on the Siuslaw River. Buchanan had been born at the Hanis village of Walitch, about a half mile to the north of Annie's mother's ancestral village of Intesedge.[32] Buchanan was at least ten years older than Annie.

Frachtenberg also had access to twelve myths that had been collected in 1903 by Harry Hull St. Clair from Tom Hollis.[33] Using the text and the interlinear translations of these thirty-one Hanis Coos myths, Frachtenberg had constructed a grammar of the Hanis language, which was first published in 1914.[34] As an appendix to his grammar, he provided two of the shorter myths with word-for-word translation. One of the myths was called "The Origin of Death."

---

* This was noted personally by the author at each of the Mid-Winter Gatherings of the Coquille Indian Tribe, Coos Bay, Oregon, in 1992, 1993, and 1994.

Annie had never heard "The Origin of Death" before. Jacobs read it to her, doing his best to accurately give voice to Frachtenberg's old-fashioned orthographic symbols. Annie translated it dutifully, but she strongly objected to some of the phraseology and style of Frachtenberg's original.[35] Her objections were to what she considered to be, according to Jacobs, "crudity, ineptitude, or improper style and phrasing."[36]

Jacobs said that this confirmed his hunch that Buchanan spoke another Hanis "provincialism." It is also likely that Frachtenberg had caused Buchanan to dictate at a very slow speed, which could easily have introduced the stylistic awkwardness that Annie objected to. The translation of the myth by Annie and Jacobs contains the same basic content as the version by Buchanan and Frachtenberg, but Annie's is much more colloquial and free-flowing. Frachtenberg, whose native language was German, always ended up with quite formal and stiff translations into English.

Jacobs had assumed that there would be enough Miluk text to construct a grammar of the language in case anyone should want to do so. In recent years a linguist by the name of Howard Berman reportedly attempted the task but failed. He concluded that Annie's command of Miluk was not good enough.[37] However, Troy Anderson, a member of the Coquille Indian Tribe trained in linguistics at Stanford University, currently believes that a grammar can be constructed. He has the entire body of the Miluk text entered into a computer program that provides a concordance of every word and phrase. With this very powerful tool, a grammar may well be possible.

Other professional linguists have expressed interest in the Miluk language. One of them is Anthony P. Grant of the University of Bradford, England. In a letter to the author he said that he believed that the Miluk material provided to Jacobs by Annie would be sufficient to build a grammar of the language.[38] He pointed out that there is a "good range of tense types, clause types and so on because there are different varieties of narrative and a fair bit of reported and quoted speech." The biggest problem in compiling a grammar is, of course, "the verb in all its complexities."

Another linguist who has expressed interest in the Miluk language is Laurence Morgan at the University of California at Berkeley[39] He has attempted to determine the relationship between Hanis and Miluk and has done some work in assessing Annie's competence in the latter. His work is in progress and due for publication soon.

By the end of September 1934, Jacobs had exhausted Annie's repertory of myth, narrative, and ethnology. Altogether, the texts formed an astonishing body of work. The myths told of a world before the coming of the Indians themselves. There were thirty-two myth texts in Miluk plus eight in Hanis and two more in Miluk and Hanis both. Among the Miluk texts was the great Coos epic of five generations of the Trickster-Transformer, "The Trickster Person Who Made the Country."[40] This text is probably unique in Native American literature.

In addition to the myths was a category of semi-mythic tales about events that had presumably occurred during relatively "recent history." That is, they occurred after the people had arrived. Annie told Jacobs sixteen texts of that kind in Miluk plus three in Hanis and one in both Hanis and Miluk. These narratives clearly show the distinction that Annie and her ancestors had placed between the "Myth Age," before the coming of the Indians, and the more nearly historic period.

Annie also told Jacobs virtually everything she knew or had ever heard concerning the ethnology of her people. There are seventy-one texts of that type, including at least seven that are biographical and autobiographical. As far as it was possible, Jacobs carefully documented the sources of all of Annie's information.

In many ways Jacobs was unique among the anthropologists of his generation and of the generation before him. He had earned his master's degree in American history, and he was ever conscious of the importance of historical documentation, a detail usually neglected by his contemporaries in anthropology. He always asked Annie from whom she had heard the myths and narratives that she was dictating, and in his footnotes to the published texts those sources are indicated.

Among her sources were her brother-in-law Daloose Jackson and her uncle Dick, both of whom were Hanis and a generation older than Annie. Among her Miluk sources were Old Tar Heels, Charlie Ned, and her good friend Cissy. She also remembered material she had heard from her mother and from her grandfather Minkws, as well as from Libby and Gishgiu, among several others. Some of the material was, as she said, the "property of all the Coos," but most of it she was able to attribute to a specific source or sources.

The students of Franz Boas, of whom Melville Jacobs was one, collected Native American texts in their original languages over a period of about fifty years. Fifty or sixty volumes of those texts were published over the years and were thus made available to scholars for further research.[41] Jacobs's work with Annie, which came toward the end of this process, has been very little studied, but it may rank among the best and most interesting of them all.

The texts of non-Western oral literature have never made for popular reading, but recently several attempts have been made to bring samples of these texts to wider audiences. Jarold Ramsey's *Coyote Was Going There: Indian Literature of the Oregon Country* (1977) is a notable example of those attempts. More recently the Oregon State University Press has published the Oregon Literature Series (1993, 1994), which contains a small sample of the oral literature of the Indians of Oregon.

The poetry volume of the Oregon Literature Series includes Annie's text of the myth "The Walkers and the Winged Things Fought" and Annie's niece Lottie's love song

"My Sweetheart," as recorded by Annie on the Ediphone wax cylinders. The autobiography volume includes Annie's own autobiography. A folklorized version of one incident from Annie's "The Trickster Person Who Made the Country" appears in the folklore volume as "Coyote and the Straw-berries." For the interested reader, an annotated listing of published works incorporating English versions of texts from the Oregon Coast Penutian languages is included here as Appendix 3.

Two of Annie's shorter myths, "White Wife of Mouse" and "Wife of Seal," are quite interesting in that they have a romantic ring that makes them easy for contemporary audiences to accept. She got both of them from Alice Johnson, whose mother had come from Annie's own mother's ancestral village of Intesedge. "White Wife of Mouse" appears in *Coyote Was Going There*.[42] Before the recent publication of the Oregon Literature Series, this was the only one of Annie's myths to have ever been incorporated into an anthology of Native American literature.

Texts recorded in the precise sounds of a non-Western language were required for scientific linguistics. Linguists, anthropologists, and folklorists all shared the perception that such texts were also superior for the study of folklore.[43] The pitifully small number of such texts that have been recorded worldwide, in relation to the thousands of non-Western languages that exist, makes Jacobs's work with Annie all the more precious and deserving of study.

Of the anthropologists who made those carefully recorded collections of myth and folklore, Melville Jacobs was one of the very few to have conducted a meaningful analysis of his material. Virtually all of the others, and there were several hundred, did no more than collect the texts.[44] They did not know what to do with the material they had recorded.

A number of scholars outside the field of anthropology were interested in mythology and folklore at that time.

Among them were the psychoanalyst Carl Jung and the folklorist Joseph Campbell. Jacobs viewed their theories with a degree of contempt. He said that they—"and a great many others"—were "out of date, pretentious, culture-bound, or rooted in untenable premises. The market is inundated with books of such kinds."[45]

Jacobs conducted an analysis of the content and style of the collection of Clackamas Chinook myths that he had obtained from Victoria Howard during the summers of 1929 and 1930.[56] In the course of his analysis he developed a theory, or framework, for conducting critical analysis of non-Western oral literatures. No one has used his methods to analyze the myths he collected from Annie, but there is every reason to believe that such an analysis would be productive.

Jacobs based his theory on his years of work with the last speakers of the languages of the Northwest states. His first premise was that the myths and folktales that he had collected were in no way analogous to the short stories and novels of Western literature. He found that the Indian texts were actually short skits, one-act plays, and sometimes longer dramatic works. The text was merely an outline or, at best, a libretto of what was in reality a performing art. Jacobs contended that no proper interpretation of the material could be made except on those terms.[47]

The content and style of the myths had multifaceted origins. The actual performances were derived from processes that were "historical, cultural, psychological, linguistic, and aesthetic."[48] They arose from features within the structure of the society and from the many ways in which people relate to one another. The myths served an important function within the society, and they were pleasurable in their own right. They tended to be about relationships of the sort that the society had not been overly successful in dealing with. The myths thus helped to relieve much societal stress.

Some of the obvious sources of such stress were the relationships of younger to elder; of nonshamans to shamans; and of wives to their co-wives, to their husbands, and to their children. Annie's myths contain examples of all of these. Humor was one of the most effective ways of dealing with these stress situations, and Annie's myths are rife with humor. They use tricks and cleverness, understatement and exaggeration, pomposity and eccentricity, humiliation and irony, as well as satire, mimicry, and wordplay. The butt of the humor within the myth is almost always a powerful personage of the type that could not be attacked directly in everyday life.

As meaningful and important as the myths were within the lives of the people of Annie's mother's generation, they were meaningless to the people of Annie's daughter's generation. Annie stood as a truly transitional figure, with no one to pass her heritage on to except a scholarly and gentle young man who hung on her every word. By the end of her second summer with Jacobs, she had exhausted her repertoire.

Annie wearing a cedar-bark dress and other items from her collection, probably ca. 1910. Photo courtesy Iola Larson.

12

The Last Years

Annie had been fortunate indeed. She had been given the chance to validate her life by passing on to the future what she knew of the accumulated experiences of generations of her ancestors. She was able to do this in her twilight years, and she could now rest, content in the knowledge that she had done what the elders of her people had been conditioned to do from the beginning of time. She must have had a feeling of satisfaction.

She had sold a part of her collection of baskets and other artifacts, and Jacobs had paid her the standard "informants fees" for two summers of work. Informants fees were quite modest. For example, Philip Drucker was paying thirty-five cents per hour at the time.[1] That may have been close to the standard fee, which is interesting when one considers that loggers were paid only $3.50 per day working in the camps on South Slough only a few miles away. Jacobs evidently paid a little better than the standard fee. According to John Peabody Harrington, Jacobs paid Annie fifty cents per hour and they worked from 1 P.M. to 5 P.M. daily.[2] During the course of the two summers, this work may have given Annie somewhere in the neighborhood of $200 in fees.

In 1934, while the world was still in the depths of an economic depression, Annie and Carl had a little extra cash. With this extra money, they were susceptible to advice on how to spend it. There was a piece of property on the hill to the south of Charleston, along the Seven Devils Road, which had been subdivided as the "Charleston Highway Tract." The developers were selling lots, and Annie and Carl invested $250 for lots 1 and 2, Block 10. Unfortunately, this does not appear to have been a profitable investment.

Annie, however, continued to enjoy herself. She grew flowers, and although she had given up on canaries, she was now raising turtles. These small reptiles were popular pets and could be bought in the five-and-dime stores of the day. Annie had quite a herd of them. Sometimes she inadvertently left the door open, and the turtles got out. She would ask the neighbor children to help find them. "Help me find my 'tuttelies,'" she would say.[3] The children liked her.

Time was again marked by fish and leaves. There was a time for crabbing and a time for catching perch. In the springtime she could still gather the tender shoots, and in the late summer she could dig the tubers that were ready. There were friends and neighbors and her daughter, Nellie, and others who could share catches of salmon, herring, and smelt with Annie and Carl. There were always clams in the mud flats just outside the door.

But there was also tuberculosis. Annie's only surviving grandson, Oscar Marlow Aasen, had been married for barely a year when he came down with the "quick TB" and died. Annie too began to feel some of the first symptoms. Her energy level was down, she was losing weight, and she had a persistent cough. Eventually she was spitting up blood.

In June 1937 she and Carl were both sick enough that they went to see Dr. Ennis Keizer in North Bend. He confirmed that they both had chronic pulmonary tuberculosis.[4] He gave the standard prescription of plenty of bed rest and fresh food. Annie was not by nature a person who could be kept at home in bed, however. After a few days she felt better and decided she needed to go to Empire, a five-mile walk. She was hiking up the road when a friend met her and said, "You're supposed to be laying still at home." Annie, very much in character, replied, "I'll lay still a long time when I'm dead!"[5] And she kept on walking.

John W. Flanagan, nephew of the John Flanagan who had helped Annie when she had arrived in Empire in 1880, was the postmaster at Marshfield. Annie once showed him her two favorite dresses. One was her well-known white buckskin dress of the Plains Indian style with its intricate beadwork, and the other was a cheap black cotton dress. She told him that she would like to be buried in the buckskin dress but had instead decided on the plain black cotton one. "If I have the other one on, White men will dig me up," she explained.[6]

A few months after they had gone to Dr. Keizer, she and Carl deeded their little lot with its beached float house at Charleston to the Coos County Relief Commission. Carl signed his name, and Annie placed her "X" on the title deed. They were to live there as long as they could, on relief, but when they were gone, the county would own it.

Annie's last visit to Dr. Keizer was on March 26, 1939. He examined her and sent her home to die. She was failing rapidly, and her last weeks were very uncomfortable. In addition to the tuberculosis, she had developed a cancer on her mouth.[7] She was unaware that, during her final month, the University of Washington published *Coos Narrative and Ethnologic Texts*, the first of the two volumes of the material she had dictated to Melville Jacobs five years earlier.

Annie was very ill indeed. At eight o'clock on the morning of May 9, 1939, she died at her little beached float house in Charleston, with her husband, Carl, at her side.[8] And that was the moment that the Miluk language became extinct.

Annie's obituaries appeared in all of the newspapers of the Coos Bay area. The *Coos Bay Times*, the big daily, printed her obituary on the front page only a few hours after she died. The weekly *Coos Bay Harbor* and the *Southwestern Oregon News* both had front-page notices. Most characteristic was the obituary written by Jesse Allen Luse, editor of the *Marshfield Sun*. He had known Annie all his life, and his father and his grandfather before him had known her relatives. After he attended the funeral he wrote:

Funeral Rites Observed

Campbell's Funeral Chapel was filled to capacity this afternoon when the last sad rites were held for Mrs. Annie Peterson, who was called to the happy hunting ground at Charleston on Tuesday of this week. There was a profusion of flowers; the Eagles lodge sent a delegation in uniform, and quite a sprinklin of the ancient dwellers of the land were present.

Deceased, a member of the Coos Bay tribe of Indians, was born on Willanch slough 83 years ago; she has lived at many points in the County, on the Siletz, but mostly in the lower bay section. There may be other pure-bloods of her tribe left, but we do not recall them at the moment.

She is survived by her husband, Peter Peterson, deep-sea fisherman of the Charleston area, and a daughter by a former marriage.[9]

Annie's age was erroneously reported as eighty-three in both the *Marshfield Sun* and the *Coos Bay Times*. She was most likely seventy-nine years old. Her husband's name was reported as "Pete" or "Peter," but his real name was Carl.

Carl was never able to recover after Annie died. His neighbors at Charleston would see him wandering dejectedly in front of the little beached float house. They sympathized, but there was probably nothing they could do to help.[10] Finally he was removed to the county farm near Coquille. He died there of tuberculosis on August 10, just three months after he had lost Annie.[11] The Eagles lodge was in charge of the graveside services.[12] The little place at Charleston went to the County Relief Commission. There is conflicting information over who got Annie's other "things."[13]

Melville Jacobs had been working on the notes he had collected from Annie. With meticulous care he had transcribed for the printer the text of her dictations, using the orthographic symbols that represent the many Miluk and Hanis sounds that do not occur in English. He did it all by hand, carefully and elegantly. Before long, his manuscript was ready for publication.[14]

The first volume of his work with Annie was published in April 1939. *Coos Narrative and Ethnologic Texts* was Volume 8, Number 1, of the distinguished University of Washington Publications in Anthropology series. Jacobs explained in his preface that he had restricted himself to the texts "dictated by Mrs. Peterson on ethnologic matters and to the semi-mythic 'narratives' or 'tales.'" The semi-mythic narratives were "about events that the natives place in a category of relatively 'recent history.'"[15]

In April 1940, the second volume of Annie's work with Jacobs was published. *Coos Myth Texts* was published as Volume 8, Number 2, of the University of Washington Publications in Anthropology. It contained forty myths and a fragment, plus Annie's translation of one of the myths that Frachtenberg had obtained from Buchanan in 1909. The two volumes comprised all of the myths that Annie could remember, including the long, epic myth entitled "The Trickster Person Who Made the Country."

Jacobs had worked with Frank Drew at Florence in October and November 1932 and had collected English versions of some of the myths from him. The English versions were added to the end of *Coos Myth Texts* because, Jacobs explained, "they offer interesting evidence of the manner in which stories disintegrate when told in an English version" by a younger informant.[16] Jacobs included a most useful appendix of abstracts of all the Coos myths, narratives, and tales that he had collected from Annie in 1933 and 1934, as well as those that Leo Frachtenberg had collected from Jim Buchanan in 1909 and those that Harry Hull St. Clair II had collected from Tom Hollis in 1903. This Coos collection constitutes one of the most interesting and varied samples of myth in all of Native American literature.

Sometime in 1939, between the publication of the two volumes, Jacobs was visited by John Peabody Harrington of the Smithsonian Institution. They spent several evenings in conversation.[17] Harrington had become a legend within the profession that both he and Jacobs practiced. An employee of the Smithsonian since 1915, he was considered to be an eccentric genius. He had spent almost every minute of his years with the Smithsonian in the field collecting notes from the last surviving speakers of most of the language groups throughout North America. In his lifetime he collected more than one million pages of field notes.[18]

Linguistics was drifting away from the minute collection of the details of individual languages, the work to which Jacobs and Harrington had devoted their lives. The linguistics of the future would be pursuing different ends. It would, however, show some interest in mass comparisons of the bewildering number and variety of languages, and much of the data used for such comparisons would be that collected by students of Franz Boas during the first third of the twentieth century. The new linguistics would use the results in helping to reconstruct the migrations and original peopling of the Western Hemisphere.[19] Jacobs and Harrington discussed these matters and came to conclusions that were strikingly similar to those reached by the most advanced linguistic thinkers fifty years later.

In the course of their conversations, Harrington expressed a strong interest in everything Jacobs had done. They talked about such specific matters as the pronunciation of the name "Coquille." Harrington noted that the whites said "kok'il," whereas the Indians said "ko'kwel."[20] And they talked about who was still alive to act as linguistic informants. Only one Alsea informant was alive and only three Lower Umpqua.[21] Among the Coos were perhaps six who could still speak Hanis, but Miluk was extinct. Two years later Harrington learned that the bulk of the knowledge remaining among the few surviving Hanis was that retained by Annie's niece Lottie Evanoff.

In 1942 Harrington finally had his chance to visit the few remaining Coos, Lower Umpqua, and Alsea Indians. He was on the Oregon Coast to find out what they knew and to write it down while they were still alive. Among the Coos he found that Frank Drew retained a fine remembrance of his youth at Yachats and Siuslaw. At Coos Bay he talked to Annie's daughter, Nellie Aasen, as well as Fanny Elliott, John Waters, and the Wasson sisters, Lolly, Nellie, and Daisy. From his notes we can infer that very little of linguistic or ethnologic value was learned from those descendants of the Indians of Coos County. It was only from Annie's niece Lottie Evanoff that Harrington struck paydirt.

Harrington filled almost 250 pages of oversize, loose sheets of paper with utterances from Lottie. The notes included a number of English-language versions of the myths and tales, the Hanis place-names of a large number of locations within the former tribal areas of the Indians of Coos County, and a remarkably rich assemblage of biographical and historical information. As Jacobs had indicated earlier, Lottie was "exceptionally well informed."[22] Fortunately for history, Harrington and Lottie were able to work well together. Harrington was evidently the only anthropological field-worker who could work well with Lottie. The Smithsonian Institution made his notes available on microfilm in 1981.

The herculean effort that had gone into the precise recording of the sounds of the original languages was not matched in the subsequent use of the material. Between 1900 and 1934, about 130 myths and tales were recorded in the then nearly extinct languages of the Oregon Coast Penutian: Alsea, Lower Umpqua, Hanis Coos, and Miluk Coos. Almost half of those myths and tales had been collected by Melville Jacobs from Annie. Yet only a dozen of the 130 myths ever showed up in publications aimed at the general public. No published analysis of their content and style was ever made. Except for grammars of the Hanis Coos and the Siuslaw (Lower Umpqua) compiled by Frachtenberg, nothing of significance to science was ever done with the exquisitely precise recording of the sounds and structure of the languages.

The work of saving those languages, myths, and ethnologic texts could be considered a monument to the futility of scholarship. But the material was not lost. It was saved. We have it, and someday—perhaps in the very near future—it might exert an unsuspected influence on life or art or science. Computerized linguistic work in Miluk has already been done by Troy Anderson of the Coquille Tribe.[23] Both the Coquille Indian Tribe and the Confederated Tribes of Coos, Siuslaw, and Lower Umpqua Indians have programs for the restoration of their cultures. If and when those programs bear fruit, one of the names to be remembered for it will be Annie Miner Peterson.

Annie in about 1910, wearing items from her collection. Photo courtesy
Ward Robertson.

Annie's grandchildren: Iola and Oscar Marlow Aasen, ca. 1925. Courtesy Iola Larson.

appendix 1

"The Trickster Person Who Made the Country"

This Coos myth, told by Annie Miner Peterson to Melville Jacobs in the Miluk language and translated jointly by Jacobs and Peterson, has been edited and annotated for general reading by Lionel Youst. It is taken from Melville Jacobs, *Coos Myth Texts* (Seattle: University of Washington, 1940), 184–222.

INTRODUCTION

Among the myths that Annie heard and remembered from her childhood was one great epic myth that describes episodes connected with five successive generations of the trickster/world-maker. Beginning with the first trickster, the "Father of the Foods," and continuing with his son and his grandson—the second and the third tricksters—the myth culminates with the fourth trickster, who becomes Coyote, and his immaculately conceived son, who ascends to the sky and becomes the "Father of the People."

Within this great epic are explanations of why the world is so arbitrarily put together. The adolescent antics of the early trickster/worldmakers established for all time how things would be, what they would be named, and their relationships to each other.

The dramatic episodes dealt especially with the tense kinds of relationships and behavior that the culture had failed to handle smoothly. Probably in any culture, sex and power are handled most poorly. One suspects that the culture from which this great epic myth emerged was no exception. Episodes of sex and power predominate, just as they do in contemporary popular culture of television, movies, novels, and comic books.

The myth explores most of the social relationships that one would expect in a preliterate culture. There are premarital and marital maneuvers: monogamous, polygamous, and polyandrous. There are deserted and tricked mates. There are incestuous relationships of all kinds. There are relationships between parent and child, between siblings, and between communities. There are relationships between individuals and their leaders, kidnappers, shamans, ogres, upper classes, lower classes, comrades, elders, and so on.

These episodes comprise the activities of dramatic characters. There are ogres, tricksters, animals, and people, but all of them are actually human or human-like. Human thinking, emotions, and relationships are projected into them. They are like the stock characters in a contemporary situation comedy. They are stereotypes, composites, eccentrics, and caricatures. They were immediately recognizable by the audience during Annie's childhood.

Although the myth itself was told only in winter, the characters and episodes within it were discussed by the community year-round. Songs are common in myths of this kind, and during the course of the year these songs might be sung at any time. During Annie's childhood everyone knew them. This myth includes three solo songs.

This myth—indeed most of the material remembered by Annie—was characterized by a rough-and-ready humor. The humor comes through in amusing songs, funny situations, clown-like personalities, laughable expressions and expletives, and, one supposes, comical vocalization by the storyteller herself. It must always be remembered that this is a *performing* art. The myth was meant to be recited dramatically to an audience by a skilled storyteller.

A certain important aspect of the worldview of Annie's ancestors comes through during the course of the telling of the myth. The mythic characters themselves are preparing a very imperfect world for the "next people to come." These next people to come are understood to be the Indians themselves. But there are also allusions to a people who are to come after the Indians. These people were understood by the generation of Annie's parents to be the whites.

Very little of what the whites did seems to have surprised the generation of Annie's parents. They could always find the explanation for whites' actions in "chapter and verse" of their myths. When the telegraph and telephone lines were first strung, they said, "The trickster knew that long ago." They remembered the trickster pulling and extending a hair in every direction and finally hearing his child who was far off. They were not surprised that occasionally an early settler would have an artificial eye. They would say, "Maybe that is what Coyote meant." They were thinking of the time Coyote put a snail shell in his eye so that he would not blink during a gambling game. When the trickster copulated with his daughters, he said: "Oh a different sort of population will come here. They will do like that even to their children." Melville Jacobs commented, "Indians perhaps used this statement of the trickster as evidence of his knowledge of what kind of people the whites would be."

The final episodes of the myth express something of a moral or religious view. Coyote copulated with his two daughters-in-law and then wiped his penis on the children's faces. When Coyote's son, the fifth trickster, returned home and discovered what his father had done, he said: "I do not like you any more. I do not want that kind of a father. They will name you coyote. You will bark at the next people." At the conclusion of the myth, the fifth trickster, with his family, returns "above." In announcer style, the myth ends: "It is he who is the father of us people. Our father still lives up above."

As for the explanatory text in the right-hand column, entries preceded by "n." were footnotes in Melville Jacobs's original.

Entries in parentheses were parenthetical statements within the text. Underlined entries are catchword titles for some of the motifs and plots indicated by Melville Jacobs in his abstracts of the folklorized Coos narratives, tales, and myths (see Jacobs, *Coos Myth Texts*, 243–58). Words and phrases preceded by "HS" are my own insertion of common Northwest Coast plot devices and humor stimuli, inspired by Jacobs's *Content and Style of an Oral Literature* (1959). Asterisked notes are my own.

Introductory Note, by Melville Jacobs

Mrs. Peterson had to give this trickster myth in installments on successive days because of its length when dictating. Since among her closer relatives only her mother's mother was a speaker of Miluk, Mrs. Peterson heard the epic more often in the Hanis dialect. But it was common property to all Coos speakers. The "tricksters" are apparently conceived of as a peculiarly powerful (supernaturally powerful) caste or type of ancient myth age people, living in certain villages in the Coos country. Five men of those trickster people, living successively in a line of descent from father to son through five generations, figure as the leading dramatis personae of this myth of the transforming of the country. It is these five whom the Coos call "worldmakers." It is only the fourth trickster, told of towards the latter part of the myth, who is turned into an actual coyote by his son who is the fifth trickster and the "people's father." These five tricksters are otherwise not specifically identified as coyotes or pictured as closely resembling coyotes, nor are any other people who are referred to in this or other myths as "trickster" tribespeople. Some myths are, however, told about a specific person called "coyote," and in each such case it is probably the fourth trickster of this myth who is meant and who is described in some episode of his life after his son had made him don a coyote garment. . . . Mrs. Peterson commented that it was bad luck to tell the long "trickster myth" in the summertime. It was told perhaps only once during the winter, not twice. And next winter it was again told just once, at about the same period of the winter as during the preceding year.

THE FIRST TRICKSTER/WORLDMAKER

1. The trickster was growing up. Now then he began to be traveling about there.[1] He was making a waterfall fish dam and then he made a fish trap basket.[2] Then he set it all in place. Now when he went down to the water his fish trap basket was already full. "Oh, it fills up too rapidly!"[3] His house was already full of fish. So then he made another house. "I always have too much. I don't want to go down to the water again. Now call out when you become full." That is what he said to his fish basket trap. Indeed his fish basket was already halooing before he finished cutting the earlier haul.[4] "Oh it is always calling out too much!" So he went to it. He never got his fish cut to dry before his basket trap was full again. "Ah, that vagina thing! that just haloos all the time!"

2. Now he went back home up from the river. And then just all his food came rolling down the trail, he was hurled aside when the smoked salmon bales hit him.[5] And then the salmon hearts too. "Oh! and you too, hearts?" Now he seized a heart, he threw the heart far away. Then he had no more food left there. Then he lay down hungry by the fire.[6]

3. "Oh well, I will get skunk cabbage." So he made a pack basket, and then he went for skunk

1. (somewhere in the Coos country)

2. *Worldmaker teaches crafts*

3. HS: exaggeration

4. Object talks

5. HS: slapstick

6. HS: irony

cabbage. His pack basket never filled up. So he looked back, and there his skunk cabbages were stretched along in a line. It was just a hole in his pack basket. So he set down and he dug large spruce roots, and he patched the basket. "Ha'ha! That is the way the next people will do it, if they have such a hole in their pack basket. That is the way they will repair it." Now he began digging again and then his pack basket filled up.

4. Now he went back home and he built a fire and he fixed the roasting stick and he put it into the ground beside the fire, skunk cabbage on the roasting stick. Now he lay down. Then he awoke. His roasting stick was merely standing there like that. "Oh that damned thing! That is how it is not cooked!" So he took it and put it down under in hot coals. Then he lay down. Now he awoke. "Mmm. I do smell something." Then he pulled out the food roasted in hot ashes. Oh they were so tender when he took them out. Now he leaped and sang,
"That is how they will cook it,
        that is how
    they will roast it in ashes.[7]
        That is the way
the next people will do it."[8]

So then he went to get more skunk cabbages again. Now he fetched a quantity and he roasted them. He

7. n. The trickster mispronounces words in the song.
8. (the Indians to come later)

collected rocks, he piled them onto the fire, and they became hot, and then he fixed the ground roasting oven. Now he cooked his skunk cabbages there. While he was cooking them that was how he was making a basket pan. Now his cooking was done. Then he put them all in the pans, and the pans were all filled.

5. But he was just all alone. He was saying, "Give this to your mother! Give this to your father! Give this to . . ." and he named all of the relations.

6. Now he thought, "Hu! I am tired of living all alone. I will make some women and then I will call them 'my children.'" Indeed so he did that. He peeled alder bark and he took it back home and he split it and he made two pieces of bark each shaped like a girl. Then he took a stick and pointed it at them and said, "Young girls, arise! Do not sleep so long! Get up! We have much to do." Indeed they arose.[9] They were quite handsome girls. "Ah, my children! You are to name me, 'My father,' and 'father!'" Then that was the way it was indeed. The young girls did work, to be sure.

9. *Image comes to life*

7. The trickster was getting up to some mischief now. "We will be going to the mouth of the stream, we will be drying salmon." So they

moved to there. He would just fail to return at times. "Where do you go, father?" "Oh, I play the stick game with the crow people. I play that with them."[10] Now then he returned shot in the back of the neck. "Ooh. I am going to die. When I have died, when you bury me do not bury my face. You are to step right over my face.[11] And if a man should arrive here, you are to take him for a husband, and then you will become many, you will have children." That is what he said to the girls. Then indeed they buried him when he died, and that is just the way they did it.

8. About five days and sure enough a man arrived.[12] The older sister was to have him already for her husband, but her younger sister said, "Older sister! He seems rather to be just like our father."[13] "Why, how could it be he? On the contrary, he must be dead." "Ah, maybe he did not die, maybe he was just playing a trick like that." Now the older sister became angry. "You are telling a lie. You are only my father, so why should I lie down with you there?" "Why I am not your father! You are two pieces of alder, you are alder bark." Now then they got ready to leave him, and then they left him there.[14] "Oh a different sort of population will come here, and that is the way they will do. They will do like that even with their own

10. (dice game)

11. n. He had himself buried with his face exposed in order to see their privates when they stepped over him.

12. *Lecherous   father; Transformation to seduce women*

13. * Youngest-smartest

14. n. The cause of their anger and departure was merely the insulting remark that they were just pieces of alder bark.

children.[15] Now then he went away too. Now he was going to go here and there, he was going to go all over the country,

9. He was going to make a waterfall. That is the way he went around. Now he got to the Columbia River, and he made a falls. "Ha. I cannot get across. I will make a bridge so that I can go across."

10. Then indeed he went about. He made dams everywhere. Now then he returned to Coos country. And he married. Then they did have a boy baby. And that child of theirs grew up and he too was a trickster. He did all sorts of things in that manner too.[16]

THE SECOND
TRICKSTER/WORLDMAKER

11. Now he was going along the ocean beach, and he came to a house. There was an old woman who was all alone in it. The children of the old woman had gone to hunt. "hmm. Maybe it is a trickster there," so the old woman thought. "Is no one at home?" The old woman said nothing, because the old woman was fearful. So he entered anyway. "Are you alone?" "Hmm," that is the way the old woman grudgingly replied. "Why did you not let me in?" "Oh, I did not hear you." "Ha. You lie." Then he threw down the old woman and he just copulated

15. n. i.e., a kind of people will come here later who will cohabit with their own children. Indians perhaps used this statement of the trickster as evidence of his knowledge of what kind of people the whites would be.

16. n. Mrs. Peterson supposed that more episodes may have occurred during the travels of the first trickster, but she remembered nothing more of him. His child became the second trickster of this epic.

with the old woman. Now foam was going out of the mouth of that old woman. Then the trickster went outside, and he went into the large men's sweat house. And there he lay down.

Now the boys returned, and just foam was coming out of her. Then one brother went to the sweat house, and there the trickster was sleeping. Now he went and told his older brothers, "That trickster is lying down there." "Good. We will take revenge on him." "But how will we take revenge?" "Oh we will get even with him well enough. We will act as if we were going out to the ocean to fish, and we will ask him to go with us."[17]

17. * revenge device

12. "Uncle! Come! We are going out to the ocean to fish." "Ahh!" That was the way he replied. "Ha'u, oh very well, nephew. Ah. I will go." "Hurry, uncle! We want to go in a hurry because the tide is running out strongly. We will have to hurry." "Ah, nephew. I will go." Indeed they went down to the water. "Get in the canoe, uncle!" So he did get into it. "You must lie down, uncle. You will have to be covered up." "All right, nephew." So then he lay down, and the young fellows covered him over.[18] Then down in the boat they got a small rope, which he could not see, and then they pushed out the canoe.

18. *Looking tabu*

Now they watched while the canoe went out to the ocean. Then the trickster arose, but when he got up he was just alone, far out in the ocean, without a paddle.[19] There was a torn basket in the boat, as well as a basket hat in it. But no paddle and not another thing.

19. *Abandonment in boat*

Now then there was a seal that approached him from out of the water. "Huh! Go away!" It would not leave. It emerged close to him again, and when it approached once more he threw the basket hat at it, so that it would drop right on its head. "When you are seen by the next people you will never do anything to a person.[20] And your head will be like the basket hat." And now a whale emerged and spouted. "Get away from here! I am afraid of you." Then he took that torn basket, the basket was somewhat rough edged and unfinished, and then he threw it into its mouth. "You will never bite anybody, you will be toothless, but it will be sticking up inside your mouth. And you will never do anything bad to anybody."[21]

20. (the Indians to come)

13. Now he was beginning to think. "Ah, I will jump into his mouth there." And indeed there he landed, and the whale swallowed him. Now those boys were watching. "He jumped into it!" So they hauled back their canoe,

21. * The gray whales of the Pacific have no teeth. Instead, they have rows of whalebone hanging from the upper jaw.

because the rope was attached to it. The trickster was inside there now, inside there in the belly of the whale. He had a little sort of knife, with it he cut at the entrails.[22] "Indeed now it will drift ashore." So he thought. Indeed then he was rolling in the surf, and then it got onto ground, it was no longer tossing. Now he got out of it through the incision he had made. He could not see a thing. So there he crawled ashore, and then he felt of a log, and he kept on crawling there, and then behind the log there he lay down.

22. *Monster killed from within*

14. He slept there a long time. "Ahh!" An odorous ant bit his penis. "Ha'! What are you doing? Biting the penis of your wealthy head man?[23] That is the way you will do to the next people.[24] You will bite them the same way. And that is the way you will also bite people from afar who will come later.[25] And in that manner you will also bite the vulvas of women." That was what woke him up.

23. *Ants bite genitals*
24. (the Indians to come)

25. (the Whites to come)

15. He wiped his eyes, and then he began to go about, and so he went towards the woods. When he had gotten to the timber, hail stormed down. So he found a hollow tree and he went inside it. "Close up!" Sure enough the tree shut about him. Then he hallooed for help, he called out to all sorts of

things. But none of them came. To others that came he cried, "Not you! I do not want you! Get away from here!" And indeed they left. Then he called out again, but none of them came.

Now red headed woodpecker arrived. It was no long time before that girl had made a hole in the tree. So now he was just up to new mischief. "Ahee, now hasn't she a fine appearance! And those breasts of hers too!"[26] Now what he did want was to touch her breasts. The girl was on the point of leaving then. "Uh', I did not want to touch them. My hand merely dropped there!" The hole was getting a little larger. So now he seized the hair of her head. "Oh! Now is not her head just so very handsome!" Then he wanted to steal some of her feathers. So the girl leaped away and left him. "Ah, my niece! Come here! I was only playing with you." But the girl never returned.

26. HS: Anatomical reference; trickiness

So he cut himself up, he sliced himself into small pieces, and he threw them outside the hole.[27] All cut up he threw himself out, because the tree hole was not large enough. Then he got out, and he collected those parts of himself. Then raven stole his entrails, and his eyes likewise, buzzard it was who stole his eyes. So he went along eyeless, and also without entrails either.[28]

27. *Disintegration*

28. anatomical reference

16. He could only hear children playing, so then he went to there and he arrived there where the children were playing. "Ha, children. Come here! Do you see that yonder? Ooh! that thing going over there?" So the children went to him. "Where is it, uncle?" "Come right here so that you can see it."[29] Indeed the children went close to the old man and then he seized one, and he took out its eyes, and he put them in for his own eyes, they became his own eyes, the eyes of that child did. "You will all be eyeless, and so they will name you snail. That is what they will call you. The next of you will all be eyeless." That is what he said to those whose eyes he had stolen. Then he went on.

17. Now he found strawberries, and he ate of them. He never got full. So he looked to the rear, and they were just in a line behind him. "Oh, I forgot I lacked entrails." Then he thought of wild parsnips. "Oh, I will have them for entrails." So indeed he gathered them, and he thrust and shoved them into his anus.[30] Oh they would not stay in. so then he thought of something. "Oh, I will put pitch on it." Then he put pitch on his anus, so that what he had thrust inside there would not fall out of his anus.[31] Now he went on.

18. Then he saw children were playing and he reached there.[32] "Ha.

29. HS: trickiness

30. HS: anatomical reference; anality

31. *Anus stopper*; n. Which is perhaps why children in play nickname a coyote "pitch-on-his anus."
32. n. Mrs. Peterson did not know who these children were.

How are you playing that?" "Oh we jump over the fire." "Oh, let me jump too." So he also leaped over the fire. But the pitch melted, and then his entrails dropped out. "Oh dear. I forgot the pitch on my anus." Then he seized one of the children, and from it he stole the entrails. Indeed then the child lacked entrails. He said, "The next people will do all sorts of things in that manner."[33]

33. (the Indians to come)

19. Then he went along, and he saw a house, and he got to there. "Ha, my younger sister! I will remain here a while, because I have come from so long a distance in order to visit you." And so then there he stayed indeed. His sister's children were young girls. One day he built a fire outside. "Come, my nieces, sit over here!" Of course they sat down there. Now he kicked the fire, and the fire fell towards them. Then the young girls tumbled backwards, and sure enough he saw their vulvas.[34] "That one with the fat thing, Ha! That is the one I will ask to accompany me." So then.

34. *Glimpses genitals*

20. "Younger sister! I am going fishing. That niece of mine, I would like to have that one go with me. She will slice the salmon for smoking. We will smoke a quantity of them." "Indeed she may go!" So then they went. Now he was getting

up to mischief. They were getting close to where they were going, and then he did tricky things. He spoke thus to a tree, "Big ones fall down! One will be to the rear, another will be ahead." Sure enough that is the way it was. Now he climbed up on one of them, but the girl could not get up on it there. "Name me! I will help you if you call me by a correct name." So then the girl called him all sorts of kinship terms. "But not that way! How did your mother name your father? Call me like that!" "Oh, my husband! Help me up over it!" "Ha'hahahaha! That is the way I wanted you to speak."[35]

35. HS: trick

Then they went on, and they reached there where the people's fishing place was, where they dried salmon. Now he made his fish dam. "Today I will just spear fish. That is the way I will obtain them." He speared quantities indeed, and the girl cut them up. Then she roasted the heads by the fire, and she roasted the tails that way too. She said, "My but I will enjoy eating them! I am hungry!" Then it was getting towards evening, and the girl went inside, and she prepared her cooking.

21. Now the trickster was getting up to more mischief. He took just dark salmon blood, and he threw the blood between her legs. "Yah! You are menstruating. You

must not eat fresh salmon!" That is
what he told the girl.[36] "Hereafter
women will menstruate. Some of
them will flow five days before they
cease menstruating. They will not
eat anything fresh until the cessa-
tion of the flow." That was how he
spoke and that was how it was to be
indeed. They do menstruate, ever
since that time women menstruate.

36. HS: trick, anatomical
reference

Now the girl wept furtively.
"Ha. So he thinks that I know
nothing. I will get away from him, I
will leave him." That is how the girl
thought. "I am going to bathe." "Do
not be away too long." "Ah, yes!"
Then she got the pitch, and she
made a torch and put it in the
ground. Then she went off. Now
she removed her clothes, and she
obtained a stick, she stuck it in the
ground alongside, and she placed
her clothes on it there. She also put
her basket hat on top of it there.
Indeed it was like a person. "Stick!
When he halloos, then you must
reply to him."

Now the girl leaped into the
water, and she swam towards home.
"Ha! Why are you so very long?"
Indeed that stick answered, "Ha! I
am still swimming around."[37] That
was how it answered. But the girl
was no longer there. She was a long
distance away. So he went down to
the water there, and he seized the
head but it was only the basket hat

37. *Magic objects talk*

that he grasped, it was only a stick there. "Ha! She thought she would go home! But she will not be able to go by the trail. She could not climb over the large logs."

But the girl had not gone by the trail. She returned home in the water, and then the girl reached home. "He did bad things to me, and he had me call him 'my husband.' And when I was finishing my cooking, this is what he said. 'Hey! you are menstruating. You are not to eat things that are fresh because you are menstruating.' That is what he told me, and that is why I ran away from him." That is what the girl explained.

22. Now the trickster returned home. "Why did you run away? Why did you leave me?" The mother of the girl replied, "Why did you do bad things to her then?" "Why I did nothing to her!" "Indeed you did all sorts of things to me!" "Ha', you lie!"[38] "I am not lying." "You are just continuing to lie." Then the girl wept. "Ah! so now you are ashamed because you are lying. You yourself named me. You said, 'my husband.' That is the way you named me. Henceforth no matter how smart women will be, they will become ashamed, and so men will vanquish them in argument." Then they told him to leave. "Go away! We want you to leave here!" To be sure, the

38. HS: dishonesty

trickster departed. That is the way he did to those people. The girl was wood-duck.

23. Now the trickster went along, he dug and picked all sorts of things, and this is what he said, "The next people will eat these." For whatever he ate, that is what he said. That is the way he journeyed along. Now he made his home at a certain place. He built a canoe, he finished making his canoe. "Ha! I will go upriver, I will trap there, I will make blankets, winter food, salmon, elk meat, acorns, myrtle nuts, and then I will have quantities of food." That is what the trickster planned to do. And indeed he went upstream, and indeed there up the river he lived. He made smoke dried food, he trapped so that he would have the hides for his clothing, and elk hides for his blankets. Indeed there he lived.

Now one day pretty near springtime he got ready.[39] "Ah. I will go downriver. I will live down toward the ocean." But he was just getting up to some mischief. Now he went downriver. "Ha, tip over, my canoe!" Indeed his canoe upset. Then he drifted on down, and he named places. "This is the way it will be named here, 'blanket-spread place.' That is how the next people will name that place. This is the way they will name 'salmon-bale-drift-

39. n. i.e., in early spring-time when wild currents bloom.

place,' thus will they name that place. 'Paddle-drift-in-place,' In that manner they will name it there. 'Where the mat-drifts-in-place,' that is how they will name that. 'Bailer-drift-in-place,' that is the way they will name that. 'Canoe-drift-ashore-place,' that is how they will name that." Now he was far downriver, there he himself drifted ashore, and he named it in this manner, "'Man-drift-ashore-place,' that is the way it will be named."[40] Then he went ashore, and he built a fire, and he made a grass-brush house, and there he lived. And he labored, he prepared foods.

24. "Ha', I will journey about." And so then he decorated himself, it was wild clover stems that he picked. "Ha'haha! You will be just like money." And he adorned himself with them. "Ha. I wonder what sort of thing will be my feathers? I will pretend they are red headed woodpecker heads, as if it is my headband." So then indeed he plucked wild current blossoms, and he made it of them, and he had that for his feathered headdress. Then he made a quiver, and he put arrows in it, and he packed his quiver, and also his large bow for big game. Then he looked into the water, and there he saw himself. "Ha'! I look fine. They will think, 'He must be a wealthy person.'"[41]

40. n. Mrs. Peterson knew nothing about the places this trickster names; she supposed they may have been places where his possessions drifted onto a rock or beach. She was neither sure of their having been names of myth sites nor of their perhaps having been actual sites known by these names to modern Coos.

41. HS. transformation

So he went on indeed. He got
to where there were people, a village lay there. "Ha! A wealthy person has arrived." That is what the
people said. "Ah! You go into there.
There the wealthy person lives."
Indeed he went there. The wealthy
man was sitting outside. "Ha! It is
good that you have come here. Do
you know where there is a good
shaman?" "Ah! I am a shaman myself!" "Ah, yes! Since you are a
shaman, my daughter is ill. If you
cure her you may have her for your
wife." "Ah! Very well."

Then he went inside. "I want
to look at her." Indeed he went in.
"Be seated there!" Now they first
gave him food, then he finished
eating, and he spoke in this manner.
"You are all to go outside. I do not
want anyone when I work on a
person. I am alone then. You are to
bring me water, and then you are all
to go outside."[42] Indeed so it was,
all the people went outside. The
sick person moaned, she ate no
food, that was just how she did,
groaning, "Penis! Penis!"[43] "Ha! I
will cure her! She is merely lusting.
She only wants to copulate. When I
do it to her she will get well."

And so indeed he copulated
with the girl. Then he bathed her.
When he finished copulation he
washed her.[44] Then he spoke in this

42. *Fake lecherous doctor*

43. n. The girl mumbled
this so that only the trickster was able to under-
stand the word.

44. HS: sex

way, "Come in! Give her food to
eat." The people entered, of course.
The girl was hungry, she wanted
food. Indeed they gave her food,
and she just ate it right up. The
shaman worked on the girl four
days. Then the fifth day when he
was going to work on the girl, one
funny-nosey woman said, "Strange
that he heals her so very quickly. I
will watch on. It may be some
different and strange sort of thing,
the way he doctors. Perhaps he is a
trickster."

And indeed then the woman
hid, and sure enough he merely
copulated with her. "So that is the
way he has been doing to her!" Why
indeed he is not a shaman at all.
He only does it to her!" Now the
shaman finished, and he merely
washed the girl. "Mmm. Sure
enough it is only that trickster!"
Then that woman went and told
them all. "He is no shaman
whatever. He is only a trickster.
He has only copulated with her.
He pretended that he was a
shaman." Then they drove him
away. "Get away from here! You are
not a person! You are a trickster."
And indeed they would have beaten
him and killed him, but he leaped
outside crying out, "Ha'hahahaha!
She was wanting copulation, so that
is why I copulated with her." He
said that as he ran off. He fled.

25. And then the girl became pregnant, and pregnant the girl wept all the time. Now she gave birth to boy children, and her parents killed her babies. They threw one of the girl's babies into the water. The trickster was doing something or other by the Coos Bay bar. And then a baby drifted down. He got it, and he took it home, and he raised the baby, he raised it by feeding it with tallow.

26. That woman just cried every day, all year long the woman wept. Her boy who lived with the trickster began to hunt. It was her he saw and he hid and he thought, "I wonder why she is weeping all the time?" But he said nothing of it, he only thought about it. The child became a young man. He heard the woman crying still. Once he went to the woman. "Who are you, you who cry here all the time?" "Oh I cannot help crying. That trickster. I did not think he was a trickster, that he could be one of the trickster people. He it was who caused me to have children, pretending to be a shaman. Indeed it was my own parents who got him, and he just made me pregnant, and so I had children. But my parents did not want them. I could not take my children's part. I was so very sick, and I did not know what they did with my children. That is why I cry

all the time. That is why you have heard me crying all the time." That is how she explained to the person who had come to her. "Oh maybe I myself might be your own child, because my father is a trickster, and I am motherless." That is what the young man said. Now they both cried. "Oh I do not like that father of mine! For having treated me like that. I will return home. You will see me tomorrow." To be sure, it was like that then.

THE THIRD
TRICKSTER/WORLDMAKER

His father returned home, he came back in the evening. Now the young man did not eat at all, he merely went to bed. And then he wept. Early in the morning he arose. "Mmm. I will kill that trickster! I do not like his having copulated with my mother!" And sure enough that is the way it was. "Father! I want you to explain something to me." "What is it I can tell you?" "How is it that I am motherless? I want to know." "Why do you want to know that?" "I just wanted to know that. I wanted to know if my mother was dead." "Hu'hu! Your mother is dead. Your mother was no good, she was a loose woman. She just wanted a penis, and so of course I copulated with her, and then I just left her." Now the young man shot his father. "Ha. You are not to speak insultingly of my mother!" And so he killed his father, and then he went to get his mother.[45] Now they buried him, they placed him in a grave. "Mother, we will go to another place." Indeed they did. They went away from there. No one knew where the girl had gone to.

27. Now the girl and her child traveled together, and they lived in all sorts of places. That is how they went along. They were going to go to a place far away. Indeed they did so. One place where they were living his mother became ill, and then his mother died. The young man journeyed about, alone. "Ha'. I too will be a trickster. I am alone. I myself will do the very same way, just as my father did. Because that was how he raised me." Sure enough that was how the young man did, he was also just like that, he took to playing tricks, he looked like his father, and indeed he did the same sorts of things. Now he got to people, all sorts of people lived there. And they took him into the house. They also were trickster people, and he remained there a long time. Then he married one, he married one of the children of a trickster. And then they moved into their own house, there he and his wife lived. It was not a long time before they had a child.

28. Different people lived in an adjacent house.[46] And now it was one

45. *Kills own father*

46. n. These particular neighbors were not trickster people but a type of water spider called colloquially "skippers, skip Jacks, water skaters."

of them who entered and said, "Ha'!
My child died. I do not want persons to die. We should not have
graves. People should not die. I am
so very sick at heart." "Ah', but let
persons die! It is nothing if they
die!" Now the wife of the young
trickster man gave birth. No long
time after, about one year, his own
child died too. Now he went to
there to the old man, his neighbor.
"Hmm! It really is so, it is true that
a person is so very sick at heart. We
should be without deaths." "Hu'.
But I do not want that now. It will
be better if they will die. My legs are
too long. If crowds of living people
were to step on them they would
break my legs. So let them die, lest
the people become too numerous, if
they did not die off.[47] I think no
more of my child. You will be like
that too, you will think no more of
him." That is why the people die.
Indeed that is how it is. He did not
think of him again.

47. *Originator of death;*
first sufferer

29. One year more, and again
his wife gave birth, her baby was a
boy. Now the young man got up to
mischief. "Oh, I will be a trickster,
I will be like my father." Sure enough
that was how he did. "I will stick a
sliver in my baby's finger there." To
be sure that was what he did. The
baby never ceased crying on account
of that. Now then "I will go for a shaman." Indeed a shaman came, and
that shaman doctored it, and he sang,

"Da'yadayadaya', da'yadayadaya."[48]

"His nose twitches up and down. a'a,
    haya hanai haya hanai.
        His ears are big,
        he has no tail,
        haya hanu."

That is how he made fun of the
shaman. Now the shaman jumped
up, he stole the baby. And even
though they pursued, they could
not catch him. The shaman leaped
into a pile of brush. He could not be
found there. Now his mother cried
all the time for the child. Another
year, and she had another child, a
girl was her child. She wept all the
time during five years.

FOURTH TRICKSTER/WORLDMAKER
30. But the young man grew up, the
young man went hunting all the
time.[49] He heard about it, all the
time he would see that woman
packing wood, she wept continually.
This is what she said when she
cried, "Han an! My child! It was
cottontail rabbit who stole my
child!" That was the way the woman
wept. One day he and his older
brothers were playing, and they just
told him what he was, saying, "You
are not my older brother.[50] You are
the trickster's child." That is how
that child told him about himself.
So then the young man lay down.
"Come here! Son! Come here!
Come and eat." "I am not hungry."

48. n. The doctoring song
of cotton-tail rabbit shaman. Joining in to help in
the singing, the trickster
tries to make cotton-tail
rabbit appear foolish by
giving a ludicrous imitation
and by mocking him in
these words.

49. (The young man who
was cared for by cottontail
rabbit)

50. (The older brothers
were real cottontails)

Then cottontail said to his own children, "Did you say anything to my trickster child?" "We did not say anything to him." "If you told him anything I would beat you." That is what he said to his children.

Now the young trickster went to hunt, the young man went away. He saw nothing to shoot, he walked the whole day long, he got not a thing. Now he was going back towards home, and he saw just a squirrel, and he was going to shoot it. But he did not kill it. He shot at it but he did not kill it, and the squirrel spoke just like a person. "Ah! You are no child of cottontail. Your father is a trickster. Cottontail stole you, he is not your father. It is your mother who is the one who has been crying all the time." That is how that squirrel spoke to him.[51] Now the young man thought thus, "I will ask his children to go to the water with me. Come here! Let us go play at the water." So they looked into the water. Indeed his appearance was different from theirs, the young man's appearance was different. The cottontail children were ugly, they had big ears. But he himself had a slender face, indeed he himself was good looking. Then they went back home. "Truly I am not the child of cottontail. My appearance is different."

Now the morning of next day the young man got ready, he went

51. n. It was so angered at being shot at that it revealed to him his poor parentage.

out to hunt. "Huh'. I will see that woman who cries all the time." Sure enough. That woman always packed wood. Now she was going to pack her basket. Then from behind her he placed his bow on the basket, and indeed she could not get up because of the weight. The young man was hidden behind a tree.[52] "Ahh! Why is that? I have been packing wood from right here for five years and my pack never got caught like that." Now she tried to lift her pack again, but again it was caught fast. And again she stood up. "What is the matter with it, for it to be caught?"

Now she looked and she looked around and there was merely a young man standing there. "Why do you weep all the time?" "Oh cottontail stole my baby when it was tiny, which is why I cry all the time." "It must be I. This is the way those children of cottontail mock me. 'Ah'! Child of trickster!' That is what they say to me. It is just I!" "Oh, my child! I have a daughter. She is having her first menses. In five days the people will come together there.[53] I am going to fix up the house. In five days, on that evening I will come to get you, because the people will be gathered there, and then you yourself will be there too. For they will do everything, have various games. That is when your sister will be raised from her bed of puberty seclusion."

52. *Surprise approach from behind*

53. n. The girl's puberty ceremonial was elaborate and involved among other things the participation of the mitadin type of shaman; after his work was done the girl was permitted to travel away from home at nights under chaperonage.

To be sure that is the way it was. Sure enough she fetched her child where he was hiding, there his mother got him. And indeed there the people were gotten together in their house. And the young man himself was also there. Now his sister had been raised, now they had gotten her up. And then the shaman fixed her. Now the girl could travel about.

31. Then one day the village people plotted. "Oh we shall war upon the cottontail people. We shall go there and fight them." Indeed they did that. She never named her older brother, though the young man named her "sister." She never did as he did, she never named her older brother.

Now the people went away, and they got to the place of the cottontail people, they watched the doors of the cottontail people, and then they killed them, and they burned their village. Now the young man went to where his sister was. His sister simply named him, "Ha, my husband! Here is one of those cottontails getting out."[54] Now the young man killed the cottontail. Then he turned back. "What did you say?" This is what he said to his sister. "Say again what you said. Is that the way you spoke? Why did you speak like that to me?" The girl said nothing. So he just shot and killed his sister.

54. *Brother-sister incest*

Then he sought his father, and he found his father. "I killed my sister. This is the way she named me, this is the way she spoke to me. 'Here is one, my husband!' That is the way she spoke to me." Now the young man walked away, and he left there. No one knew, there was no one who knew where the young man went. He went away from there, and he went about all alone. He built a home far back on the prairie, and there he lived. He remained there a long time.

32. "I will seek people." Indeed he found people, he stayed there a while, and he obtained a wife. He took his wife back home to where he lived. They lived there a long time. He and his wife never slept together. He just lay in the large men's sweat house. He never slept in the living room. The girl remained alone in the house.

About five years after they were married, one day he spoke thus to his wife, "Find lice on my head!"[55] Indeed the girl worked on his head, she even parted his hair in small strands, but she never found a thing. One day when she was working on his head, and it was getting nearly evening, she found a baby louse, a cute little louse. She showed it to her husband. "Ha'! That is what I want, what you have found. Do not bite it! You must just

55. *Lousing*

swallow it. So sure enough the girl did that. She swallowed that baby louse. He never slept with his wife. And now the girl got large, and now she was pregnant.[56] Then the girl gave birth. When she gave birth to her baby the girl died. Thus the husband became alone, and alone he raised his baby. So that is how it got big, it began to walk, and it grew up.

56. *Conception from eating*

The Fifth Trickster/Worldmaker (Father of the People) and his father, The Fourth Trickster/Worldmaker (Coyote)[57]

33. His father made arrows for him, and the child grew. Then his father told him this, "Even though your arrow drop yonder there, you are not to go and get it." His father told him that continually. Indeed he did not go to there. Now the child grew to be a young man. His arrows constantly fell at that place yonder. "Hmm. I wonder why he does not want me to go to the end of the prairie there?" So he felt. His father again told him the same thing. "You must not go to the end of the prairie there." But the young man felt about it this way, "Oh I will go there! I wonder why he does not want me to go there to whatever is there, which my father does not want me to go to."

Then the young man went. As he went along he shot, and sure

57. n. Note that the father is the fourth in this myth line of tricksters, and his immaculately conceived son is the fifth and last. It is the latter who is called by the Coos the "people's father" or "God." He had two birds or two types of birds that worked for him; one was "stork," the other was the monster so-called "angel-bird."

enough every one of his arrows dropped at that place. So he went on to there anyhow, and he got to the end of the prairie there. It was merely a woman digging there, that woman was digging camas. "Ha', my husband! I have been waiting for you every year here, I have been collecting your arrows." That is what the woman said. "Let us go home, my husband." Though the young man did not want it, he followed her anyway.[58] Indeed they went on homewards, and they reached the woman's house.

58. n. Mrs. Peterson commented, "He could not help himself. She worked a charm on him, she took his mind along with her."

She was cooking a type of large frog, and she gave it to the young man to eat. But he could not eat it. "Ha'. No one else is here! What are you jealous about?" However, the young man was not jealous, he just could not eat frog. Without a garment on, she lay on her back with her legs apart.[59] The young man did not do it to her. And each morning the young man went away, the young man went out, he tried to go back to his home, and he went along, and he only returned to there again.

59. *Vagina dentata*

One morning he went to the creek to bathe. Oh the creek was just full of salmon. so then he killed two of them, and he cooked them, and he ate them. Then the woman returned. "Mmm." This is what she said. "I smell a type of water lizard."[60]

60. * the poisonous western newt; n. Seeing this kind of black lizard is evidence that you are going to suffer some sort of bad luck. To the woman in the myth the salmon was water lizard.

That is what she did. The next day
she went away, and the young man
also went down to the water. And he
bathed, and when he finished
bathing he again caught some of
those salmon. Then he cooked
them and ate them. One whole salmon he lay outside the door. Now
the woman returned. "Ha . . . , I
am frightened. Take away that water
lizard. Take it away! I am afraid of
it!"[61] Of course the young man took   61. *Fish thought ogres*
it away. "Hu'!" And the woman
jumped up and down, she was so
afraid of the salmon. "Ah'. The awful
thing! Do not put that horrible
thing near here." The young man
was there a long time. There the
woman lay on her back with her legs
apart, without clothes on she lay.
But that young man never noticed
her. Then she went away.

34. Now then some person
reached there, and he entered.[62]   62. n. Mrs. Peterson did
"Ha. What are you doing here?" "I   not recall who this visitor
cannot get away from here." "Huh,   was.
she is an ogress woman, ogress
women are bad people. Five days
from now we will come here, and
then we will take you back home.
Even though she be without clothes
and act wrongly, do not copulate
with her. For as long as five days we
will gamble with her, and when we
quit she will sleep a long time, she
will not quickly awaken. In that
manner we will get you away."

Indeed that was how it was. Five days later she said to him, "Hide over here. There are many people coming to gamble. I do not want them to see you." "Ah! I will hide." That was what the young man said to her. Indeed that is the way it was. Now sure enough the people arrived. Indeed that ogress woman hid the young man. And the people came together there. Now they began to gamble, and they played the hand game. "Have you not something hidden? I smell something." "Ah. You do not smell anything. I have nothing hidden." Now indeed they gambled five nights. And then the men were going to return home.

The woman lay down, and of course she was snoring at once. Indeed they came back again then, and they doctored the young man, because she had been keeping his heart. "That is why you could not get away to anywhere." So they fixed the young man, they got his heart from her. Indeed that is how it was then. All those men had packs of pitchwood. "Take all her money outside." So the young man did that. He took outside all the woman's money.[63] She never awoke, she slept so very soundly. Then they fixed bunches of pitchwood in the house, they stood it on the ground all around there. They also

63. n. The woman had become wealthy from the possessions appropriated from the wealthy young men she killed when she enticed them into copulating with her; she had a "dagger vagina" of two blades, one on each side, and they cut off a penis.

placed it around outside, all in and
about her house. Pitchwood was
placed all about there, and then
they set it all on fire, and they
fastened her door tightly. Indeed
her house set on fire, and then it
burned. Now she awoke. She
jumped ᷃nd jumped at the door.
"Where are you, my husband? You
will be burned also, you too will be
burned, my husband." Now they
killed the ogress woman.

When she was burned her
heart leaped out, and they caught it.
When this child of hers, her heart,
grew up she too was no good, so
they killed her because she was bad.
She was just like her mother, no
good. Even though raised by good
people, she was still no good. That
is why they killed her also. And now
that is why there are no more ogress
women, because they killed them
all. Now they took the young man
back to their village.

35. The trickster's father, the
young man's father, began to think
about him. "Ha! Something must
have happened to my child. I will
pull one of my head hairs." Now he
stretched and extended it, he
extended that hair of his in every
direction.[64] Indeed that is what he
did. Then he extended it in that
direction. "Ha! Fine! I heard my
child! The next people will find
people in that manner, when a person

64. The Coos attitude up-
on introduction of the telegraph and telephone was
one of matter of fact accep-
tance, "the trickster knew
that long ago." These in-
ventions were exactly what
the trickster had been able
to do himself in hearing
his son over a head wire.

is gone like that. Each day one will just extend out his head hair in that manner, and indeed he will find out where his child is."

36. Now the people made ready, and they told the young man, "We are all going to go to all sorts of different places, to there we will go. We will gamble, we will play shinny, we will play all kinds of games." That is what they said to the young man. Now the people went, men, women, girls, all of them went. And to be sure they arrived where there were people.

Now the people played shinny. All those women there were enamored of the young man, but he never noticed them. And when the people finished shinny then they were going to invite into the houses the visitors who had come to play. And they had sitting mats. And one of these was put down just for the young man, so that he could sit there. Now the visiting player people entered. They watched for the young man, but he was not seen to enter at the door. He was already seated there! They saw him already in the house seated on his mat. Just as if he were a ghost, no one had seen him enter. That is the way the young man was. For ten days the people danced there, and then they went back home.

37. Then they again went off to a different place. But now when they got to there the people there were poor, lacking food, without fire, without water, without anything! "Ha, how is it that these people are so poor?" asked the trickster. "We must all get together, we will have to fight, we will have to gamble with him. And if we cannot win over him we will fight. You must all have your large bows when you go." Indeed that is what the people did.

Then they sent word to the trickster's head man.[65] He was told thus, "People will come and play, shinny, target shooting, all sorts of things. The people will play. They will gamble too, with you." Indeed that is the way it was. "Ha, very well. If you wish it you may come." The person who took the news went back, and he returned. "Very well." That is what that head man said. "You may come." And of course the people then were going to go.

"You are all to do it well. I will arrange everything that is needed.[66] Rat, mouse will be ready. Beaver will be the one to open up the water dammed up there. Then the mice will cut the bow strings. The rats will be cutting other things. The yellowhammers will be boring holes in the canoes, with the red headed woodpeckers. Everyone must work

65. n. The trickster's head man referred to is actually head man of the trickster people where the fourth trickster (the father of the young man) still lives. This trickster head man has so confined water and foods that people in other villages lack elemental necessities; he does not know that among his visitors will be the young trickster man (the fifth trickster).

66. n. The young trickster makes these birds and animals and assigns them tasks, before they all set out.

at all the different things. The winged one, the birds, all will take care of all kinds of fruits and berries. They will carry them all over, so that all will have them for food." That is how it was indeed.

Now then the people went off, and then indeed the people reached there. For five days they gambled with their eyes.[67] Now he put a snail shell into his eyes, and indeed he appeared to be open eyed. The young man slept thus propped up for two nights. Indeed that assisted him. Then he took out the snail shell eyes. He said, "Another kind of people will have that kind of eye, an artificial sort of eye. Indeed that is how it will be. The next people will see that kind of snail shell eye." They gambled playing the motionless eye game ten days, and they were still playing.

They made all sorts of things, flies, so that the maggots would get on him, on that person who had everything dammed up. And still they did not beat him at this game. So that young man made a giant snake, and then he made a giant lizard. Now these screamed from either side. To be sure now they had beaten the wealthy trickster head man.[68] Then he would have fought, but he had no bow, nothing of any sort.[69]

67. n. The contesting sides sat in two rows, opposite one another, watching one another as in the hand game. The loser was that first person who was observed to blink, wink, roll, or close an eye. n. When some early white settlers were found to have artificial eyes the Coos said, "Maybe that is what coyote meant."

68. n. The cries of the snake and lizard so perturbed the man that he at last rolled his eyes and lost the game.
69. n. The rats and mice had ruined his weapons.

"Leap away with the fire!" Now they pursued the person who had stolen the fire. Then the young man spoke thus, "Throw the fire on willows, they will be our fire drills." Indeed he did so. And now another (perhaps robin) dashed on with the fire, but they were still pursuing.[70] So he threw the fire on cedar.[71] "You too will be for making fire. From now on people will use you for making fire." Indeed the people use it for making fire.

70. n. Mrs. Peterson thought the young trickster told deer to "leap away with the fire."
71. *Theft of fire*

This is what the young man now said. "Winged things! Cast the berries and fruits all over.[72] Water! Flow all over to the ends of the country. Flow everywhere, so that all may drink you." And so they took all sorts of things. "Many years from now it will be like that again, there will be a trickster person again, from somewhere such a trickster person will come. Then it will be like that again." Indeed water flowed all over the land.

72. *Release of foods; Release of water*

And now they went home. They all had something or other. None of the people were hungry for food.[73] There was plenty of all sorts of things. No one was hungry any more. Before then the younger people had to dance, whatever food they had they held under their armpits, that was how they had cooked whatever foods they had. And the older people had just sat on it, so

73. n. In the future there will be wealthy people again who will appropriate the foods and the poor will have little to eat. It is not impossible that this thought of Mrs. Peterson is taken from or at least somewhat affected by what she had observed of the economic situation of 1933–34, rather than wholly from Coos mythology.

that it would become warm. That was how they had cooked. Then when the young man took all the things, then indeed they became fine, and they had all sorts of things for food. That was how the young man was good to them, he pitied the pitiful people. Now indeed water flowed everywhere, indeed everyone could drink. And then the young man spoke thus, "In a future day it is going to be like that again."

38. Now the young man was going to return to where his father lived. And he took two wives, and he was given all sorts of things by his in-laws. Then he returned to his father's place. He lived there a long time. After he returned his two wives gave birth.

Now his father was getting up to mischief. He went off to defecate.[74] Indeed he defecated, and he examined his feces. Half was bloody. "Hey, my feces! You are bloody. Hey!" He tapped it. "Move around!" He poked at it with a little stick. And he just kept on doing that to it. And then to be sure it began to fly.[75] "Little tree!" And sure enough a tree grew up. "My feces! Fly up on that tree!" And indeed his feces now became a sapsucker and flew up.

Then he was figuring out mischief. "Children! Tell! Tell your father there is good luck money, it is

74. HS: scatological

75. *Excrement becomes bird*

pecking at the tree. Go get your
father!" So the children ran home.
"Father! Our grandfather wants
you." So the young man went. "Son!
A good-luck-thing is ascending
there. You climb up it, you ought to
be able to catch it. Do not shoot it!
Just catch it." That is what he said
to his child. "Climb up it!"

So the young man climbed up.
He almost had caught it when it
ascended just beyond his reach.
"Grow up! My tree!" Whispered the
grandfather.[76] Sure enough the young   76. *Stretching tree to*
man followed the thing that was   *upper world*
climbing. He got to quite a height
above, and still he kept following
the thing that was climbing. At
length he got above on top, he got
up to another country. Then the
grandfather trickster, "Return! My
tree!" And to be sure the tree came
back down. Then he dashed to the
house, and he copulated with both
his daughter's-in-law. Then the
children entered, and he just wiped
his penis on the eyes of the chil-
dren.[77] "The next people will have   77. HS: regressive behavior
matter in their eyes, that will be its
name, that semen of mine that I
have wiped there, matter will be its
name then."

39. Now the young man went
about here and there, he went on a
prairie. And he went a distance.
Pretty near straight up noon, and he
saw smoke, in the middle of the

prairie. So he went to there, and he got there. Just an old couple lived there, their heads were as if scorched, they were like charcoal.[78] "Hey, grandson! What are you going around here for? A bad thing eats here, it eats here at straight up noon."

78. n. They are a type of large and poisonous spider, and they are scorched by the daily hot visits of sun girls.

Sure enough he heard it coming. Something jingled. "You must hide." That is what the old people said to him. Indeed they hid him. "Sun girl is no good, she is too hot. That is why we fear her." Sure enough she entered. She was quite a handsome girl. And now she was going to eat. Each time she went to put food into her mouth she just struck herself outside on her face. Then she became enraged.[79] "Take out the person you have hidden!" That is what the girl said.

79. (She was angry at being unable to find her own mouth)

"Uh! She is so awfully hot!" That is what the young man thought. "Hey, but I myself am a trickster! I will do it to her! And then she will not be so hot any more." Now the girl dashed outside, she was angry. And she went and ran on. "Ha, I myself am a trickster! I am like my father. I will copulate with her with an iced penis, and then she will not be so hot any more."[80]

80. *Iced penis*

Indeed that was how it was. She shivered from the cold penis, like salmon, when the young man copulated with her. Then the girl said as follows, "Hey my husband! I never stay at home, I travel all the time. Go to my younger sister, go to her there, she stays at home once in a while." Then the girl went on.[81] She was not any longer as hot when she went on. Since that time the sun has not been as hot as it was before Coyote cooled it, because the sun is this girl.

81. n. Said Mrs. Peterson, "She had to go right on then, because she is the sun."

40. Now the young man went back to the old people, and he went inside. "Grandson!" He told the old people about it. "She told me to go to there, there where her younger sister lives." "Ha. those people are bad.[82] You must take care and watch. Here! take these five yellowhammer tailfeathers, lest he do bad things to you. Watch him with care, because they are bad people, and his wife is bad too. Do watch him. If you have to go salmon spearing, you must watch him carefully. When salmon come downriver do not spear them until the first five have passed by, lest you be dragged in and drowned, and then you may spear them. And when you do catch them, you are to insert those yellowhammer tail-feathers in their navels. Do that to them all, to as many as you spear, do it thus to them all. And when he tells you like this, 'Oh there is an elk!' then shoot him on his ankle. Then he will just become himself, he will become a person again—

82. * The spider couple warn him of most of Sun girl's sister Moon's tests given by her parents, telling him how to survive them.

otherwise he will kill you. And when he will speak to you thus, 'Let us go fix my fish trap,' then you must take care! He will drop that maul of his, and when you dive down for it you may not be able to come back up because he will spread ice over the top of the water. But then you will break it with your maul." To be sure that is just what the young man did. One thing he did not tell, the old man forgot to tell him that a whale would be stranded. That was what the old man did not tell him, he did not tell the young man that, because he had forgotten it.

41. Now then indeed, so the young man went on. Then he got to there. "Hey' my son-in-law. Go into the house!" To be sure the young man went inside. "Hmm. My son-in-law. Sit down there beside your wife." So he sat there. Now the old woman was going to give him food. The old woman climbed above to get food, and then she dropped a maul, and the young man dodged it. Indeed it dropped right beside him. She failed to hit the young man.

Then she got something else, and then she spilled on him inside-bark-splinters. But that young man just blew them up, and her vagina was filled with them when the young man blew up the bark-splinters. And the old woman tumbled, she fell on her back, kicking there in

pain. Then the young man said,
"Go wash your mother with water."
Indeed then the moon girl washed
her mother with water, and then the
old woman was all right. Now the
young man said, "Hereafter such
stickers will be on the ocean sand,
they will be seen there, they will
grow there." Indeed that is the way
it is, that thing, that sticker bush
does grow on the sand beaches.
"Ha. Now he is going to be my son-
in-law." Indeed so it was.

42. Now the old man said,
"My son-in-law, let us go fishing."[83]
Indeed they went, and then they got
to there. When the first five salmon
were to come downriver, the young
man would certainly not spear
them. Then five passed by, and now
the next one the young man did
spear. And still more came downriver, so he speared another. And
into the salmon navels he inserted
yellowhammer tailfeathers. Indeed
more in just that manner until he
had killed five, and inserted just five
yellowhammer tailfeathers. Now that
was so much of that. Then they
went home.

43. And the next day that old
man asked him to come along. "We
will repair a place that is bad." So
they went off. And then he said to
his son-in-law, "My maul fell in.
Dive down in there for it." The
young man thought, "It is just as he

83. *Son-in-law tests*

told me. Now I believe." So the young man did dive in, sure enough he found the maul. Then the young man leaped up, but to be sure he could not get through the ice.[84] So he dropped down again, and then he leaped again, and he struck with the hammer, and the ice broke.

84. * The surface had been magically iced over.

Sure enough the old man was already going on downriver. "Hey! Why are you leaving me?" "Hoh. It is just my canoe that has drifted away." So then the young man deliberately dropped the hammer. "You will have to. I did not get it. You will have to dive for it." "Ah. Son-in-law! I will dive." So then indeed the old man dived. The young man watched him, and also made ice magically. Then it bubbled. Now the young man broke the ice, and he took hold of the nearly drowned old man, and he placed him in the canoe. Then they went back.

44. Now the next day, "Ah, my son-in-law. I saw an elk. You kill it!" "Oh, I know about that. It really is just what my grandfather told me about. Indeed I will shoot him right there." And to be sure he shot at the ankle. Indeed there the young man shot him, and sure enough it was only the old man.[85] "Oh you shot me!" "Well why were you pretending to be an elk?" "Oh I was only testing you."

85. HS: transformation

45. The next day then he was going to fell a tree. Then this is what he said to his son-in-law, "You work on the other side of it." The young man pretended to do so. Now the tree was going down. The young man stealthily went around it, and hurled a chunk of wood, and indeed he hit him so well that the old man fell and thought he was pinned under the tree. "Oh a stick dropped on you." That is what he said to him. Now they went back. He had not yet killed the young man.

46. So the next day, "Oh my son-in-law. A whale came ashore." Indeed they went down to the water. The old man had forgotten, he had forgotten to tell him about this. That is why the young man did not know how to watch out for it. Then they cut it up, and he said to him, "Go to the other side, go to the water side." The young man looked, the young man saw when he looked that he was out in the ocean. He floated on the ocean five days, inside the belly of the whale.[86] There was a log jutting out, and he drifted toward it, and the young man stood on it. Then he wept. "Oh I am just here voluntarily doing this!" To be sure the young man just remained there like that. After staying there five days, he saw somebody, persons coming in a canoe, two persons in the canoe.

86. *Whale boat*, or *Abandonment in boat*

"What are you doing, grandson? where are you from?"

"Oh I am just here, just here!"[87]

87. n. When singing, coyote pretends that he would not have to be there if he did not want to be.

"But what are you doing there?" "Oh I cannot get back. You take me into the canoe." "Why no. The next persons will take you in." Now the young man wept again. He stayed there a long time, before another one came along. They sang in just the same manner.

"What are you doing, grandson? where are you from?"

"Oh I am just here, just here!"[88]

88. HS: understatement

"Oh what are you doing there?" "I cannot get back. Take me into your boat." "Why no. The next persons will take you." And they went on. Then the young man wept. He stayed there a long time, and then another came along. It was the very same way again. They did not take him either. "The next persons will take you." Four of them passed him by. Now he saw another, and they too sang like that, and they took in the young man. "Lie down!" The young man lay down of course.[89] "Now arise!" They had brought him back to where he had left.

89. *Looking tabu*

47. He heard his wife crying, and he got to her. "What are you crying about?" "I am crying about

my husband." That is what the girl said. "My parents are not good. They do all sorts of bad things to people. That is why I am weeping here." "It is I! They did not kill me then. I have come back." Now they went inside. "Ay, my son-in-law. Ay, so you have come back. I could not get hold of you to save you. That is why you drifted away on the whale. Now the moon man did not do anything further to him.

48. Then the trickster said to his wife, "I have children, I have two wives on the country down below. I will go back there now, I will go for those two wives of mine, and then all of us will live here." So the young man went, and he got to there where the two old spider people were, and he said thus, "Grandfather! I want to go back home. I want to fetch my wives and my children." "Uh. We will make you a basket. After five days we will go get your wives." And so it was.[90] Five days later the young man got back to them, and indeed they did so. They got into the basket there, and they went back down towards home. To be sure they arrived there, they got down below there.

90. *Spider web sky rope,* or *Spider web basket*

49. The children ran to there, matter in their eyes. The children could hardly see. Then he went in, both his wives wept. "Your father has humiliated us. He copulated

with us both."[91] That is what they told him, and this is what they informed him of. "When he finished copulating with us he wiped his penis on the children's faces." That is what his wives told him.

Now the young man was enraged. No longer did he like his father. "Grandfather! Come! My father wants you." "Hu', oh indeed really? So it is your father? Why he could not get here! That could not be your father around here." "Oh come anyway! You will see him." So sure enough the old trickster went. And, to be sure, it really was his child.

The younger said to the older trickster, "Ha'. Come in! You may eat." And he gave his father food. "But first just put this on." So he put it on, a coyote fur hide. Then he gave him food to eat. Now he finished eating, and he spoke to him thus, "Go far down towards the water, there you will attempt to dodge arrows." Then they made ready, and they got into the basket, and they started to go up.

Now the old trickster saw them ascending. "Hu. I forgot about that spider." Then he ran, and he grabbed at it, and he cut two of the strings. Indeed their basket almost spilled down. Now this is what the young man said. "I do not like you

91. HS: humiliation; inappropriate behavior

anymore. I do not want that kind of
a father. They will name you coyote.
You will bark at the next people."[92]
That is how he spoke to his father.
Indeed that is what he became.

50. Now the young man
returned above. It is he who is the
father of us people. Now the young
man said, "A different type of
people will use this sort of basket
for travel.[93] The next people will see
that." Now he went home. Our
father still lives up there.

92. (the Indians who
will come later); HS;
transformation

93. n. This is possibly another thought introduced
by the modern Coos survi-
vors who could manage to
find page and line, so to
speak, in their mythology,
for all the inventions and
queer ways of the white
people.

appendix 2

Kinship Charts

O = female; △ = male.

Vertical line = descent.

Single horizontal line = sibling.

Double horizontal lines = marriage. Note: no distinction is made among the various kinds of marriage relationships: Indian marriage; common-law marriage; legal marriage. All are indicated by double horizontal lines.

Permanent separation by a cause other than death is indicated by a diagonal line.

Primary sources of kinship data: Harrington, *Alsea/Siulsaw/ Coos Field Notes*; Jacobs, "Coos Ethnologic Notes"; Jacobs, *Coos Myth Texts*; Jacobs, *Coos Narrative*; Coos County, Oregon, marriages in Coos County; and Larson, interviews.

ANNIE MINER PETERSON
Ancestry, Descent, and Marriages

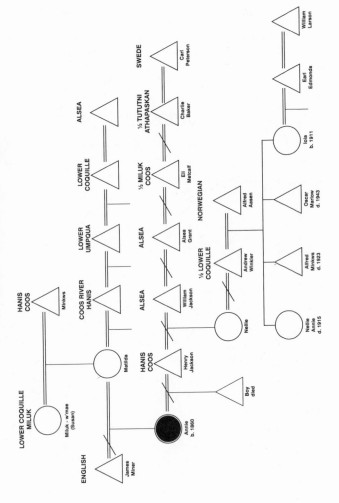

ANNIE'S "HUSBANDS"

1. *Henry Jackson (Coos).* Nephew of Daloose Jackson. In this traditional Indian marriage at Yachats, Annie was about fourteen years old. She had a son by Henry. After about two years she left but was forced to return. She later left him again, also leaving their son, who died a few years later.

2. *William Jackson (Alsea).* From a large and prominent Alsea family. Annie had a daughter, Nellie, by William. She left him at Siletz after about two years, taking the daughter with her when she moved to Siuslaw.

3. *Alsea Grant (Alsea).* A well-known "affair" of Annie's at Siletz, reported by several informants to John Peabody Harrington. Alsea Grant was brother to U. S. Grant, a prominent Alsea at Siletz. After this liaison, there is an eighteen-year period during which very little is known about Annie's love life. She remained silent on the subject in her autobiography.

4. *Eli Metcalf (1/2 Miluk Coos).* Legally married Annie in Coos County on August 31, 1898. Annie was thirty-eight years old at the time of this marriage. She carried the Metcalf name until she married Charlie Baker in 1910.

5. *Charlie Baker (1/2 Tututni Athapaskan).* Son of Ione Baker, last of the Euchre Creek band of the Tututni of Curry County. Annie was fifty years old at the time of this marriage, which ended in divorce on January 2, 1918.

6. *Carl Peterson (Swedish immigrant).* Married Annie in Portland after her divorce from Charlie Baker. Annie was then fifty-eight years old. This was a good relationship that lasted until she died in May 1939. Carl died three months later.

KINSHIP AND AFFINITY
of Annie Miner Peterson with Other Hanis Coos Linguistic Informants

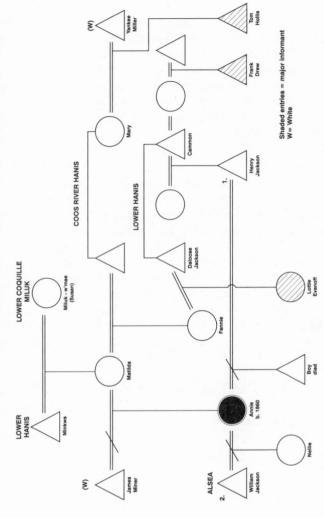

Shaded entries = major informant
W = White

Annie Miner Peterson. Hanis and Miluk Coos informant to Melville Jacobs in 1933 and 1934.

Tom Hollis. Hanis Coos informant to Harry Hull St. Clair II in 1903. He was the son of Annie's mother's first husband's sister; thus he was a first cousin to Annie by marriage.

Lottie Evanoff. Annie's niece, the daughter of her half-sister Fannie and Daloose Jackson. Lottie was a Hanis Coos informant to John Peabody Harrington in 1942.

Frank Drew. Annie's brother-in-law when she was married to Henry Jackson. He was a Hanis informant to Leo J. Frachtenberg in 1909, to Jacobs in 1932, and to Harrington in 1942.

James Buchanan. The only significant Coos informant whose relationship to Annie is uncertain. He was said to have been related in some degree to Daloose Jackson's people. He was a Hanis informant to St. Clair in 1903, to Frachtenberg in 1909, and to Jacobs in 1932.

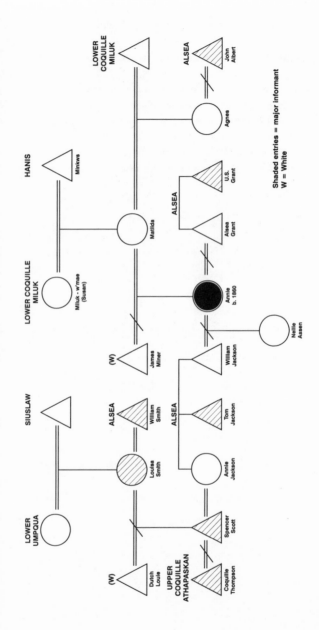

KINSHIP AND AFFINITY
of Annie Miner Peterson with Alsea, Umpqua, and Other Major Linguistic and Ethnologic Informants

Shaded entries = major informant
W = White

ALSEA

John Albert. First husband to Annie's half-sister Agnes. He was an Alsea informant to John Peabody Harrington in 1942 and to others.

Thomas Jackson. Annie's brother-in-law when she was married to William Jackson, the father of Annie's daughter, Nellie. Thomas was an Alsea informant to Leo J. Frachtenberg in 1910.

William Smith. Second husband of Louisa Smith, the mother of Annie's one-time brother-in-law Spencer Scott. He was an Alsea informant to Frachtenberg in 1910.

U. S. Grant. Brother to Annie's one-time paramour Alsea Grant. He was an Alsea informant to Frachtenberg in 1910.

Alsea George. The only significant Alsea informant for whom the relationship to Annie is uncertain. He was an Alsea informant to Livingston Farrand in 1900.

LOWER UMPQUA (SIUSLAW)

Spencer Scott. One-time brother-in-law to Annie. Spencer was the husband of Annie Jackson, sister of William Jackson, who was the father of Annie's daughter, Nellie. He was a Lower Umpqua informant to Harrington in 1942.

Louisa Smith. Mother of Spencer Scott. She was a Lower Umpqua informant to Frachtenberg in 1911.

UPPER COQUILLE ATHAPASKAN

Coquille Thompson. First (divorced) husband of Annie Jackson, sister to William Jackson, and thus one-time brother-in-law to Annie. He was an informant to Elizabeth Derr Jacobs in 1934, to Harrington in 1942, and to others.

appendix 3

Published Works Incorporating English Versions of Texts from the Oregon Coast Penutian Languages

FROM JEROLD RAMSEY, ED., *COYOTE WAS GOING THERE: INDIAN LITERATURE OF THE OREGON COUNTRY* (SEATTLE: UNIVERSITY OF WASHINGTON PRESS, 1977)

"Coyote and the Two Frog Women," 152. Obtained in Alsea by Leo J. Frachtenberg from Tom Jackson at Siletz in 1910. This myth was first published in a literal translation in Frachtenberg, "Myths of the Alsea Indians of Northwestern Oregon," 72–74. Tom Jackson was Annie's brother-in-law when she was married to William Jackson, the father of her daughter, Nellie.

"How the Coos People Discovered Fire," 144–46. Obtained in Hanis by Leo J. Frachtenberg from Jim Buchanan at Florence, Oregon, 1909. This myth was first published as "The Stealing of Fire and Water" in Frachtenberg, *Coos Texts*, 39–42. It was subsequently published in Frachtenberg, *Coos: An Illustrative Sketch*, 427–29, and reprinted in Boas, *Handbook of American Indian Languages*, 419–29.

"The Magic Hazel Twig," 153. Obtained in Alsea by Livingston Farrand from Alsea George at Siletz, 1900. This was first published in Frachtenberg, *Alsea Texts and Myths*, 237–39.

"The Revenge of the Sky People," 170–73. Obtained in Hanis by Harry Hill St. Clair II from Tom Hollis at Siletz, Oregon, 1903. It was first published in Frachtenberg, *Coos Texts*, 149–57. Most recently it was reprinted in Jones and Ramsey, *The Stories We Tell* (see below), 67–69.

"Thunderstorm Exorcism," 144. Obtained in Alsea by Leo J. Frachtenberg from William Smith at Siletz, 1910. For Smith's relationship to Annie, see below, page 269. This tale was first published in Frachtenberg, *Alsea Texts and Myths*, 231.

"The White Wife of Mouse," 161. Obtained in Miluk by Melville Jacobs from Annie Miner Peterson at Charleston, Oregon, 1933. Annie had heard this myth from her friend Alice Johnson, whose mother was from Intesedge, the same Hanis village that Annie's own mother was from. Annie had also heard this tale from her mother-in-law Ione Baker, a Tututni Athapaskan of the Euchre Creek band. It was originally published in Jacobs, *Coos Myth Texts*, 165–66.

"The Woman Who Married a Merman," 150–52. Obtained in Hanis by Harry Hull St. Clair II from Tom Hollis at Siletz, Oregon, 1903. First published in Frachtenberg, *Coos Texts*, 157–63, it was subsequently reprinted in Clark, *Indian Legends*, 197–99 (see below). This myth is set at Takimiya, the Coos River village of Annie's mother's first husband. The story was also told in English by Annie's niece Lottie Evanoff to John Peabody Harrington at Coos Bay, 1942.

FROM THE OREGON LITERATURE SERIES, A PROJECT OF THE OREGON COUNCIL OF TEACHERS OF ENGLISH (PUBLISHED BY OREGON STATE UNIVERSITY PRESS, CORVALLIS, 1993–94)

"A Coos Indian Woman Looks at Life," in Beckham, *Many Faces*, 152–59. This is Annie Miner Peterson's autobiography, obtained in Miluk by Melville Jacobs from her at Charleston, Oregon, 1933. It was originally published in Jacobs, *Coos Narrative and Ethnologic Texts*, 104–14.

"Coyote and the Strawberries," in Jones and Ramsey, *The Stories We Tell*, 125–30. This folklorized version by George B. Wasson Jr. of an episode from the Coos myth cycle had been published as "The Trickster Person Who Made the Country" in Jacobs, *Coos Myth Texts*, 184–222. Wasson said that the story was told by his relatives (in English) over the years. The incidents within the episode are strikingly similar to Jacobs's version, but Wasson's story has lost the typical stylistic features of the Indian oral literature of the Northwest. It is another interesting example of the manner in which stories disintegrate when retold in an English version by a generation less "Indian" in mind and manner than previous generations, which had told the story in the original language.

"The Girl Who Married a Sea Otter," in Jones and Ramsey, *The Stories We Tell*, 262–63. This is a folklorized version by Susan Wasson Walgamott of a recurrent theme from the Oregon coast of mortals marrying seals, killer whales, and other undersea creatures—usually mammals. Related examples are in Jacobs, *Coos Myth Texts*, 149 ("The Wife of Seal"), Frachtenberg, *Coos Texts*, 55 ("The Woman Who Married the Seal") and 157 ("The Woman Who Married the Merman"), and Harrington, *Alsea/Siuslaw/Coos Field Notes* ("Killer Myth").

"Moon Eclipse Exorcism," in Wendt and St. John, *From Here We Speak*, 11. Reprinted from Rothenberg, *Shaking the Pumpkin*, 45. First published in Frachtenberg, *Alsea Texts and Myths*, 226–27.

"My Sweetheart," in Wendt and St. John, *From Here We Speak*, 25. Obtained in Hanis and recorded on Ediphone wax cylinder by Melville Jacobs from Annie Miner Peterson at Charleston, Oregon, 1933. Annie had heard the song from her niece Lottie Evanoff. It was a parody of Grizzly Bear's mourning song in a myth that Annie had heard from Lottie's parents (Annie's half-sister Fannie and Daloose Jackson). The myth and song originally appeared in Jacobs, *Coos Myth Texts*, 152–55.

"The Origin of Face Rock at Bandon," in Jones and Ramsey, *The Stories We Tell*, 203–4. This is a folklorized version by Susan Wasson Walgamott of the Coquille legend recorded originally from Coquille Mary, ca. 1909. See "A Potlatch on the Oregon Coast," in Clark, *Indian Legends*, 124–26.

"The Revenge of the Sky People," in Jones and Ramsey, *The Stories We Tell*, 67–69. This myth, first published in Frachtenberg, *Coos Texts*, 149–57, was also reprinted in Ramsey, *Coyote Was Going There*, 170–73.

"Thunderstorm Exorcism," in Wendt and St. John, *From Here We Speak*, 12. Reprinted from Ramsey, *Coyote Was Going There*, 144. First published in Frachtenberg, *Alsea Texts and Myths*, 231.

"The Walkers (Animals) and Winged Things (Birds) Fought," in Wendt and St. John, *From Here We Speak*, 24. Obtained in Hanis by Melville Jacobs from Annie Miner Peterson at Charleston, Oregon, 1933. Annie had heard this myth from her Hanis-speaking uncle Old Dick, among others. It was originally published in Jacobs, *Coos Myth Texts*, 232–33.

OTHER REPRINTED VERSIONS OF TEXTS

Baldiyasa: The Beach Shore People, by Lionel Youst. Historical pageant performed for the Friends of South Slough National Estuarine Sanctuary and for the Coos County Educational Services District, Charleston, Coos Bay, Myrtle Point, and Bandon, Oregon, 1988–89. One scene depicted Melville Jacobs interviewing Annie, with her narration of "A Man Obtains Fir Power," "Bluejay Shaman," and "Wife of Seal."

"Bluejay Shaman," in Peterson and Powers, *A Century of Coos and Curry*, 260. Obtained in Miluk by Melville Jacobs from Annie Miner Peterson at Charleston, Oregon, 1933. Annie had heard the myth from her uncle Dick and from other Hanis and Miluk speakers. The Bluejay shaman's song was recorded on Ediphone wax cylinder and on RCA Victor pregrooved record. That song, along with several others from Annie, was transcribed in 1982 by Susan Johnson of Lewis and Clark College and published in Beckham, Toepel, and Minor, *Native American Religious Practices*.

"Coyote and Two Frog Women," in Erdoes and Ortiz, *American Indian Myths and Legends*, 384–85. The editors do not give a source for this myth other than to say that it was based on an Alsea tale from 1901. It was in fact collected by Leo J. Frachtenberg from Annie's one-time brother-in-law Tom Jackson in 1910. See the entry (above) under Ramsey, *Coyote Was Going There*.

"Moon Eclipse Exorcism," in Rothenberg, *Shaking the Pumpkin*, 45. This is an English version by Armand Schwerner from text obtained in Alsea by Leo J. Frachtenberg from William Smith at Siletz in 1910. The relationship between Annie and William Smith is tenuous but real. While Annie was married to (Alsea) William Jackson, her sister-in-law Annie Jackson was married to Spenser Scott, who was later an important Lower Umpqua informant to John Peabody Harrington. Scott's stepfather was William Smith.

"The Mortal Who Married a Merman," in Clark, *Indian Legends*, 197–99. Obtained in Hanis by Harry Hull St. Clair II from Tom Hollis at Siletz, Oregon, 1903. Tom Hollis had probably heard it from his Hanis-speaking mother, a former sister-in-law of Annie's mother.

"A Potlatch on the Oregon Coast," in Clark, *Indian Legends*, 124–26. Obtained in English by Otellie K. Kronenberg from Coquille Mary at Bandon, Oregon, ca. 1909. Coquille Mary, a Lower Coquille Miluk, was related in some degree to Annie's maternal grandmother.

Notes

ABBREVIATIONS

MJNB Melville Jacobs, "Coos Ethnologic Notes," Notebooks 93–104, Melville Jacobs Collection, University of Washington Archives, Seattle.

JPH John Peabody Harrington, *Alsea/Siuslaw/Coos Field Notes* (John Peabody Harrington Papers, National Anthropological Archives, Smithsonian Institution, Washington, D.C.; New York: Kraus International Publications, 1981), microfilm, reels 22–30.

PREFACE

  1. Oregon State Board of Health, "Certificate of Death, Annie Miner Peterson."

  2. Jacobs, *Coos Myth Texts*, 221–22.

  3. Thompson, *To the American Indian*; Hopkins, *Life among the Piutes*.

  4. Jacobs, *Coos Narrative*, 104–14.

CHAPTER 1. CONTACT

  1. MJNB 93:44.

2. Parrish, "Report," 109.

3. JPH 22:1155.

4. Douthit, *Guide*, xv, and "Hudson's Bay Company," 33–36.

5. Ibid. 23:933.

6. Van Kirk, *Many Tender Ties*, 75–94.

7. Douthit, "Hudson's Bay Company."

8. Harris, "Reminiscences," 129.

9. Frachtenberg, *Lower Umpqua Texts*, 101–2.

10. JPH 23:932.

11. Ibid. 24:936.

12. Flanagan, "Chief Jackson."

13. Jacobs, *Coos Narrative*, 4.

14. MJNB 93:67.

15. Jacobs, *Coos Narrative*, 115 (in the Miluk text).

16. JPH 23:895.

17. Ibid. 22:1113.

18. Larson, interview, October 31, 1991; JPH 23:895; Cybulski, "Human Biology," 52.

19. Jacobs, *Coos Narrative*, 58–59.

20. Atwater, Stuiver, and Yamaguchi, "Radiocarbon Test," 156–57.

21. Nelson, letter, December 15, 1992.

22. MJNB 93:46.

23. Ibid. 93:37.

24. Jacobs, *Coos Narrative*, 72.

25. MJNB 97:24.

26. JPH 24:184.

27. Ibid. 24:102.

28. Jacobs, *Coos Narrative*, 104.

29. Beckham, *Land of the Umpqua*, 74–75.

30. JPH 22:1126; Sengstacken, *Destination*, 116; Flanagan, "Patrick Flanagan."

31. JPH 22:1126.

32. Flanagan, "Patrick Flanagan," 5–6.

33. Beckham, *Land of the Umpqua*, 74–76.

34. Baldwin, "Wreck of the Captain Lincoln," 117.

35. Beckham, *Coos Bay*, 6.

36. Harris, "Reminiscences," 131.

37. Lockhart, "Recollections," 350.

38. Van Kirk, *Many Tender Ties*, 74–94.

39. Harris, "Reminiscences," 130; Parrish, "Report," 108.

40. Bensell, *Yamhill*, 131.

41. Harris, "Reminiscences," 133.

42. Coos County, Marriages, Book 1, #A-44.

43. JPH 22:1165; Zenk, "Siuslawans," 572–73.

44. Dodge, *Pioneer History*, 133.

CHAPTER 2. THE WAR

1. Beckham, *Requiem*, 134–35.

2. JPH 22:1130.

3. Ibid. 22:1126.

4. Ibid. 23:969.

5. MJNB 100:84.

6. JPH 26:348–49.

7. Ibid.

8. Ibid. 24:940.

9. Ibid.

10. Ibid. 24:938.

11. Ibid. 24:994.

12. Beckham, *Indians of Western Oregon*, 134.

13. JPH 24:21.

14. U.S. Congress, *Siletz Restoration Act*, 270–81.

15. Harris, "Reminiscences," 135–36.

16. Court of Claims, Case #K-345, Mrs. William Waters, in JPH 24:836.

17. MJMB 101:26.

18. JPH 24:273.

19. Sengstacken, *Destination*, 116.

20. MJNB 93:75, 101:25; Larson, interview, November 10, 1991.

21. JPH 23:596.

22. Ibid. 23:612.

23. Ibid. 23:755.

24. Ibid. 23:595.

25. Ibid. 24:702–4.

26. Beckham, *Indians of Western Oregon*, 155.

27. JPH 24:238; Boyd, "Demographic History," 139.

28. JPH 24:914.

29. Jacobs, *Coos Narrative*, 104.

30. JPH 23:997.

31. Ibid. 24:40.

32. Ibid. 24:206, 207, 124, 488.

33. Ibid. 24:40.

34. Ibid. 24:124.

35. Ibid. 24:185.

36. Ibid.

37. Jacobs, *Coos Narrative*, 105.
38. Ibid.

CHAPTER 3. ANNIE'S FIRST YEARS

1. JPH 22:1041; Frachtenberg, *Illustrative Sketch*, 305. For an account of the Oregon coastal sand dunes, see Lund, "Oregon Coastal Dunes," 73–92. Mileages were estimated using DeLorme Mapping, *Oregon Atlas*, 32–33.
2. Bensell, *Yamhill*, 142 n.
3. Ibid., 142.
4. JPH 23:605–6.
5. Schwartz, "Sick Hearts," 230.
6. JPH 24:316.
7. Ibid. 23:979.
8. Jacobs, *Coos Narrative*, 106.
9. MJNB 93:43–44.
10. Ibid. 95:160.
11. JPH 24:942.
12. Jacobs, *Coos Narrative*, 118–120.
13. JPH 24:942.
14. MJNB 93:51.
15. Bensell, *Yamhill*, 126 n.

CHAPTER 4. CHILDHOOD

1. Bensell, *Yamhill*, 133 n.
2. Jacobs, *Coos Narrative*, 103.
3. Court of Claims, Case #K-345, Annie Peterson.
4. Bensell, *Yamhill*, 147–49.
5. Ibid., 145.
6. Ibid., 150.
7. Ibid., 146.
8. JPH 23:979.
9. Ibid. 24:457.
10. Jacobs, Ediphone cylinder recording 14603b.
11. Bensell, *Yamhill*, 147 n.
12. Ibid., 150.
13. Court of Claims, Case #K-345, Annie Peterson, in JPH 24:954.
14. Bensell, *Yamhill*, 146.
15. Nelson, *Haynes*, 1.
16. Saling, "History of Allegany," 215.
17. Jacobs, *Coos Narrative*, 67.

18. MJNB 93:34.

19. JPH 24:635.

20. Larson, interview, May 20, 1994.

21. Bensell, *Yamhill*, 141 n.

22. Jacobs, *Coos Narrative*, 107.

23. JPH 24:401.

24. Jacobs, *Coos Narrative*, 99.

25. JPH 24:238.

26. Beckham and Munnick, *Church Records*, 34, 39, 46.

27. MJNB 99:10.

28. Jacobs, *Coos Narrative*, 29–30.

29. Ibid., 28–29.

30. JPH 22:1194.

31. Ibid. 24:670.

32. Jacobs, *Coos Narrative*, 92.

33. Ibid.

34. MJNB 93:87.

35. Ibid. 93:88.

36. Ibid. 93:84.

37. Ibid. 100:96.

38. Ibid. 93:85.

39. Ibid. 98:124.

40. Ibid. 98:126.

41. Ibid. 98:118.

42. Ibid. 98:114.

43. Ibid. 98:122.

44. Ibid. 98:98.

45. Jacobs: Ediphone cylinder recordings; RCA Victor pregrooved recordings.

46. Jacobs, *Coos Narrative*, 96.

47. JPH 24:936.

48. Jacobs, *Coos Narrative*, 26.

49. MJNB 93:76.

50. Jacobs, *Coos Narrative*, 26.

51. Ibid., 26–28.

52. JPH 24:1022.

53. Ibid. 24:726.

54. Hays, *South Lincoln County*, 36.

55. JPH 23:275.

56. Hays, *South Lincoln County*, 36.

57. Schwartz, "Sick Hearts," 231.

CHAPTER 5. YACHATS

1. MJNB 93:67.
2. Ibid. 94:56.
3. Jacobs, *Coos Narrative*, 67.
4. Ibid., 66.
5. MJNB 93:33.
6. Ibid., 93:34.
7. Ibid. 98:96.
8. Ibid. 99:178.
9. Bensell, *Yamhill*, 148.
10. JPH 24:748.
11. MJNB 93:105.
12. Ibid. 93:102.
13. Ibid. 93:103.
14. Hays, *South Lincoln County*, 30.
15. MJNB 94:54.
16. Jacobs, *Coos Narrative*, 110.
17. Larson, interview, May 20, 1994.
18. JPH 23:174.
19. Ibid.
20. Hays, *South Lincoln County*, 36.
21. JPH 22:1173.
22. Ibid. 24:420.
23. Ibid. 24:236.
24. Ibid. 24:237.
25. Ibid. 25:755.
26. Ibid. 24:759.
27. MJNB 96:130.
28. Ibid. 93:49.
29. Ibid. 99:30.
30. Ibid. 101:25.
31. Jacobs: Ediphone cylinder recording 14580(7), RCA Victor pregrooved recording 14610b(4).
32. JPH 24:1034.
33. Jacobs, Ediphone cylinder recording 14579c.
34. Jacobs, RCA Victor pregrooved recording 14614b.
35. Ibid. 14615a.
36. Jacobs, *Coos Narrative*, 63.
37. Du Bois, *Ghost Dance*, 36–37.
38. Ibid., 26. This quotation was from the *Corvallis Gazette* 10, no. 10 (February 8, 1873).
39. Ibid., 34.

40. Ibid., 135–39.

41. Jacobs, *Cultural Anthropology*, 394–95.

42. Jacobs, *Coos Narrative*, 3.

43. Jacobs, *Coos Myth Texts*, 147–48.

44. Ibid., 183.

45. Ibid., 173–74.

46. Ibid., 130.

47. MJNB 94:35–36.

48. Ibid. 93:135.

49. Jacobs, *Coos Myth*, 143–46.

50. Gogol, "Traditional Arts," 17–19.

51. Jacobs, *Cultural Anthropology*, 291–93.

CHAPTER 6. WOMANHOOD

1. Beckham, Toepel, and Minor, *Native American Religious Practices*, 42–45.

2. MJNB 93:109. "Gishgiu" is the spelling used by her great-grandson George B. Wasson Jr. Melville Jacobs spelled it "t'cigi'yu." Her nickname was Gekka.

3. Beckham, Toepel, and Minor, *Native American Religious Practices*, 42; MJNB 93:30–31.

4. MJNB 93:29.

5. Ibid. 93:33.

6. Ibid. 91:53–54, in Beckham, Toepel, and Minor, *Native American Religious Practices*, 44.

7. JPH 24:499.

8. Ibid. 24:635.

9. Jacobs, *Coos Narrative*, 110.

10. Ibid., 72.

11. MJNB 93:81.

12. JPH 24:498.

13. MJNB 101:26.

14. Jacobs, *Coos Narrative*, 107.

15. JPH 24:703.

16. Jacobs, *Coos Narrative*, 74.

17. Ibid., 75.

18. Ibid., 71–72.

19. Ibid., 107.

20. Hays, *South Lincoln County*, 36.

21. Jacobs, *Coos Narrative*, 107.

22. JPH 24:427.

23. Hays, *South Lincoln County*, 37.

24. MJNB 93:52.

25. Jacobs, *Coos Narrative*, 72–73.

26. MJNB 93:57.

27. Jacobs, *Coos Narrative*, 107.

28. JPH 24:465.

29. Thornton and Stutzman, *Indians of the Oregon Coast*, 31; JPH 24:247.

30. MJNB 101:20, 28, 30.

31. JPH 23:870.

32. Hays, *South Lincoln County*, 36.

33. Schwartz, "Sick Hearts," 238.

34. Ibid., 258.

35. JPH 27:541.

36. Ibid. 23:36.

37. Ibid. 24:704.

38. Ibid. 24:682.

39. Ibid. 24:704.

40. Ibid. 23:36.

41. Court of Claims, Case #K-345, George Wasson, in ibid. 27:540.

42. JPH 27:539.

43. Court of Claims, Case #K-345, George Wasson, in ibid. 27:450.

44. Jacobs, *Coos Narrative*, 108.

45. JPH 24:946–47.

46. Ibid.

47. Ibid.

48. Ibid. 23:36.

49. Ibid. 23:561.

50. Ibid. 23:163.

51. Ibid. 24:740.

52. Ibid. 24:266.

53. Ibid. 24:683.

54. Ibid.

55. Jacobs, *Coos Narrative*, 114.

56. Du Bois, *Ghost Dance*, 32–34.

57. Beckham, Toepel, and Minor, *Native American Religious Practices*, 98–101.

58. Ibid.

59. Du Bois, *Ghost Dance*, 35.

60. Ibid., 33.

61. Ibid.

62. JPH 23:944.
63. MJNB 95:40.
64. Jacobs, *Coos Narrative*, 97.
65. MJNB 95:107.
66. Lomax, "Shipping and Industry," 32.
67. JPH 24:688.
68. West, interview, October 21, 1994.
69. Skinner, "Florence," 27–28.

CHAPTER 7. RETURN TO COOS BAY

1. JPH 24:305.
2. Ibid. 23:605.
3. Ibid. 24:971.
4. Ibid. 24:40.
5. Ibid. 24:207.
6. Ibid. 23:944.
7. Ibid. 23:997.
8. Ibid. 23:893.
9. Flanagan, "Chief Jackson."
10. Murkel, "Empire Boys," n.p.
11. JPH 24:369.
12. Dodge, *Pioneer History*, 466.
13. Jacobs, *Coos Narrative*, 109.
14. Ibid.
15. Ibid., 110.
16. Ibid.
17. Douthit, *Coos Bay Region*, 60.
18. Larson, interview, May 20, 1994.
19. JPH 22:1194.
20. Ibid. 24:439.
21. Jacobs, *Coos Narrative,* 110.
22. MJNB 96:142.
23. Larson, interview, October 31, 1991.
24. Jacobs, *Coos Narrative*, 110.
25. JPH 23:895.
26. Ibid. 24:365.
27. Ibid. 23:1004.
28. Ibid. 23:885 and 24:948 provide examples.
29. Jacobs, *Coos Narrative*, 117–18.
30. JPH 24:994.
31. Jacobs, *Coos Narrative*, 110.
32. Ibid., 118.

33. Ibid., 111.
34. Ibid.
35. Ibid., 63.
36. Peterson and Powers, *Century*, 358–59.
37. JPH 23:922.
38. Beckham, *Coos Bay*, 55.
39. JPH 24:684.
40. Jacobs, *Coos Narrative*, 111.
41. Hall, *Coquille Indians*, 78.
42. JPH 23:919.
43. Beckham, *Indians of Western Oregon*, 180–81.
44. JPH 24:975; "Col. C. H. Holden" (obituary).
45. Beckham, *Indians of Western Oregon*, 180; JPH 24:937.
46. Larson, interview, May 20, 1994.

CHAPTER 8. BIG CREEK

1. JPH 23:1021.
2. Ibid. 24:124; Coos County, Marriages, Book 1, #A-39.
3. JPH 24:124.
4. Douthit, *Coos Bay Region*, 22.
5. Larson, interview, May 20, 1994.
6. Ibid.
7. Collins, interview, April 24, 1990.
8. MJNB 101:37.
9. Caldera, newspaper clipping.
10. Hall, *Coquille Indians*, 80–81.
11. MJNB 93:109.
12. JPH 23:1030.
13. Ibid. 23:922.
14. Ibid. 24:465, 933, 969; Jacobs, *Coos Narrative*, 115–17.
15. Jacobs, *Coos Narrative*, 56–8.
16. JPH 24:272.
17. *Coos Bay Times*, "Old Indian," 6 Jan 1907.
18. Douthit, *Coos Bay Region*, 97–105.
19. Bensell, *Yamhill*, 217.
20. JPH 27:574.
21. Ibid. 24:235.
22. Jacobs, *Coos Narrative*, 63.
23. JPH 22:1022.
24. Wasson, Jr., "Redwood Canoe," 100–101.
25. JPH 24:1019, 27:560.
26. Ibid. 27:616.

27. Ibid. 23:710.

28. MJNB 93:89.

29. Larson, interview, May 20, 1994.

30. Gogol, "Traditional Arts," 20.

31. Jacobs, "Oral Literatures," 90–99.

32. Jacobs, *Coos Narrative*, 112.

33. JPH 22:1050.

34. Jacobs, *Coos Narrative*, 112.

35. Ibid.

36. Larson, interview, May 20, 1994.

37. Ibid.

38. Ibid., 31 Oct. 1991; 20 May 1994.

39. Collins, interview, October 31, 1991, and May 20, 1994.

40. Douthit, *Coos Bay Region*, 103.

Chapter 9. Portland

1. Peterson and Powers, *Century*, 488.

2. Jacobs, *Coos Narrative*, 113.

3. Ibid.

4. U.S. Department of Commerce, *Fourteenth Census*, vol. 21, E.D. 92, Sheet 8, Line 85.

5. Ibid.

6. Jacobs, *Coos Narrative*, 113.

7. Ibid.

8. Ibid.

9. Larson, interview, October 31, 1991.

10. Ibid., December 8, 1994.

11. Beckham, *Indians of Western Oregon*, 183.

12. JPH 27:627.

13. Barnett, *Indian Shakers*, 43–85.

14. Golla, letter, November 7, 1995.

15. MJNB 95:1.

Chapter 10. The 1931 Court of Claims

1. Jacobs, *Coos Narrative*, 114.

2. MJNB 101:10.

3. JPH 24:177.

4. Ibid. 23:35.

5. Larson, interview, May 20, 1994.

6. "Indians Prepare."

7. "Indians' Claims."

8. Beckham, *Indians of Western Oregon*, 181.

9. JPH 24:993.

10. Ibid. 23:885.

11. "Probe Indian Land Claims."

12. JPH 24:792.

13. Court of Claims, Case #K-235, George Barnett, in ibid.

14. JPH 23:590.

15. Ibid. 24:792; Jacobs, *Coos Narrative*, 3.

16. Court of Claims, Case #K-235, Mrs. William Waters, in JPH 24:792.

17. Court of Claims, Case #K-235, Laura Metcalf, in JPH 24:954.

18. Court of Claims, Case #K-235, Lottie Evanoff, in JPH 23:804.

19. Court of Claims, Case #K-235, George Wasson, in JPH 24:846, 919, 956.

20. The quotations in the following paragraphs are from Court of Claims, Case #K-235, Annie Peterson.

21. JPH 23:35.

22. Beckham, *Indians of Western Oregon*, 181–89.

23. Jacobs, *Coos Narrative*, 4.

24. Thompson, "Melville Jacobs."

CHAPTER 11. THE ANTHROPOLOGISTS

1. JPH 28:401.

2. Thompson, "Melville Jacobs," 642.

3. Frachtenberg, *Illustrative Sketch*, 307–9.

4. Jacobs, *Cultural Anthropology*, 130.

5. Thompson, "Melville Jacobs," 641.

6. Jacobs, *Cultural Anthropology*, 93.

7. Ibid., 95.

8. Ibid., 93.

9. Ibid., 95–96.

10. Ibid.

11. Boas, "Letter to Professor Holmes."

12. Jacobs, *Coos Narrative*, 4.

13. MJNB 101:1.

14. Jacobs, *Coos Myth Texts*, 129.

15. Mills, *Papers*, 1:78–79.

16. JPH 28:401.

17. Ibid. 28:342.

18. Drucker, "Coos Ethnographic Fieldnotes."

19. Du Bois, *Ghost Dance*, v.

20. Ibid., 142.

21. Ibid.

22. Ibid., 25.

23. Ibid., 17.

24. Jacobs, *Coos Myth Texts*, 129.

25. Jacobs, Ediphone cylinder recording 14601b.

26. Jacobs, RCA Victor pregrooved recording 14614a.

27. Jacobs, *Coos Narrative*, 100.

28. Thompson, "Melville Jacobs," 642.

29. Jacobs, *Coos Narrative*, 100.

30. MJNB 94:77.

31. Jacobs, *Coos Narrative*, 100 n.

32. JPH 22:1165, 23:975.

33. Frachtenberg, *Coos Texts*, 1.

34. Frachtenberg, *Illustrative Sketch*, 297–429.

35. MJNB 104:7, 17.

36. Jacobs, *Coos Myth Texts*, 135 n.

37. Seaburg, personal communication, May 27, 1995.

38. Grant, letter, June 7, 1995.

39. Morgan, conversation/interview, April 25, 1996.

40. Jacobs, *Coos Myth Texts*, 184–221.

41. Jacobs, *Cultural Anthropology*, 321.

42. Ramsey, *Coyote Was Going There*, 161.

43. Jacobs, *Cultural Anthropology*, 321.

44. A notable exception is Radin, *The Trickster*.

45. Jacobs, *Cultural Anthropology*, 344.

46. Jacobs, *Content and Style*, v.

47. Ibid., 7.

48. Ibid., 3.

CHAPTER 12. THE LAST YEARS

1. Seaburg, personal communication, May 27, 1995.

2. JPH 28:401.

3. Garrett, interview, October 20, 1994.

4. Oregon State Board of Health, "Certificate of Death, Annie Miner Peterson."

5. Larson, interview, May 20, 1994.

6. "Annie Peterson, Elderly Indian."

7. JPH 24:947.

8. "Annie Peterson Called."

9. [Luse], "Funeral Rites."

10. Garrett, interview, October 20, 1994.

11. Oregon State Board of Health, "Certificate of Death, Carl Peterson."

12. "Death Takes Carl Peterson."
13. JPH 24:947, 498; Larson, interview, May 20, 1994.
14. Seaburg, personal communication, May 2, 1995.
15. Jacobs, *Coos Narrative*, 3.
16. Jacobs, *Coos Myth Texts*, 239.
17. JPH 30:4–53 contains Harrington's notes of the conversations.
18. Mills, *Papers*, 1:i–viii; Hinton, "Ashes, Ashes," 194–209.
19. See, for example, Greenberg, *Language in the Americas*.
20. JPH 30:32.
21. Ibid. 30:10, 31.
22. Jacobs, *Coos Myth Texts*, 129.
23. Anderson, "A Miluk Lexicon."

Bibliography

UNPUBLISHED SOURCES AND GOVERNMENT DOCUMENTS

Anderson, Troy. "A Miluk Lexicon." B.A. thesis, Linguists Department, Stanford University, 1990.

Barnett, Homer G. "Coos Ethnologic Fieldnotes." In Philip Drucker, "Coos Ethnographic Fieldnotes" (copy), folder 65–22, box 65. Melville Jacobs Collection, University of Washington Archives, Seattle.

Caldera, Melody. Newspaper clippings, various. Personal collection.

Coos County, Oregon. Circuit Court, Docket No. 4833, Annie Matilda Baker vs. Charles Manter Baker. January 2, 1918.

———. County Clerk. Deeds.

———. Marriages in Coos County.

Drucker, Philip. "Coos Ethnographic Fieldnotes" (copy). Folder 65–22. Box 65. Melville Jacobs Collection. University of Washington Archives, Seattle.

Flanagan, J. W. "Patrick Flanagan Biography." Special Collection. University of Oregon Library, Eugene.

Jacobs, Melville. "Coos Ethnologic Notes." Notebooks 93–104, 1933–34. Melville Jacobs Collection. University of Washington Archives, Seattle.

———. Ediphone cylinder recordings of Annie Miner Peterson, 1933. Melville Jacobs Collection. University of Washington Archives, Seattle. Cassette tapes, Library of Southwestern Oregon Community College, Coos Bay, Oregon.

———. RCA Victor pregrooved recordings of Annie Miner Peterson, 1934. Melville Jacobs Collection. University of Washington Archives, Seattle. Cassette tapes, Library of Southwestern Oregon Community College, Coos Bay, Oregon.

Larson, Iola. Photographs and newspaper clippings, various. Personal collection.

Oregon State Board of Health. "Certificate of Death, Alfred Aasen" (State Registered Number 146). Coos County, Oregon. June 10, 1916.

———. "Certificate of Death, Annie Miner Peterson" (State Registered Number 102). Coos County, Oregon. May 19, 1939.

———. "Certificate of Death, Carl Peterson" (State Registered Number 183). Coos County, Oregon. August 10, 1939.

———. "Certificate of Death, Eli Metcalf" (State Registered Number 263). Umatilla County, Oregon. October 22, 1936.

U.S. Congress. Senate. Subcommittee on Indian Affairs. *Siletz Restoration Act*, appendix B. 94th Cong., 2d sess., 1976. S. 2801.

U.S. Court of Claims. Case #K-345. Testimony of Annie Peterson, 1931.

U.S. Department of Commerce, Bureau of the Census. *Tenth Census of the United States, Coos County, Oregon, Schedule No. 1: Population, 1880.*

———. *Twelfth Census of the United States, Coos County, Oregon, Schedule No. 1: Population, 1900.*

———. *Thirteenth Census of the United States, Coos County, Oregon, Schedule No. 1: Population, 1910.*

———. *Fourteenth Census of the United States, Multnomah County, Oregon, 1920.*

U.S. Executive Order Number 9. 34th Cong., 3d sess., 1855.

INTERVIEWS AND PERSONAL COMMUNICATIONS

Collins, Ann. Interview by Melody Caldera, Coos Bay, Oregon. April 24, 1990 (videotape). October 31, 1991; May 20, 1994; October 4, 1994.

Garrett, Midge. Interview by Melody Caldera, Coos Bay, Oregon. October 20, 1994.

Golla, Victor, Humbolt State University. Letter to the author. November 7, 1995.

Grant, Anthony P., University of Bradford, England. Letter to the author. June 7, 1995.

Larson, Iola. Interviews by the author, Bandon, Oregon. October 31, 1991; November 10, 1991; May 20, 1994; June 1, 1994; December 8, 1994; February 28, 1995.

Morgan, Laurence, University of California (Berkeley). Conversation/interview by the author concerning Miluk language. North Bend, Oregon. April 25, 1996.

Nelson, Alan R., U.S. Geological Survey. Letter to the author. December 15, 1992.

Seaburg, William R. Personal communications with the author. April, May, June 1995.

West, Victor. Telephone interview by the author. October 21, 1994.

ARTICLES AND BOOK CHAPTERS

"Annie Peterson Called Tuesday." *Coos Bay Harbor*. May 11, 1939, 1.

"Annie Peterson, Elderly Indian Called Home." *Coos Bay Times*. May 9, 1939, 3.

Atwater, Brian F., Minze Stuiver, and David K. Yamaguchi. "Radiocarbon Test of Earthquake Magnitude at the Cascadia Subduction Zone" (letter). *Nature* 353 (1991): 156–58.

Baldwin, Henry H. "Wreck of the Captain Lincoln." In Dodge, *Pioneer History*, 114–25.

Beckham, Stephen Dow. "History of Western Oregon since 1846." In Wayne Suttles, ed., *Northwest Coast*, 180–88. Vol. 7 of *Handbook of North American Indians*. Washington, D.C.: Smithsonian Institution, 1990.

Boas, Franz. "Letter to Professor Holmes, July 24, 1905." In George W. Stocking, ed., *A Franz Boas Reader: The*

Shaping of American Anthropology, 1883–1911, 122–23. 1974. Reprint, Chicago: University of Chicago Press, 1982, 1989.

Boyd, Robert T. "Demographic History, 1774–1874." In Wayne Suttles, ed., *Northwest Coast*, 135–48. Vol. 7 of *Handbook of North American Indians*. Washington, D.C.: Smithsonian Institution, 1990.

Clark, Ella E. "The Bridge of the Gods in Fact and Fancy." *Oregon Historical Quarterly* 53 (March 1952): 29–38.

"Col. C. H. Holden" (obituary). *The West* 22 (December 27, 1912).

Cybulski, Jerome S. "Human Biology." In Wayne Suttles, ed., *Northwest Coast*, 52–59. Vol. 7 of *Handbook of North American Indians*. Washington, D.C.: Smithsonian Institution, 1990.

"Death Takes Carl Peterson, 68, at Coquille Today." *Coos Bay Times*. August 10, 1939, 3.

Douthit, Nathan. "The Hudson's Bay Company and the Indians of Southern Oregon." *Oregon Historical Quarterly* 93 (spring 1992): 25–64.

Flanagan, J. W. "Chief Jackson and Wife, Coos Tribe." *Coos Bay Harbor*. May 25, 1939, 3.

Frachtenberg, Leo J. "Myths of the Alsea Indians of Northwestern Oregon." *International Journal of American Linguistics* 1 (1917–20): 72–74.

Fuhrman, Frederick A. "Tetrodotoxin." *Scientific American* 217, no. 2 (1967): 60–71.

Gogol, John M. "Traditional Arts of the Indians of Western Oregon." *American Indian Basketry* 4, no. 2 (1984): 4–28.

Hall, Roberta L. "Language and Cultural Affiliations of Natives Residing near the Mouth of the Coquille River before 1851." *Journal of Anthropological Research* 48 (1992): 165–84.

Hall, Roberta L., and Don Alan Hall. "The Village at the Mouth of the Coquille River: Historical Questions of Who, When, and Where." *Pacific Northwest Quarterly* 82 (July 1991): 101–8.

Harris, W. H. "Reminiscences of Capt. W. H. Harris." In Dodge, *Pioneer History*, 126–36.

Hinton, Leanne. "Ashes, Ashes: John Peabody Harrington—Then and Now." *Flutes of Fire: Essays on California Indian Languages*. Berkeley, Calif.: Heyday Press, 1994.

Hussey, John A. "The Women of Fort Vancouver." *Oregon Historical Quarterly* 92 (fall 1991): 265–308.

"Indians' Claims to be Presented." *Coos Bay Times*. November 14, 1931, 1.

"Indians Prepare to Offer Claims." *Coos Bay Times*. November 5, 1931, 1.

Jacobs, Melville. "The Fate of Indian Oral Literatures in Oregon." *Northwest Review* 5, no. 3 (1962): 90–99.

———. "Areal Spread of Indian Oral Genre Features in the Northwest States." *Journal of the Folklore Insititute* 9, no. 2 (1972): 10–17.

Kinkade, Dale M. "History of Research in Linguistics." In Wayne Suttles, ed., *Northwest Coast*, 98–106. Vol. 7 of *Handbook of North American Indians*. Washington, D.C.: Smithsonian Institution, 1990.

Lawton, Harry W. Foreword to *Encounter with an Angry God*, by Carabeth Laird. Riverside, Calif.: Rubidoux Printing Co., 1975.

Lockhart, Esther M. "Recollections of Early Days." In Dodge, *Pioneer History*, 349–60.

Lomax, Alfred L. "Early Shipping and Industry in the Lower Siuslaw Valley." *Lane County Historian* 16 (1971): 32–38.

Lund, Ernest H. "Oregon Coastal Dunes between Coos Bay and Sea Lion Point." *Ore Bin* (State of Oregon Department of Geology and Mineral Resources) 35, no. 5 (1973): 73–92.

[Luse, Jesse Allen]. "Funeral Rites Observed." *Marshfield Sun*. May 11, 1939, 3.

Murkel, Margaret Stauff. "Empire Boys of the 1880's." In Emil Peterson, ed., *Early Day Stories*. North Bend, Oreg.: Coos-Curry Pioneer Historical Association, 1945.

O'Brien, A. R. "Friends of Princess Lottie Jackson in Tribute to Last of Coos Indians" (letter). *Coos Bay Times*. April 1944 (clipping).

"Old Indian Passes Away." *Coos Bay Times*. January 6, 1907, 1.

"Oregon Squaw Only Living Person Who Knows Old Tongue."
    Newspaper clipping in possession of Iola Larson.
    [1934?].

Parrish, J. L. "Report of J. L. Parrish, Indian Agent." In Dodge,
    Pioneer History, 104–11.

Pierce, Joe E. "Hanis and Miluk: Dialects or Unrelated
    Languages." *International Journal of American
    Linguistics* 31 (1965): 323–25.

————. Genetic Comparisons and Hanis, Miluk, Alsea, Siuslaw,
    and Takelma." *International Journal of American
    Lingusitics* 32 (1966): 379–87.

"Probe Indian Land Claims." *Coos Bay Times*. November 11,
    1931.

Pullen, Reg. "Stone Sculptures of Southwest Oregon:
    Mythological and Ceremonial Associations." In Nan
    Hannon and Richard K. Olmo, eds., *Living with the
    Land: The Indians of Southwest Oregon*, 120–24.
    Medford, Oreg.: Southern Oregon Historical Society,
    1990.

Saling, Elwin. "History of Allegany." In Youst, *Above the Falls*.

Schwartz, E. A. "Sick Hearts: Indian Removal on the Oregon
    Coast, 1875–1881." *Oregon Historical Quarterly* 92 (fall
    1991): 228–64.

"Six Year Old Boy Is Drowned." *Coos Bay Times*. April 30, 1923,
    1.

Skinner, Mary Lou. "Florence: The 'Fir-Clad' City." *Lane County
    Historian* 16, no. 2 (summer 1971): 25–31.

Thompson, Laurence C. "Melville Jacobs, 1902–1971" (obituary).
    American Anthropologist 80 (1978): 640–49.

Wasson, George B., Jr. "Memory of a People: The Coquilles of the
    Southwest Coast." In Carolyn M. Bruan and Richard
    Lewis. eds., *The First Oregonians*, 83–87. Portland:
    Oregon Council for the Humanities, 1991.

————. "Gishgiu's Escape," "Gishgiu and the Sugar Thief," "The
    Redwood Canoe," and "Coyote and the Strawberries." In
    Jones and Ramsey, *The Stories We Tell*.

Whereat, Don. "Chiefs." *Newsletter of the Confederated Tribes
    of Coos, Siulsaw, and Lower Umpqua Indians*,
    November 1994, 9–11.

Whereat, Don, and Stephen Dow Beckham. "Captured Heritage: Confederated Tribes of Coos, Lower Umpqua, and Siuslaw Indians." In Carolyn M. Bruan and Richard Lewis, eds., *The First Oregonians*, 77–82. Portland: Oregon Council for the Humanities, 1991.

Zenk, Henry B. "Alseans" and "Siuslawans and Coosans." In Wayne Suttles, ed., *Northwest Coast*, 568–79. Vol. 7 of *Handbook of North American Indians*. Washington, D.C.: Smithsonian Institution, 1990.

PUBLISHED BOOKS AND MONOGRAPHS

Barnett, Homer G. *Indian Shakers: A Messianic Cult of the Pacific Northwest*. Carbondale: Southern Illinois University Press, 1957.

Beckham, Stephen Dow. *Requiem for a People: The Rogue Indians and the Frontiersmen*. Norman: University of Oklahoma Press, 1971.

———. *Coos Bay: The Pioneer Period, 1851–1890*. Coos Bay, Oreg.: Arago Books, 1973.

———. *The Indians of Western Oregon: This Land Was Theirs*. Coos Bay, Oreg.: Arago Books, 1977.

———. *Land of the Umpqua: A History of Douglas County*. Roseburg, Oreg.: Douglas County Commissioners, 1986.

———, ed. *Many Faces: An Anthology of Oregon Autobiography*. Oregon Literature Series, Vol. 2. Corvallis: Oregon State University Press, 1993.

Beckham, Stephen Dow, and Harriet Duncan Munnick. *Catholic Church Records of the Pacific Northwest*. Vols. 1 and 2, *Grande Ronde*. Portland: Binford and Mort Publishing, 1987.

Beckham, Stephen Dow, Kathryn Anne Toepel, and Rick Minor. *Native American Religious Practices and Uses in Western Oregon*. University of Oregon Anthropological Papers No. 31. Eugene: University of Oregon Department of Anthropology, 1984.

Bensell, Royal A. *All Quiet on the Yamhill: The Civil War in Oregon*. Ed. Gunther Barth. Eugene: University of Oregon Books, 1959.

Boas, Franz, ed. *Handbook of American Indian Languages*. Part 2, Bureau of American Ethnology Bulletin 40. Washington, D.C.: Smithsonian Institution, 1922.

Brumble, David H., III. *An Annotated Bibliography of American Indian and Eskimo Autobiographies*. Lincoln: University of Nebraska Press, 1981.

Caldera, Melody, ed. *South Slough Adventures: Life on a Southern Oregon Estuary*. Coos Bay, Oreg.: South Coast Printing, 1995.

Clark, Ella E. *Indian Legends of the Pacific Northwest*. Berkeley: University of California Press, 1953.

DeLorme Mapping. *Oregon Atlas and Gazetteer*. Freeport, Maine: DeLorme Mapping, 1991.

Dodge, Orvil, ed. *Pioneer History of Coos and Curry Counties, Or.* 1898; reprint, Bandon, Oreg.: Western World, 1969.

Douthit, Nathan. *The Coos Bay Region, 1890–1944: Life on a Coastal Frontier*. Coos Bay, Oreg.: River West Books, 1981.

———. *A Guide to Oregon South Coast History*. Coos Bay, Oreg.: River West Books, 1986.

Du Bois, Cora. *The 1870 Ghost Dance*. University of California Anthropological Records, Vol. 3, No. 1. Berkeley: University of California Press, 1939.

Erdoes, Richard, and Alfonso Ortiz, eds. *American Indian Myths and Legends*. New York: Pantheon Books, 1984.

Frachtenberg, Leo J. *Coos Texts*. Columbia University Contributions to Anthropology, Vol. 1. New York: Columbia University Press, 1913.

———. *Lower Umpqua Texts and Notes on the Kusan Dialects*. Columbia University Contributions to Anthropology, Vol. 4. New York: Columbia University Press, 1914.

———. *Coos: An Illustrative Sketch*. Bureau of American Ethnology Bulletin 40 (extract). Washington, D.C.: Smithsonian Institution, 1914.

———. *Alsea Texts and Myths*. Bureau of American Ethnology Bulletin 67. Washington, D.C.: Smithsonian Institution, 1920.

Gill, John. *Gill's Dictionary of the Chinook Jargon*. 18th ed. Portland: J. K. Gill and Co., 1960.

Greenberg, Joseph H. *Language in the Americas*. Stanford: Stanford University Press, 1988.

Hall, Roberta L. *The Coquille Indians: Yesterday, Today and Tomorrow*. Lake Oswego, Oreg.: Smith, Smith, and Smith Publishing Co., 1984.

————, ed. *People of the Coquille Estuary*. Corvallis, Oreg.: Words and Pictures Unlimited, 1995.

Harrington, John Peabody. *Alsea/Siuslaw/Coos Field Notes*. John Peabody Harrington Papers, National Anthropological Archives, Smithsonian Institution, Washington, D.C. New York: Kraus International Publications, 1981. Microfilm.

Hays, Marjorie H. *The Land That Kept Its Promise: A History of South Lincoln County*. Newport, Oreg.: Lincoln County Historical Society, 1976.

Hopkins, Sarah Winnemucca. *Life among the Piutes*. Ed. Mrs. Horace Mann. 1883; reprint, Reno: University of Nevada Press, 1994.

Jacobs, Melville. *Coos Narrative and Ethnologic Texts*. University of Washington Publications in Anthropology, Vol. 8, No. 1. Seattle: University of Washington, 1939.

————. *Coos Myth Texts*. University of Washington Publications in Anthropology, Vol. 8, No. 2. Seattle: University of Washington, 1940.

————. *The Content and Style of an Oral Literature*. Chicago: University of Chicago Press, 1959.

————. *Pattern in Cultural Anthropology*. Homewood, Ill.: Dorsey Press, 1964.

Jones, Suzi, and Jarold Ramsey, eds. *The Stories We Tell: An Anthology of Oregon Folk Literature*. Oregon Literature Series, Vol. 5. Corvalis: Oregon State University Press, 1994.

Krupat, Arnold, ed. *Native American Autobiography: An Anthology*. Madison: University of Wisconsin Press, 1994.

Mills, Elaine L., ed. *The Papers of John Peabody Harrington in the Smithsonian Institution, 1907–1957*. Vol. 1, *A Guide to the Field Notes: Native American History, Language, and Culture of Alaska/Northwest Coast*. New York: Kraus International Publications, 1981.

Nelson, Ines. *Haynes Inlet Memories, 1870–1940*. North Bend, Oreg.: Wegford Publications, 1979.

Peterson, Emil R., and Alfred Powers. *A Century of Coos and Curry*. Portland: Binfords and Mort, 1952.

Radin, Paul. *The Trickster: A Study in American Indian Mythology*. New York: Bell Publishing Co., 1956.

Ramsey, Jarold, ed. *Coyote Was Going There: Indian Literature of the Oregon Country*. Seattle: University of Washington Press, 1977.

Rothenberg, Jerome. *Shaking the Pumpkin: Traditional Poetry of the Indian North Americas*. New York: Alfred Van Der Marck Editions, 1986.

Seaburg, William R. *Guide to Pacific Northwest Native American Materials in the Melville Jacobs Collection and in Other Archival Collections in the University of Washington Libraries*. Seattle: University of Washington Libraries, 1982.

Sengstacken, Agnes Ruth. *Destination, West!* Portland: Binfords and Mort, 1942.

Thompson, Lucy. *To the American Indian*. 1916; Reprint, ed. Julian Lang, Berkeley: Heyday Books, 1991.

Thornton, Jim, and Esther Stutzman, eds. *Indians of the Oregon Coast: The Ancient and Original Inhabitants*. Coos Bay, Oreg.: Coos County Education Service District, 1978.

Van Kirk, Sylvia. *Many Tender Ties*. Norman: University of Oklahoma Press, 1980.

Ward, Beverly H. *White Moccasins*. Myrtle Point, Oreg.: Myrtle Point Printing, 1986.

Wendt, Ingrid, and Primus St. John, eds. *From Here We Speak: An Anthology of Oregon Poetry*. Oregon Literature Series, Vol. 4. Corvallis: Oregon State University Press, 1993.

Winterbotham, Jerry. *Umpqua: The Lost County of Oregon*. Brownsville, Oreg.: Creative Images Printing, 1994.

Youst, Lionel. *Above the Falls.* Coos Bay, Oreg.: South Coast Printing, 1992.

Index

Minor, Annie, 120
Mixed-bloods, 164, 167; at
  Chemawa, 158; employment,
  127, 133
Montavilla (area in Portland), 154
Morgan, Laurence (linguist), 187
Moving people. *See* Whites
Music: bawdy songs, 74, 143;
  dance band, 119; recording
  of, 172, 176–77; social and
  love songs, 74; "Song of
  Ma'lu'c," 182; "The
  Sweetheart," 188–89
Mussel Reef, 131
Mythology: analysis of, 189;
  "The Bears," 184; "Bridge of
  the Gods," 159n, 159–60;
  "Butterball duck," 78; cautionary tales, 77; characters
  in, 76; in English, 200, 201,
  265–69; function of, 190–91;
  "He eats human children,"
  133; introduction to Coos,
  205–208; from Jim Buchanan,
  185; "Origin of Death,"
  185–86; as performing art,
  190; "Pheasant," 78; publication of, 199–202; published
  texts, 188; from Tom Hollis,
  185; "The Trickster Person
  Who Made the Country,"
  187, 189, 200, 209–56;
  "Two Loose Women," 80–81;
  in unexpurgated form, 180;
  "The Walkers and the
  Winged Things Fought,"
  188; "White Wife of Mouse,"
  189; "Wife of Seal," 189

Names: Annie's, 152; Annie's
  grandchildren, 138, 142;
  Annie's naming ceremony,

54–55; "Coquel," 201; given
  by whites, 25–26; "Jackson,"
  89; persons named for villages,
  11, 171; place-names, 113
Natural disasters: earthquakes,
  12; forest fires, 8, 53, 71;
  tsunami, 12
Ned, Charlie (Lower Coquille
  Miluk), 131, 165, 188;
  storyteller, 76, 80
Nellie (Annie's half-sister): birth
  of, 14; death of, 60; and
  shamanistic healing, 59
Nellie Agnes (Annie's
  daughter). *See* Aasen, Nellie
New River, 168
North Bend, 29, 109, 133
North Slough, 15, 143

Old Lady Sam (Alsea shaman),
  60
Oregon George (Ione Baker's
  brother), 137
Orton, Molly (Takelma Indian
  woman), 180

Palmer, Joel (Supt. of Indian
  Affairs), 24, 75, 166
Palmer, Nancy, *124*
Parrish, J. L. (Indian agent), 18
Peterson, Annie Miner, *124,
  146, 161, 162, 192, 194,
  203*; acquaintances, 15;
  attends dances, 118, 119;
  attends first Ghost Dance at
  Alsea, 93; attends Indian
  meetings, 121; aunts, 18, 42;
  basketmaking, 138; cancer,
  197; Carl (Annie's fifth
  husband), 149, 150, *161,
  162,* 163–64, 172, 180;
  clothing, 122; consorts with